F*CK YOUR DIET

AND OTHER THINGS MY THIGHS TELL ME

CHLOÉ HILLIARD

GALLERY BOOKS

New York   London   Toronto   Sydney   New Delhi

Gallery Books
An Imprint of Simon & Schuster, Inc.
1230 Avenue of the Americas
New York, NY 10020

Note to readers: Certain names and characteristics of people portrayed have been changed.

First Gallery Books hardcover edition January 2020

GALLERY BOOKS and colophon are registered trademarks of Simon & Schuster, Inc.

For information about special discounts for bulk purchases, please contact Simon & Schuster Special Sales at 1-866-506-1949 or business@simonandschuster.com.

The Simon & Schuster Speakers Bureau can bring authors to your live event. For more information or to book an event, contact the Simon & Schuster Speakers Bureau at 1-866-248-3049 or visit our website at www.simonspeakers.com.

Interior design by Davina Mock-Maniscalco

Photographs courtesy of the author's friends and family

Manufactured in the United States of America

10   8   6   4   2   1   3   5   7   9

Library of Congress Cataloging-in-Publication Data

Names: Hilliard, Chloé, author.
Title: F*ck your diet : and other things my thighs tell me / Chloé Hilliard.
Other titles: Fuck your diet
Description: First Gallery Books hardcover edition. | New York : Gallery Books, 2020.
Identifiers: LCCN 2019031745 (print) | LCCN 2019031746 (ebook) | ISBN 781982108618 (hardcover) | ISBN 9781982108625 (paperback) | ISBN 9781982108632 (ebook)
Subjects: LCSH: Hilliard, Chloé. | African American women, comedians—Biography. | Body image in women—United States—Humor. | Self-esteem in women—United States—Humor. | United States—Race relations—21st century—Humor.
Classification: LCC PN2287.H516 A5 2020 (print) | LCC PN2287.H516 (ebook) | DDC 818/.602—dc23
LC record available at https://lccn.loc.gov/2019031745
LC ebook record available at https://lccn.loc.gov/2019031746

ISBN 978-1-9821-0861-8
ISBN 978-1-9821-0863-2 (ebook)

To Mom and Dad for your love, support, and fat genes.
This book isn't a grandchild, but it's close.
P.S. Don't read chapter 15.

———

To my amazing friends who indulged me during a Fat Girl Moment
without judgment and those who smacked food from my hand
because I was supposed to be eating clean.
Your understanding means the world to me.

———

And lastly, to any person who's looked in the mirror
and hated the skin they're in—don't shrink when you really should soar.

contents

CONTENTS

DIABETES FOR BREAKFAST

I had a perfect body once. I was five. Ever since, I've been consumed with trying to fit in, both literally and figuratively. Standing six foot one, fluctuating between fat and thick since the age of twelve, "big" was my unofficial nickname. It's funny how people consider that to be a compliment.

"Wow, you're a *BIG* girl!" delivered with a smile as if they hadn't publicly questioned my ability to walk away from a plate. Understandably, they had no idea that the giant before them was an impressionable, introverted child with no say in what or how much was on her plate. No one wants to admit it, but a person doesn't get fat by themselves. I didn't come out of the womb craving McNuggets and Oreos. The system planted that gluttonous seed in my malleable mind. It was "The Man" with buckets of fried chicken deals and $1 pizza slices. Meanwhile, an organic apple comes with a credit check.

*F*ck Your Diet* is the chronicle of nearly forty years of failures mixed with conspiracy theories, supported facts, and many TMI moments. I'm stirring the pot and exposing, what I believe to be, the history of government policies and corporate capitalism that's affected my waistline, self-esteem, and body image.

As if American economics and policies didn't do enough to screw up how and what we eat, society's unrealistic expectations of beauty are strongly suggested at every turn. We want slim waists and muscles when our meals are extra-large and full of fillers. Whatever damage the system didn't do, there was always land mines at home. Early-childhood eating habits, often created by parents who didn't know how to break the processed-foods cycle, laid the foundation for a lifetime of nutritionless and emotional eating. Take my earliest memories of breakfast, for example.

A BOWL OF SUNSHINE

When I was growing up, my mother was my beauty icon—stunning, petite, long black hair that flowed down her back. She is the reason I told people "I have Indian in my family," when in actuality she was born and raised in Bed-Stuy, Brooklyn, by parents who landed here by way of the Great Migration. During my ugly years, I was furious with her for not giving me more of her genetics. Where was my light brown skin, high cheekbones, and small waist? Yes, I know it sounds absurd, a prepubescent girl comparing herself to her grown mother—but we were already damn near the same height, so I figured our appearance should match. Convinced I was adopted, I'd stare at photo albums of my parents and imagine what their real biological kid would have looked like.

PROLOGUE

Each morning at school, all the little boys would make it a point to say, "Good morning, Chloé's Mom!" That was the only time they'd glance my way.

During the week, breakfast wasn't a big production. I'd sit at the table alone. Mom placed a bowl in front of me containing the finest instant maple and brown sugar oatmeal. Steam still rising. A pat of salted butter melted over the mound. Then came a cup of cold whole milk, which I slowly poured over the top, mixing the hot and cold together. My yin and yang, if you will. It was as if I were a Michelin-star chef presenting some deconstructed meal to the rich and pretentious. "The milk represents the cold reality we face when we step out into the world and the warmth of the oats is what grounds us to nature. Feast upon this and feel as if you just pissed on yourself in an air-conditioned car." And last—it's embarrassing to write this—a generous drizzle of Hershey's Chocolate Syrup was added, elevating the flavors to juvenile diabetes. You don't understand. This was the only way I would eat oatmeal.

"Mom, I need more chocolate syrup!"

"There's no more," she'd yell from the kitchen.

"What!" I'd whine. "It tastes nasty."

"Girl, it's not nasty. You have enough stuff in there already."

"I don't want it."

"You are going to eat it. I'm not playing with you."

———

Honestly, I don't even remember how the concoction came to be. My mother was probably rushing one day and I threw a fat-kid tantrum over breakfast. Since she liked never throwing out good food and that "chocolate" was legit my first word, she threw some syrup on it and thus began my bad eating habits. Despite how crazy this sounds, this shouldn't reflect badly on my mom. Yes, she was potentially taking years off my life, but this was the only way she knew how to tame the beast. I lived for breakfast cereal. I still have an affinity for it today. Honey Nut Cheerios with some rice milk is my jam. Although my childhood oatmeal recipe was gag worthy, my mother (ironically) refused to buy me the trendy sugar-filled cereals that targeted kids.

"That's too expensive!" she'd say as my hand would reach for the box with horseshoes, marshmallows, or pebbles on the front. Then the next morning she would turn around and add a half of banana and a tablespoon of white sugar to my cornflakes.

SERVED WITH A SIDE OF SHAME

John Kellogg was probably rolling in his grave. The inventor of cornflakes was a devout Seventh-Day Adventist who shunned all sugars, soda, drugs, and sex. He lived to ninety-one. Fun fact: Kellogg invented cornflakes as a solution for masturbation. Kellogg believed, and finessed thousands of others into believing, that a vegetarian diet led to a longer, healthier life (correct) and removed the urge to rub one out because apparently eating burgers is the only thing that makes you want to flick your bean (so wrong). The married father of eight never consummated his marriage, choosing to adopt.

Kellogg was one of many Seventh-Day Adventists who opened and operated sanitariums around the country. These health spas and resorts were popular among the wealthy, pushing a vegetarian diet, daily exercise, and abstinence. America's Gilded Age produced a bustling new class of the 1%. And history proves, the 1% loves nothing more than wasting their money on schemes to extend their lives. (Watch *A Cure for Wellness*.) In 1906, at its height, Kellogg's sanitarium—not to be confused with sanitorium for the mentally insane—in Battle Creek, Michigan, housed over seven thousand well-to-do visitors, and due to his charitable and religious leanings, some poor sick patients who couldn't afford treatment elsewhere. He would describe his system as "a composite physiologic method comprising hydrotherapy, phototherapy, thermotherapy, electrotherapy, mechanotherapy, dietetics, physical culture, cold-air cure, and health training." Translation: You would pay Kellogg to dunk you in water, expose you to UV light, heat, electric shock, massages, sit outside in the freezing Michigan cold, jog, lift weights, and of course eat his cereal.

Vegetarianism was a drastic shift for the wealthy who flocked to Kellogg to recharge. A standard breakfast in the 1900s consisted of rice, cold leftover or jellied meat; usually a poor cut of beef that on its own would've been indigestible. Later in the century fruit juice, toast, eggs, bacon, and grits gained popularity. Kellogg believed that spicy or sweet food led to illicit passions, not just masturbation. What if he wasn't too far off? Is there a connection between India having asshole-burning spicy foods and the *Kama Sutra*? Could wasabi be the cause of Japanese tentacle porn?

Soon after his artisanal cereals took off, Kellogg's younger brother, William, bought the rights to cornflakes, scrapped his brother's Captain Save-A-Ho mentality, dumped a shit ton of sugar into the mix, and made millions pushing new sweet cereal to kids across the world. Of course, it was still marketed as a healthy way to start the day. As a kid I always wondered what "part of a complete breakfast" meant at the end of cereal commercials, not realizing it was the industry standard of saying, "This shouldn't be considered a meal on its own 'cause it has no nutritional value, but this cute white kid smiling and chewing is going to make you ignore this audible fine print." Later, William, probably riddled with guilt, launched the W. K. Kellogg Child Welfare Foundation, which, ironically, battles malnutrition and eating disorders.

General Mills, Post (C. W. Post was a patient of the elder Kellogg's and was so impressed with cornflakes he developed his own cereals), and Quaker rounded out the top four cereal makers who made it their mission to send kids out into the world with a day's worth of sugar intake swirling around in their bellies. By 1953, Kellogg's Sugar Smacks was 56 percent sugar. The original mascot was a white-faced, red-nosed, bald clown. The brainwashing was in full effect.

It would be centuries before people realized, or at least admitted, sugar is a drug. Studies have shown it causes the same response in the brain as nicotine, cocaine, heroin, and alcohol. And they wonder why kids were bouncing off the walls one minute and comatose the next.

———

"Mrs. Hilliard, Chloé has a hard time staying alert in class."

"Really? I don't understand why."

"I'm afraid that it causes her to fall behind in some subjects. I know she's a smart girl, but I need to see it."

On the way home from a parent-teacher conference my mom

would give me a loving yet stern speech, and the next morning she'd place that big bowl of oatmeal or sweetened cornflakes in front of my face again.

It would be years—filled with bouts of depression, heartbreak, mild eating disorders, discovering what self-confidence was, and so on—before I was able to rehabilitate my negative relationship with my body and food. What changed my life was the realization that my issue with weight wasn't entirely my fault. I, like most Americans, am the result of the working class who survived on processed foods, fast-food chains, and a lack of education when it came to nutrition and exercise. *Did this woman just say that society is the reason why she had a double chin and bad knees?* You damn right! You just read about my torrid love affair with cereal. It's not like I was rolling maze by my damn self. What I mean is, you're only as healthy as your options, and for me, those options were determined by socioeconomics; culture; ill-informed, deep-rooted traditions; and my zip code. Otherwise known in the public health sector as "social determinants of health." Chitter-lings, anyone?

I'm happy to say, I'm no longer enlisted in the battle of the bulge. That's not because I'm currently walking around with a six-pack. I just don't give a shit about trying to be skinny. Now I can reflect back on my successful careers as a journalist and comedian, relish in my detach-ment from food as an emotional crutch, and call out the bullshit sold to us by the food industry and society. Long gone are the days when I thought being able to look down and see your pelvic bones made you more valuable as a person. I have a lot of skinny friends and I'm doing way better in life than most of them.

I wrote this book for those who've failed diets, hid under baggy clothes, declined invitations to go out into the world, or contemplated ending their life when a sugar coma wasn't enough. I'm sharing my embarrassing and empowering moments for those who prayed for a faster metabolism or winning the Lotto so they could afford liposuction. I've been where you are. I once prayed for the Lord to give me a tapeworm so I could fit in a pair of jeans that only closed by attaching a key ring to the zipper hole, which I then secured around the top button and fastened. MacGyver should have been a plus-size woman. You become very crafty when you're fat and in a jam.

Look, perfection is overrated and impossible to achieve. Understanding that frees you up to focus on being healthy, unique, and confident. That is my prayer for you. Plus, tapeworms are expensive to remove.

———

P.S. My mother is still very beautiful.

1

RONALD REAGAN CAN DO HIS OWN PUSH-UPS

As an only child, I spent an absurd amount of time home alone, watching TV and eating snacks. I didn't realize how much bigger I was than my peers until it was time to take President Ronald Reagan's nationwide fitness exam. With the Cold War nearing its end, America's patriotism was on steroids. What better way to show the world that we were number one than to have kids continue an antiquated fitness analysis originally designed to test military servicemen in the 1950s? As if I needed another reason to be bullied, struggling to do sit-ups when my belly got in the way did not need to be one of them.

This is not a competition, but if it were, I would've been in the bullied kids Hall of Fame, circa 1986–1989. My crime: I was chunky, and that automatically classified me as being inferior. Without fail, my classmates figured out a way to put me in my place, reminding me that I would never be one of them by nicknaming me "Ugly," "Nasty," and "Ill, Chloé." Ill being the 1980s slang for "gross," not today's definition of "dope, fresh, sweet." Whenever they addressed me, their faces screwed up like they'd smelled a fart. I had chicken bones thrown at me. My personal items tossed into city trash cans. I was hit across the face with a wire Double Dutch rope. Adults downplayed my complaints because of my size. Whatever abuse I received, they thought I exaggerated it or was big enough to handle it. On really bad days, I'd be teased to tears, yelling, "Just leave me alone." Satan's spawns would sing back Michael Jackson's 1987 hit "Leave Me Alone" and say I was shaped like the elephant bones that danced in the music video. They hated me and used my favorite pop culture moments to torment me.

Every year until I turned twelve, I had growth spurts, so Mom never splurged on clothes. If she bought designer jeans they'd be high-waters in a few months. Also, it wasn't in the family budget. Some of my clothes were bought by the pound. Whenever my penny-saving grandma picked me up from school, we'd go to Domsey's—a no-frills, multilevel, secondhand department store near the old Domino sugar factory in my neighborhood of Williamsburg. Now that area is full of luxury apartments, but back then, the only folks strolling through the cobblestone industrial strip were the mob, drug dealers, prostitutes, and their respective clients. You couldn't pay people to walk there at night. The waterfront was a dumping ground for body parts and trash. Going "down to the water" meant I'd get to play kid detective in search of a gruesome discovery instead of enjoying the Manhattan skyline across the East River.

There were two ways to shop at Domsey's. Either you walked in the front door and shopped off the racks like a normal person. Or you went around to the back and looted the wears before they were sorted and given price tags. I loved Indiana Jones and looked at this as an adventure; instead of missing treasure, I searched for clothes without holes and stains. Grandma's take-no-prisoners bargaining skills made her lots of enemies. She once argued the price down from $27 to $15 on a thirty-pound bag of clothes. "They smell moldy!" she complained before winning the bid and stuffing them in her trunk. The latest shipments arrived on Tuesdays. Grandma and I, partners in thrift, would be there to receive them. "Chloé, climb on into that bin for Grandma and throw some clothes down." The crown jewel was anything name brand, but usually we ended up with dusty corduroys and combustible polyesters.

When Mom did spend money on clothes, they were from the nearby Jewish stores. Let me clarify. I don't mean clothing stores that happened to be owned by Jewish people. We're talking clothing stores that catered to the black and navy-blue, hem-to-your-lower-calf, heavy-wool-blend, ultraorthodox Hasidic Jewish enclave of Williamsburg. Wedged between the East River and the black and Italian Brooklyn that people imagined when you used to say, "I'm from Brooklyn!", Williamsburg is its own world. I grew up seeing the Twin Towers from the back of our apartment complex. On the Fourth of July we'd walk to the water and watch the fireworks. Crack was ravaging the city but it barely registered in the sprawling apartment complexes my Jewish neighbors and I called home. In fact, my classmates made fun of me because I didn't know what a crack vial was.

"Look down, idiot." The school playground was littered with hundreds of clear vials with red, yellow, or blue tops. "What you think all those are?" I don't know, I thought they were pretty though, like fish tank gravel. My naïveté is what bothered my classmates the most. I was Rose Nylund to their Dorothy Zbornak (can't pass up a *Golden Girls* reference). That was part of the problem. I watched *The Golden Girls* and listened to Al Jarreau. I knew nothing about hip-hop or high-top sneakers. I was a bully's dream.

Living among Hasidic Jews had perks. Our community was safe, my neighbors were friendly, and they paid me with kosher treats when I did things for them. Sundown on Friday till sundown on Saturday was their Sabbath. Their faith required they not touch any modern technology during that time, so if they needed a light turned on, the fire on the stove adjusted, or one of their dozen kids pushed in a stroller to the nearby emergency clinic, I was their *goy*. Filled with anticipation, I'd rush home from school on Fridays, listen out for their sundown alarm that marked the start of their holy time, and wait for a knock on the door.

"Mom, Dad, I got it." No point in looking through the peephole, I knew who it was and what they wanted. "My people need me." I'd open the door and a Jewish neighbor would motion with their hand "Come this way." And I went. This wasn't a Chris Hansen sort of deal. We trusted each other. More importantly, I trusted I was going to get some good treats as payment. After doing the Lord's work for his cho-sen people, I'd count my kosher confectionaries. *Dare I say it? The Jews made me fat.* Chocolate rugelach is my shit.

Back at school, I was struggling to fit in. Picked last in every team activity, ignored on the playground, blamed for everything, I'd go home and complain to my mom about being the only child. How come I didn't have any older siblings or hood-ass cousins who could come and beat my haters up? An incident that stuck with me was when the popular girls demanded I pay fifty cents in order to play with them. And not just any old nickel, dimes, or quarters would do. These monsters wanted my coveted John F. Kennedy fifty-cent piece before agreeing to let me play "house" with them. I handed it over, desperate for friends, and was assigned the role of maid.

My third-grade teacher, Mrs. Hirsch, knew I was having trouble in class but couldn't have known it was to this degree. Whenever she could, she made me feel special, like on school trips. Field trips were the only time we inner-city kids rode a yellow school bus. The morning of, my classmates jockeyed for seat partners and negotiated who would get the window. Mrs. Hirsch always saved me from the embarrassment of sitting alone.

"Chloé, would you sit next to me?" Her asking—in front of everyone—made all the difference in the world. I hoped that her doing so would show the others how cool I was. It didn't, because I wasn't. I got on the bus and grabbed the first row across from the driver. Mrs. Hirsch had teacher stuff to do, so our conversations were stop-and-go throughout the ride. I didn't mind. I always got the window seat, and if that didn't hold my attention, I'd memorize the bus's four-digit number located above the windshield. Don't feel too sorry for me. My memory came in handy during one trip to the aquarium. The parking lot was a sea of yellow buses. "Class, tell Chloé thank-you for remembering the bus's number."

"Ill, Chloé . . . thank you."

Mrs. Hirsch was a plump, tiny women. Her skin soft, like risen dough. She was probably in her thirties, but when you're a kid everyone seems ancient. Her thick, frizzy auburn hair was cut into a blunt Edward Scissorhands–style bob with feathered bangs, which bounced as she wrote on the chalkboard. Since it was the eighties, her oversize turtleneck sweaters swallowed most of her body, and wherever she went a trail of White Diamonds perfume lingered behind.

"All right, Class, next week during gym you will be taking a fitness test. President Ronald Reagan wants to see how big and strong you all are." The classroom buzzed with their excitement and my fear. "To get you ready, I'll be taking your measurements and weight in class today."

In the early eighties, President Ronald Reagan amended the Physical Fitness and Sports Executive Order. One of its directives included the advancement of ". . . physical fitness of children, youth, adults, and senior citizens by systematically encouraging the development of community recreation, physical fitness, and sports-participation programs." Let me tell you, there was no systematic encouragement.

Mrs. Hirsch produced a scale and placed it next to her desk, at the front of the room. She started calling students up alphabetically. *Okay, my last name starts with an H.* My little brain was working overtime. *Ask to go to the bathroom; you can pee out the milk and chocolate syrup from breakfast.* I loved food too much to throw it up. I stood in front of the sink, washing and rewashing my hands, staring at myself in the foggy mirror. *Chloé, how did we get here? Why does the president want to know how much I weigh?* I would've escaped out the window, like every kid on TV did when why they got into hot water, but this was Brooklyn. There were bars on the windows. Ramona Quimby would never have had to deal with this. If Mom had sent me to boarding school like I'd begged, I could've been living it up like Tootie on *The*

Facts of Life. Skating around all day, that's exercise. I would've lost weight in no time.

President or not, Ronald Reagan was now Enemy #1. I didn't know then, but his policies would impact my life for years to come. Of course, everyone knows about the shit show that was and continues to be the GOP's obsession with "trickle-down economics" (fun fact: it never works), but this man felt very strongly about kids' fitness and school lunches (we'll get to that later).

———

President Dwight "Ike" Eisenhower introduced the President's Council on Youth Fitness in 1956. Sounds cool, but when you read between the lines, this initiative was nothing more than nationalist propaganda. Eleven years after World War II, the U.S. was engaged in the Cold War with the Soviet Union. The two nations had risen from the ashes as the leading superpowers and proceeded to spend the next four decades playing "Whose dick is bigger?" Replace "dick" with "nuclear weapons arsenal" and you really see how dangerous of a time it was. When a study appeared in the *New York State Journal of Medicine* showing that America's children were slower, fatter, and weaker than their European counterparts, the president sprang into action. These results—58 percent of American kids failed compared to 9 percent of European kids—led to funding legislation that forced students age 6–17 to be tested twice a year.

A military man, Eisenhower served in the U.S. Army for forty-six years, rising to five-star general. Ironically, he never saw a single day of combat, but took his personal health and diet very seriously. He hoped the country would feel the same way about being wartime ready. However, after two world wars, the majority of the country's interest had shifted. Eliminating the evil axis meant the country was free to chill. Families had disposable income and spent it on fast food, vacations, and convertibles. Food rations were replaced with TV dinners. Backbreaking farm work was ditched for city life. The only place people were running to was the burger joint for a shake and a double stack. No one gave a damn about having abs.

While in the bathroom, my classmates had taken bets that I would be too heavy for the scale. The scale went to 300 pounds. I told you, kids are assholes. At eight years old, I was nearly five feet tall and wore a size 8 women's shoe. With one big inhale, I stepped on the scale, wishing I'd become light as a feather, and waited for her to read the number. She didn't. The class was extra quiet. Mrs. Hirsch was nice enough to use a folder to hide the number from peeping eyes. I looked down and saw the red needle bobbing around 100. Fine, okay, past 100. I couldn't count the little dashes for a more accurate reading. I didn't want to bend over, redistribute my weight, and have it go higher. She leaned over and whispered in my ear, "We've got to get that down, okay?" I gave a fake grin and nodded my head in agreement. As I turned back to my seat, I caught eyes with the entire class. Some were bold enough to ask me how much I weighed. I wasn't about to help any of them win their bets. I kept the number to myself until I forgot it. I don't even think I mentioned it to my parents when I got home. I prayed that no one but Mrs. Hirsch and Ronald Reagan would know what the scale said.

In 1988, the average eight-year-old American girl weighed 65.7 pounds and stood at four foot three. I was the supersize version, dragging ass at the back of the line as we headed down two flights of stairs to the gymnasium for the government-approved gauntlet erected to break our preteen psyches. Already winded from walking down the steps, I had no chance in hell of making it through the next forty minutes. My mom always said to call on the name of Jesus if I was afraid; however, this fitness test required something stronger. I had watched my fair share of *Bewitched* reruns and decided to call upon black magic. I'd never attempted to tap into my inner witch, but I'd seen Samantha and her daughter do it countless times. The concept of TV magic escaped me.

Please let me do good on this test. Wiggle, wiggle. *I promise I won't eat another Oreo Big Stuf even though rapper Heavy D is in the new commercial and I really like him 'cause he's fat like me but he always has a smile on his face and he's a really, really, really good dancer.* Wiggle, wiggle. *I'm going to run so fast they won't be able to see me. Like the Bionic Woman.* Wiggle, wiggle.

We spilled into the gym where Mr. Pell was none too happy about having to play drill sergeant. He blew his whistle and clapped his hands to get our attention from the death course laid out before us. "All right, kids, listen up." Mr. Pell's shirts were always skintight. His pecs jumped as he spoke, his veins protruded, and his pimple-covered biceps bulged. His hair was slicked back like the Fonz, and he wore track pants that swished when he walked. Hey, it was the eighties, man. "For the next week, we are going to be participating in the president's fitness test. Each day we will do some exercises and I will record your scores."

The test included:

* **A Timed One-Mile Walk:** This was Brooklyn, there was no track *or* field. Want to bore kids to death? Ask them to walk laps around the gym without music.

* **Push-Ups:** The boys braced on their hands and toes while the girls could push off their knees, to lighten the load. Thank God feminism wasn't popping back then. You know they would not stand for girls getting different treatment due to our lack of upper-body strength.

* **Sit-Ups:** Yes, we did sit-ups before folks realized we were probably fucking up our necks and backs. No one held your feet; you had to use those adolescent abs on your own. The goal was 38+ in one minute.

* **Shuttle Run (Sprint):** The teacher placed a wooden cube in the middle of the floor and you took turns running to it, picking it up, and running it back to where you came from. Repeat until you throw up.

* **V-Sits:** Lie flat on your back with your legs open in a V-shape, then sit up and reach over as far as you can.

* **Softball Toss:** Because every kid should know how to throw a grenade in a time of war.

When people talk about repressing childhood trauma into the dark crevices of their mind, I wonder if those memories include not being able to complete a one-mile walk. Mom taught me to look for the silver lining, which in this case was I didn't die. That didn't stop me from praying for a way out via, preferably, asthma. I'd daydream about having an inhaler and whipping it out in slow motion right before Mr. Pell ordered us to do jumping jacks. The dream ended with my being excused and watching my classmates get in formation from my comfortable bench. First I had to convince him I had asthma.

"Mr. Pell, my chest hurts. I can't breathe. I think I have asthma."

"Chloé, you're fine. We've only stretched. Go back to your spot."

"I think I need to go to the nurse."

"Chloé, if you had asthma you wouldn't be able to talk right now. Now go back to your spot. You're holding up the class. "

"If I pass out you know why."

Push-ups were not happening. Even on my knees it was too much for my arms. Why did they expect city kids to have muscles anyway? We weren't working on farms before school started. There's no lakes to skip rocks across. We had a murky river with floating debris and bodies. There were no trees to climb. We called it the concrete jungle for a reason. Don't get me started on the sit-ups. What did they expect me to do with my stomach? Two inches, max, that's how far I could get my head and neck off the hard, cold, dusty floor. My shoulders never lifted. I would get up and a dust angel would be left in my place where I had shimmied as best I could off the ground. I did not get an A for effort.

___

At the time, President Reagan was the latest in a long line of fragile white men in the Oval Office who used propaganda to get Americans to accomplish the physical feats they themselves could not. It was commendable when President Eisenhower launched the fitness tests. He was a war vet, had a strict diet, and was coming off the heels of World War II. Those who followed suit couldn't say the same.

When John F. Kennedy took office in 1961, he was so impressed with an old military order of soldiers completing fifty miles in twenty-four hours that he introduced it to the nation, who ate it up as a sign of patriotism and vigor. Then a six-minute song entitled "Chicken Fat" was released and played in schools across the country as an exercise how-to. The lyrics dictated what moves to do: "Touch your toes! 10 times. Push-ups! 10 times!" The best was the hook: *Give that chicken fat back to the chicken / Don't be chicken again.*

It was the precursor to the "Cha Cha Slide" but without the fun and heavy on the body shaming. Meanwhile JFK could barely put on his own shoes as a result of his osteoporosis and took a cocktail of medications that included codeine, Demerol, and methadone.

President Lyndon Johnson raised the stakes, giving presidential awards to the top 15 percent of students. However, the Texan dined on steaks most days, eating chipped beef with cream for breakfast.

Fast-forward to Reagan, who got serious about his health after his two assassination attempts and made an old-fashioned Hollywood propaganda push for the fitness test in the eighties. The threat of the Russians beating our ass helped. Later, presidents didn't give the same attention to the program. President Bush, who loved pork rinds, was too busy with Desert Storm to care about fat kids. President Clinton made sure we saw him jogging daily, but the cameras stopped rolling when he'd made it to McDonald's for breakfast. President G. W. Bush loved to cycle. And the most athletic president of our lifetime, President Obama, hooped in the White House and graciously ended the program in 2012, rebranding it "Let's Move"—an awardless, less-pressurized push for the generations that didn't believe in first-place winners but rather participation medals.

Our presidents' efforts were in vain. For the last fifty-six years, Europe could give a shit about us doing more push-ups. Warfare shifted from hand-to-hand combat to flying drones five thousand miles away. The chickens, along with their fat, have come home to roost. Now we have a fat president who lies about his weight and has doctors embellish the quality of his health. He drinks Diet Coke by the gallons and eats ice cream every night. I vote we bring back the Presidential Fitness Test, but let it be for the actual president. If you can't do a pull-up, you can't pull this nation together.

2

STARVING KIDS IN AFRICA

Before the internet, we used to be alerted to a world crisis via telethons, concert fund-raisers, and catchy celebrity-sung anthems. I loved a good telethon—celebrities answering phones, the corny host in a tuxedo, bad variety acts, and that massive counter that showed how much money had been raised. Whenever they reached their goal, confetti would drop from the ceiling. Even though I was never allowed to call in, I still felt like I was contributing to the cause by cheering from home. That's how most of us do it. If you can't open your wallet, you send some positive vibes. It's not real currency but it gives you the false sense of offering a helping hand. Hence, society's favorite ways to fix a problem: money or thoughts and prayers. My family did a lot of the latter. Often these prayers were led by my holier-than-thou grandmother, who made it a point to make us simultaneously feel guilty and grateful for our blessings by comparing our lives to those much less fortunate. In the early 1980s, her source material came from the motherland.

"There are kids starving in Africa who wish they had food to eat." Mothers across America heard news of the famine in East Africa and decided to not only inform us kids about it but also use it to make us appreciate whatever we had and force us to eat every bite of food they put on our plate. Somehow, a humanitarian effort resulted in us binge eating.

I was in preschool and my grandmother placed the lives of millions of people on the tip of my fork. I felt like Horton hearing a Who! (Dr. Seuss's well-intentioned elephant who took it upon himself to save a small world living on a speck of dust.) Talk about pressure. There was no further explanation. She wasn't about to break down the social and political conflict that was killing hundreds of thousands, possibly millions. *Africa? Starving kids? I'm a kid. I don't want to starve. Wait, what's "starving"? Where is Africa? I haven't started school yet, so I haven't learned about Black History Month and the ships and shackles.* The Lion King *doesn't come out for a while, so what is this Africa you speak of, Grandma? Grandma, you got brand-new Tupperware. If the kids are starving, can't we just send these chicken gizzards and cow peas over to them?* All my tiny brain could gather was that if I ate all my food, I was somehow *helping* people in a place I never knew existed.

The Jedi mind trick was in full motion. As Christian as she was, my grandmother didn't really care about those kids in Africa. In theory, yes, her heart sympathized; but in reality, she wasn't about to start sending my table scraps or buying extra food to ship overseas.

"I don't want any more," I'd whine, all of four years old.

"You don't want it? After I slaved in this kitchen—it's one hundred degrees in here." Then she would reason with herself. "Well, give it here. You're gonna eat this for dinner, and if your mother comes before then, you'll have it tomorrow for lunch." The longest she'd saved my plate was four days. Each time we sat at the table, we'd repeat the same dance.

"Don't play around with that food." I'd be lost in the tiny color TV positioned on the counter right behind her, her sternness snapping me back. A highlight was getting to adjust the rabbit-ear antennas and adding aluminum foil to the tip to get better reception. During the day, it was just the two of us and countless reruns of old TV shows. "You gonna sit right there until it's gone." I'd move my food around with my fork to stall.

———

Handcrafted wood, rectangular with room for ten, the dining table in my grandmother's kitchen was massive. It was so special, she covered it with three tablecloths. The last of them, of course, being plastic. On the rare occasion I'd catch a glimpse of the smooth, naked wood, its beauty was blinding. It felt like that scene in *Indiana Jones* when the Nazis opened the Ark of the Covenant and their faces melted. She hated when I watched "sinner" movies like *Indiana Jones*. If it wasn't Christian, *The Cosby Show*, or a classic black-and-white show where all the women were actual housewives, like she was, it was banned from her house. When my mother was pregnant with my younger brother in 1995, Grandma scolded her for watching *Star Trek*, for fear that my brother would come out looking like a Klingon.

The cornerstone of the family, Grandma ruled with an iron fist that was saved, sanctified, and filled with the Holy Spirit. Her table reminded me of *The Last Supper*. However, in this picture, she was seated at the center with her husband and seven children surrounding her. Grandma referenced Jesus so much I thought she knew him personally. She answered the house phone "Praise the Lord" and had a calligrapher stencil "He Is Holy" on the back of her Astro van. We dubbed it the "Jesus-mobile."

From morning until after dinner was served, the dining table was my grandmother's office, food-prep station, library, gossip hub, you name it. I was her first grandchild; she took care of me while my parents worked. She didn't sing to me or entertain my blissful glee. There was no playroom dedicated to me. I barely remember having any toys there. There were rules, and I was to follow every one of them. Her word was my gospel, and the biggest sermon always revolved around food.

Franks and beans. Chicken gizzards. Lima beans. Smothered liver. Collard greens. Pork chops. Grandma's Southern roots would not allow her to just make a sandwich, and if she did, the cuts of meat were at minimum one-inch thick, since she'd cut it off the carcass. A deli sandwich was a myth to me. *There's a real place where they'll make you a sandwich with all the things you want, and the meat comes in paper-thin slices? I can have mayo and mustard on it? They have rolls instead of Wonder Bread that sticks to the roof of your mouth like a ninja hiding from your tongue? And I can have it hot!? You're lying.*

Dorothy Stevens grew up on a South Carolina sharecropping farm owned by a white man. She was the youngest of seven and the bossiest. All the pets she had would eventually become the family's dinner.

"There was no point in naming them," she'd say. Once, she told me about the time a car hit a calf that had wandered away from their farm. Her father put it out of its misery, and her mother made sure all the families, black and white, that worked on the land got some of the meat. "Oh, it was so tender!" My grandma is eighty-nine years old and remembers it like it was yesterday.

Going back centuries to my ancestors first stepping foot on this continent, food held a very special place as the center of the black American home and community. Black cuisine often consisted of us making the best out of the worst. It told our history, fueled revolutions, and rebuilt spirits. When someone made you a plate, it was assurance that you were in a safe place, welcome, cared for, and loved. It's called soul food for a reason. Some people had generational wealth; we had recipes. Grandma's "hard-earned" food was our inheritance.

The three greatest loves of my grandmother's life are Jesus, my grandfather, and food. If she could cook my grandfather a huge supper including a cake made from scratch while listening to the Old Testament on tape, she'd be in nirvana. A stay-at-home mom, she raised seven kids, making sure they had "food on their plate, clothes on their backs, and a roof over their heads." That was her favorite phrase to deliver whenever us kids complained. She was old-school. The concept of compromise was unfamiliar to her. Kids were to be seen and not heard. It was either her way or her way. Everything was hers—her food, her plate, her house—you just got to partake in it for the moment. Lunch, dinner, whatever she put on *her* table had to be completely consumed. You'd better figure out how to unhook your jaw and shove everything down your throat, or welcome death. Those were the only two options. Even then, my grandmother would lean over the table and check your pulse to make sure you weren't faking it, while saying, "You better be dead!"

———

From 1983–85, the East African country of Ethiopia suffered a famine that led to an estimated 400,000 to 1 million deaths. More than a decade of civil war combined with a drought created a crisis that caught the attention of Europe and the U.S. And what do first worlders do when we see people in need? We write, perform, and sell a song about it. In 1984, some of Europe's biggest pop stars teamed up to record "Do They Know It's Christmas?," a song that would bring international attention to the famine in East Africa. Feather-haired singers such as Boy George, Bono, George Michael, and more delivered these lyrics over a synth pop beat: *Where nothing ever grows / No rain or rivers flow / Do they know it's Christmas time at all?*

Real quick, let's address the audacity of these lyrics. The narrative that nothing grows in Africa is bullshit. If nothing grew in Africa, the continent wouldn't have been a go-to destination for European countries who raped and pillaged their way across the continent, stockpiling its natural resources and people and leaving behind crumbs. Yet the singers of "Do They Know It's Christmas?," who lived in some of the same countries who contributed to Africa's problems, could never see it that way. Although ground zero of the 1980s famine, Ethiopia has a rich history. It holds the honor of being the only African country to never be colonized. (Sorry, Wakanda doesn't count.) Ethiopia is considered the birthplace of the coffee plant, so when you drink that morning cup of joe, make sure to thank its African origins. See, something does grow there. Sixty-three percent of the population is Christian, so famine or not, it's safe to say Ethiopians know when Christmas is. White-savior gaze aside, the intent of the song's organizers was pure. They hoped to raise £70,000 for humanitarian and food relief, but surpassed all expectations and by 1989 sold 11.7 million copies, taking in £8 million.

Not to be outdone by the blokes across the pond, singer/actor/activist Harry Belafonte enlisted Lionel Richie, Michael Jackson, and Quincy Jones to come up with a song featuring a diverse group of America's top artists. The group, United Support of Artists for Africa, or USA for Africa, would go on to sell 20 million copies, win three Grammys, and raise $63 million ($141 million in today's money). "We Are the World" debuted in March 1985. Soon, the entire world would be singing *We are the world / We are the children / We are the ones who make a brighter day, so let's start giving.*

The stage was set. Pop culture was going to do the work that policy and Mother Nature could not. The sweet voice of Michael Jackson was supposed to raise the social consciousness and end world hunger. People cared for a minute, but the popularity of the song overshadowed the real issue. The song took on new meaning, and soon every graduating class from pre-K to postgraduate sang it as a sign of hope for their own personal future. Americans are the best at making everything about us. We turned a song about compassion and helping others into a narcissistic theme song. It was perhaps the worst game of telephone.

"There's a big famine happening in Africa. We've got to do something."

"There's a big festival happening in Attica. We've got to shoot something."

"There's a Big Mac at McDonald's. We've got to supersize it."

Only in America would people eat more because they've heard about someone else starving. It's as if we were voodoo dolls and our consumption made it into the bellies of Ethiopians. The fight to end world hunger translated into: "Eat your food. There are starving kids in Africa."

———

The most the famine in Ethiopia got out of Grandma was "My God. That's a crying shame," and she'd turn her head away from the TV newscast of gaunt brown faces and back to her pots. Dinner prep started at 5:00 p.m. and she'd have everything piping hot for my grandfather when he came home from work an hour later. Sunday dinners were even more elaborate. She'd start cooking in the morning before heading to church. A table was erected just to hold her pies and cakes. Industrial rolls of aluminum foil were there so you could take a plate home, and nap spots were assigned for when the "itis" hit. (That's postprandial somnolence, for all you squares.)

God bless my grandmother. What she didn't realize was her attempt at teaching me compassion only taught me how to overeat. My little belly expanded with every extra bite. To add insult to injury, I wasn't allowed to burn off the extra calories. My grandmother wasn't doing Jazzercise or taking me to the park so I could play while she power walked.

"Don't run in this house! You ain't gonna be tearing up my good furniture." *Lady, I'm hyped up on sweet tea and pot roast. For the love of God, let me skip.*

Her idea of fun was watching you eat her food. Then once you left, she'd tell everyone, "That child eats way too much! She's gonna be big as a house." I developed a habit of eating everything on my plate and sitting down somewhere. I attribute those days of being quiet and still to the reason I have laser focus. There were no stimulants around, just gospel music, gossip, and silence. Grandma would enlist me in her meal prep. I got really good at snapping green beans and shelling peas. We'd sit in the backyard and assess whatever random produce or meat relatives and neighbors dropped off. This may have been Bed-Stuy, Brooklyn, but it felt like every part of the sharecropping farm Grandma lived on. Mr. Johnson would come by with the fresh fish he caught in the wee hours of the morning off the Long Island Sound. Mr. Thompson would drop off a peck basket of cow peas his cousin brought up from their farm in Virginia. Cousin Jimbo delivered a hunk of deer meat he shot last winter. "It was just sitting in my freezer. Aunt Dot, I figured you could do something with it." She always did.

Like most women from the South, she considered herself to be the best cook in the world. When I was with her, I wasn't allowed fast food. According to her, she made better burgers than McDonald's, better chicken than KFC, and better fried rice than the "Chinese man." Dorothy is not a humble woman. She did buy me pizza because that was the one thing she couldn't make at home. On the other hand, deer meat was easy. She'd slice it into cutlets. We'd line the table with newspaper and wax paper. I'd run to the drawer and bring back her meat pounder. We'd roll up our sleeves and take turns beating the wilderness out of that deer. Bambi who? Next came the flour and cast-iron skillet. Country-fried deer meat, cow peas, and Uncle Ben's rice was on the menu. I remember going home and bragging to my mom about manhandling deer. I don't know what Mom said when she talked to Grandma that night, but there was no more deer meat for me.

I've never gone a day without food. There've been times I didn't feel like eating, or later on as an adult I was too broke to buy something, but there was always a can of something, a cup of pasta, or a bowl of cereal I could scrape up. Even when I'd tried the cayenne pepper cleanse, I'd break down and cheat. My mind can't let me go without food. *Girl, you have things to do tomorrow; you need your energy. Just go to the corner store and get you a hero sandwich. You're a grown-ass woman. Treat yourself.*

The concept of starvation is foreign to America. Sure, we learn about the Great Depression, with its soup kitchens and bread lines, but people didn't die because they didn't have food. They jumped out windows after losing their life savings. We have so little empathy for those suffering that I remember seeing those Sally Struthers commercials asking us to sponsor a child, and thinking, "Well, why didn't the camera guys give them some food?" Sally would be walking around some shantytown, thicker than a Snickers. Sis couldn't toss them food from her trailer? We lack empathy because we don't realize that America has its own problem with feeding its people, and not because of lack of food, either. Due to poverty, one in eight adults and one in six children face hunger. In total, that's an estimated 42 million Americans. This from a country that's home to the value meal and the highest rate of adult obesity in the world.

If ever Americans' rib cages started to show, which country would record a song for us? Which celebrities will harmonize these heartfelt lyrics?

They thought they had it all.
Then their country began to fall.
They didn't believe the ozone was depleting.
Their carbon footprint really soared.
Now they're really hungry. They're not starving just yet.
But they're down to Doritos and Twinkies
And still refuse to eat kale.

Of course I'm not wishing for famine, but the way this country values or devalues food needs to change. There's probably a mother sitting in a displacement camp with her kids as they share a portion-controlled meal, warning them about us. "Okay, kids, don't eat too much. There's a fat kid in America stuffing their face right now. They're overcome with greed. So here, slowly chew each grain and think about those tubs of lard."

Revisiting the Ethiopian Famine, I understand that their crisis came down to issues America is now facing—global warming, government mismanagement, and civil unrest. Famine is the result of a perfect storm, yet this country's arrogance leaves us to believe we are immune. We're just a drought, flood, stolen election, misappropriated funds, and AR-15–fueled war away from fighting over bags of rice and Funyuns.

3

LET THEM EAT KETCHUP

There's a common belief among black people that the government is trying to poison our food via chemicals that can cause cancer or make us sterile. This paranoia doesn't seem without merit once you begin to pull back the layers on the food industry and all the corners they are allowed to cut in order to increase their bottom line. Poisoning us isn't the goal, but it's definitely an ignored side effect. Yes, I know I sound like a Hotep; however, you have to understand that my caution stems from President Ronald Reagan once again interfering with my childhood for his own shits and greedy giggles.

Each school year, parents provided their income, and based on that, kids received free, reduced, or paid full price for lunch. My mom worked part-time at a luxury department store. From kindergarten to fourth grade, my dad was "Upstate." In the Polaroid pictures he'd send home he was wearing a uniform, so I thought he was working in a factory. Our weekly phone calls weren't complete until I asked, "Daddy, when are you coming home from work?" With him gone, the family's financial situation was tight. We were on welfare, which automatically qualified me for free lunch. At school I was in the majority. It really wasn't something to be ashamed of, but like I said, kids are like sharks sniffing for blood in the ocean.

I *thought* my family was middle class. Once Mrs. Hirsch taught us about upper, middle, and lower class, us third graders became obsessed with proclaiming our statuses. There are few things more intense than elementary school kids coming to verbal blows about a topic they don't fully grasp. "Nuh-huh" and "So!" were tossed into the air like daggers. For a solid week the lunch table conversation was dominated by us trying to count our parents' money. There was no way I was going to let my classmates call me poor, so I declared and made a solid case for my family being "upper lower class." I always had a way of putting words together.

"Nun-uh, I'm not lower class," I said. "My mom *and* dad work. I'm upper lower class." Somehow that "upper" made a world of difference to me.

"Fine, you upper lower class, but your sneakers still ugly." Sandy was my harshest critic. "I'm middle class 'cause my dad gets a new car every year." If only I knew what a lease was, I could have demolished her brag.

"How you middle class when you get free lunch?" An astute observation from William. His parents were, by black standards, well-off. They summered in Martha's Vineyard. His dad wore loafers with no socks. We trusted what he had to say about wealth and status.

"So!" Sandy replied.

"If your parents don't have money, you get free lunch."

"Ooooh!" The kids at the table turned into a chorus.

I never considered us to be poor. I often heard "no" when I asked for things, but my mom made sure birthdays and Christmases were pleasant. Since I was born three days after Jesus, I usually got one big present for both. I never went to bed hungry unless I was boycotting the menu. My clothes didn't have holes in them until I tried to rip the knees like everyone else was doing. My mother wasn't having none of that. She promptly sewed them back together by hand.

"I don't care what the other kids are doing. No child of mine is walking around with tears in their clothes." Also, we didn't stink. I'm not saying all poor people have an odor, but there was definitely an aroma that was associated with not having the ability to wash your clothes properly. I knew poor kids. I would beg my mom to adopt them so I could finally get bunk beds in my room. I wanted a sibling so bad I was willing to share my toys. Hunny, I had name-brand toys. Further proof that I wasn't poor. My favorite was a black, bald-headed Cabbage Patch Doll my dad bought before going away. I named her Willie Mays, after the Hall of Fame baseball player.

———

In 1981 Reagan's Omnibus Budget Reconciliation Act slashed the public school food budget by 25 percent. Just the year before, in his last year in office, President Carter reduced spending by 8 percent in a cost-saving measure that focused mostly on cutting monies given to the food and beverage industry via grants and contracts. Reagan's amendment targeted schools, parents, and kids. His $1.46 billion in cuts doubled the price of reduced lunch to $.40 a meal and full price to an estimated national average of $1.30. It may not seem like a lot even with inflation, but to more than half of the 26 million kids who paid for lunch, it was enough to make their parents start packing lunch or force kids to skip the meal altogether. The thought of American kids going to school hungry shouldn't sound too foreign to you. Yes, we are a first-world country, but 1 in 5—that's 16 million—kids lack enough food.

School lunch shaming, as it's referred to, has scarred kids across the country by subjecting them to dehumanizing treatment, all because their parents couldn't afford to pay. Documented tactics include:

* Getting "I Need Lunch Money" stamped on their arm.

* Hot food being confiscated and thrown out so the student in debt couldn't have it.

* Wristbands that labeled the kid's outstanding payment.

* Children being forced to clean cafeteria tables during their lunch period in exchange for their meal.

* A cold cheese sandwich instead of a regular hot lunch.

A few years ago, I remember coming across the story of a lunch worker who was fired for giving cheese sandwiches to hungry kids at her school who couldn't afford lunch. After media coverage and over

100,000 signatures demanding she get her job back, the Idaho school district was guilted into taking her back.

I don't remember the lunch ladies I came across being that caring. Maybe they were to some of my smaller-framed classmates, but if I tried that "Please, ma'am, may I have some more" Oliver Twist shit with them, they would have looked at my double chin and shooed me away. They were a group of Southern black women you didn't mess with. Not a single smile in the kitchen. Their white uniforms—button-down dress, apron, corrective shoes, and hair nets—were crisp and unstained even as they slang candied carrots and spaghetti on our trays. You could've easily mistaken them for church ushers on Communion Sunday, marching for the Lord.

———

Pizza day was the best day in elementary school. Word would spread. The boys would race to the front of the lunch line. Our aggressive happiness didn't faze the women behind the counter. On normal days, we'd slide our trays down and pick out what we wanted. But pizza day was different. Everyone wanted pizza. We even made sure to say, "Thank you, Lunch Lady!" on pizza day. That cement block of dough, two Basquiat paint brushes of tomato paste and cheese that never fully melted. It just stared at you: "You're gonna get sick when you're fifty 'cause this is not real cheese." According to President Reagan, pizza was a balanced meal featuring three of the five basic food groups: carbs, dairy, and vegetables. That's right, President Reagan tried to reclassify ketchup as a vegetable in his plan to cut school lunch spending. Thankfully, he received so much pushback, they abandoned the idea.

The second-best days in elementary school were school trips. I would dust off my *Sesame Street* lunch box made from real metal with characters imprinted on the sides. One swift swing and I could jack someone up. After kindergarten, my lunch box came out only for special appearances. Lots of planning and begging went into what was going inside of it.

"Mommy, I want a peanut butter–and–apple-jelly sandwich for my trip lunch. Can you cut it in a triangle and cut the crusts off?" I had seen the new girl in my class eat her sandwiches like that and I became obsessed. That's the one thing about being an only child, you're constantly watching other kids to see what is on trend. This week was triangle sandwiches. The week before, painting my nails with magic marker. The following week, side ponytails. I was a sponge.

At the start of fourth grade a miracle happened; well, two. We got our first black teacher, Mrs. Stewart, and two new girls joined the class. I had been with the exact same group of gifted and talented kids since kindergarten. Every September, I would come in the first day of school, confident that the summer had cured whatever made the majority of the kids in class dislike me so much. By the week's end they'd go right back to snapping on my clothes, hair, height, weight. At the risk of sounding like I have Stockholm syndrome, not all the kids were my tormentors. There was a core group of popular girls whose only joy came from making me miserable. Then there were the followers. Whoever wanted to cozy up to the popular girls would pick up their beef with me to solidify their allegiance.

But with Shelly and Alexandra joining the class, I thought I'd have a chance to make new friends, unsullied by the others' history with me.

Shelly was taller than me, stealing my spot at the end of the size order class line and I couldn't have been happier. One day during lunch, she did the unimaginable. She sat next to me, on purpose.

"Shelly, eww, don't sit next to Chloé!" the ringleader of the popular girls yelled across the lunch table. I looked down at my tray, trying my best to shrink.

"You're not my boss," Shelly responded.

You could hear a pin drop. Even I didn't believe she knew what she was saying. I almost felt compelled to explain to Shelly what she was risking by standing up to the popular girls. Shelly was the epitome of "unbothered" before it became a trend. Her dad was a jazz musician, which is what I attribute her coolness to. Shelly was the first to invite me to a sleepover. Thirty years later, she and I are still dear friends.

Alexandra was unlike any black girl I'd come across. She smelled like shea butter and wore pigtails and dresses damn near every day. She didn't eat school lunch. Her parents were well-off. They ate organic and shopped at a food co-op in Park Slope where you brought your own bags, decades before it became common practice. By the time we got back from collecting our unsavory chow from the lunch line, she was already a third into her lunch. She would open her lunch bag and lay everything out in front of her like a blackjack dealer. Box juice, fruit, pretzels, sandwich cut in triangles, of course, and a look of contentment that gave my tray of canned green beans and nuggets the appeal of dog food. Seeing Alexandra enjoy her lunch made me realize TV moms yelling to their kids, "Don't forget your lunch!" as they rushed to catch the school bus was a real thing.

Continuing my "I'm not poor" campaign, I begged Mom to start sending me to school with fancy packed lunches. "Alexandra's mom makes her lunch." Alexandra was my latest inspiration. "Don't you love me?" My mother loved me, all right. She loved me so much that she decided her pudgy daughter needed a jump start in the weight-loss department. My days of sitting on the sidelines while my peers ran timed miles were numbered. Mom handed me a can wrapped in foil.

"Drink this for lunch."

"What is it?"

"A milkshake."

"Where's the rest of my lunch?"

"That's it."

I may have been nine, but I wasn't a dummy. Something about this didn't feel right. I peeled the foil, revealing a huge "S."

"Mom, this is SLIMFAST!"

"So what, you're drinking it!"

I was so disappointed in my mother; not only was she ignoring my request for better food to take to school but she also was insulting my intelligence by not thinking that I, queen couch potato, wouldn't recognize the weight-loss shake. SlimFast commercials were on all the time. I still know the original slogan: "Give us a week, we'll take off the weight." All I wanted was a turkey sandwich and some chips in my lunch box, instead Mom handed me a hand grenade that was sure to blow up in my face once the kids saw it.

Sold in vanilla, chocolate, and strawberry, the canned milky concoction was supposed to replace two meals a day. It was at the forefront of a shit ton of new "get slim quick" products that flooded the late-eighties' market right alongside the oat bran boom and weight-loss clinics. Oh, Mom and I had a huge blowup that and every morning thereafter when she'd hand me that awful shake. When I'd yell, "I hate you!" I really meant it. Dad, who recently returned home from being "Upstate" for four years, played referee. Our morning shouting matches didn't make for a great welcome back home. Time out on the yard made him a stellar mediator. He'd had plans of being a lawyer before his life took a turn. Since I was Daddy's little girl, he sided with me, becoming defense attorney to Mom's vicious prosecutor. He'd shuffle into the kitchen while tying his tie and stand between us.

"The girl doesn't want the shake." His observation was keen. "Why are you forcing it?"

"Either she takes this shake or she'll get nothing."

"Chloé, please take the shake to school." At a certain point his marriage had to come before his child. "Do it for me, please." That "do it for me" was the difference between him heading to work in peace or having to battle my mom for the rest of the day over his disloyalty to their united parental front.

I was happy that my dad had my back. I was also angry with him because it was his genes that did this to me. I inherited his "slow metabolism," and everything I was going through he'd been through it as a chubby kid growing up in Indiana. He'd crack jokes trying to lighten the mood, but I was angry and hungry. And when I wasn't angry, I was melancholy. I didn't know what the word meant until much later, but it was clearly the reason I was emotionally connected to the cartoon character Charlie Brown. Winnie the Pooh's Eeyore was a close second on my list of animated icons. It was hard for a kid to explain their complex feelings about their weight issues, especially in the eighties, long before anyone gave a rat's ass about children having feelings. Kids were viewed as empty vessels created to store their parents' made-up philosophies on life. That meant I had to go to school with a can of SlimFast in my bookbag, which felt like a brick. If I jumped in the Hudson, I'd surely sink to the bottom.

Adding insult to injury, by the time lunch came, my shake was room temperature. I'd take a seat next to Alexandra. She and I were bonding over our "homemade" lunches. She'd pull out each item from her bag, I'd peel back the foil from the top of my can, careful not to remove it from the sides. My sips were small, to prolong my consumption of 190 calories. Alexandra was too into her organic tuna fish sandwich and plum to look over at my meal. The other kids would return with their trays of President Reagan's cosmic slop, and in between bites of their pizza and burger wondered out loud what I was drinking.

"It's a milkshake," I lied. I was a terrible liar. My mother was a born-again Christian, we went to church every Sunday, and the only reason I was allowed to wear pants instead of a skirt like all the other Pentecostal girls was because my thighs chafed. My lie worked for maybe a week. The idea of the fat girl in class being sent to school with a milkshake sparked everyone's interest. Kids who never talked to me now wanted to sit next to me at lunch.

"Why is it covered in foil?" they asked.

"To keep it cold," I replied.

"Why is it in a can?"

"So it doesn't spill in my bookbag."

"How does your mom get it in a can?"

I had no more answers left, plus by the time the interrogation heated up I'd excuse myself to go toss my can/evidence and rejoin my classmates as they ate their newly approved servings of protein, veggies, and dairy. Translation: A soy-laced burger with cheese and ketchup.

Those SlimFast days were some of my darkest. Exhausted, famished, and mercilessly bullied, I'd come home to an empty house and contemplate ending it all. First step was consulting the encyclopedia to look up suicide. I had a hard time finding it since I was only nine and sounded it out as "*S-e-w* . . ." On TV, people always stuff their mouth with pills. My medicine options were Tylenol and Flintstone vitamins. I went with the latter for taste, of course, but you can't swallow a Flintstone pill, you have to chew them. I stood in the bathroom mirror, crunching on several. *God, I hope this calcium stops my heart.* Before I could finish, my guardian angel whispered in my ear, "No, Chloé, don't do it. Tomorrow is pizza day!"

Yes, thank you, pizza day. I'm going to live.

That wasn't the last time I thought about ending it. Another time, my dark thoughts were cut short when I remembered there was Häagen-Dazs in the freezer. Food has literally saved my life.

Childhood obesity rates rose under President Reagan and exploded by 1994, with nearly 20 percent of kids ages 6–19 classifying as overweight. Reagan's budget cuts decreased the portion size of meals and allowed for a massive drop in the quality. In order to come under the new budget, food suppliers were allowed to add fillers to food, such as soy, yogurt, high fructose corn syrup, and reduce whole grains and vitamins. Flavored drinks full of sugar were offered, and the big dairy industry won contracts to get milk cartons handed out with every meal. Sugar, fat, and salt dominated school-meal offerings.

It would be years before we'd learn about the negative impact excessive soy products had on us. I was one of the last in my group to get my period at twelve. Some started theirs as early as nine. To date, several of my girlfriends have had severe fibroids that needed to be surgically removed. Men, don't think you're not affected. If you're a child of the eighties or later and wonder why your manly chest is more of an A or B cup, chances are those fun bags are a result of President Reagan rolling back food restrictions. Soy protein carries genistein and daidzein, which have been scientifically proven to be responsible for elevated levels of estrogen in men if consumed in large quantities. That school cheeseburger sadly came with an option of man boobies. For the record, I'm no scientist, but this theory feels right. This, my friends, is how you blame "The Man."

President Obama attempted to undo the damage, signing the Healthy, Hunger-Free Kids Act of 2010, which included mandates on the minimum of fruit, vegetables, and whole grain servings as well as a max on sodium, sugar, and fat percentages. Not surprisingly, his successor has undone every measure in order to appease business shareholders, confirming that kids are just helpless pawns set on a path that leads to a life of meds and elastic-waistband pants. My personal takeaway from all this is: Don't have kids unless you can afford to send them to school with a tasty and poison-free lunch. Shake not included.

4

CHAMPIONS TRAIN; LOSERS COMPLAIN

In the summer of 1990, my mother enrolled me at a camp that offered only physical activities. It wasn't a "fat camp," but the choice of curriculum did feel suspicious. I'm sure the reason for the curriculum, or lack thereof, was due to the fact that the counselors were 19–24 years old and could only instruct us on how to play basketball, handball, hip-hop, dance, and so on. I decided I wanted to take on modern dance and tennis. My parents loved tennis and kept talking about these two girls: the Williams sisters. They were the epitome of Black Girl Magic before we even knew what that was. Since the girls were my age, I figured I could learn to play tennis too. Forget genetics, practice, skill, endurance, and dedication. I had my dad's old tennis racket and lots of naïveté. This had to be part of my destiny—why else would God make me so big and tall? This was his plan, to let the Williams sisters kick down the door, so I could walk through it. We three would showcase our Black Girl Magic to the world.

Magic mag·ic ['majik] (noun):
the power of apparently influencing the course of events by
using mysterious or supernatural forces.

Black Girl Magic. I wish I had had this phrase growing up so I knew how magical I was instead of trying to deny my poise, beauty, intuition, problem-solving, and strength. Some of these gifts are inherent, but most were the by-product of being a double minority. Left to our own devices, black women, often invisible, are forced to come to terms with who we are. That freedom and understanding of self leads to the creation of extraordinary things. Remember, not all coal produces diamonds. Just the ones who receive the most pressure.

———

Every August, New York City is covered with images of the goddess Serena Williams. Weeks leading up to the U.S. Open, massive billboards, buses, subway cars, and cabs are plastered with the face and body of the greatest tennis player, male or female, in the history of the sport. Disagree? Who else could give birth, almost die, return in less than a year, and—let's not forget—play in those loud, hard-ass beads? No wonder she's mastered having thick skin, her neck was being tenderized every time she stepped on court.

Serena Williams is the poster child of a "Strong Black Woman." That was our go-to slogan for centuries, but then all the black women in America got together for a sip and paint and decided it was time to update the brand to something just as powerful yet metaphysical, hence "Black Girl Magic." Those who don't possess it try to undermine it when they secretly wish they had it for themselves. They tell us our hair is ugly, our lips big, our butts offensive—killing our joy; and once they see the glimmer of hope leave our eyes, they go out and get all the things they trashed us for having.

If you are sensitive about the term "Black Girl Magic" and want to ride in on your "why not all women" pale horse, let me explain something. Throughout American history, black women have been stripped of dignity, freedom, education, and wealth. We turned to mantras, affirmations, and prayers to cope with whatever bullshit has been thrown at us from everyone else. Oppression can be debilitating, its physical and psychological effects passed down to children in the womb. The American Psychiatric Association even began linking PTSD to victims of racism. Black women deal with a lot, and you don't see us shooting up a mall. So yeah, excuse the fuck out of us if we turn to our inner magic.

There are two types of people in this world: Those who have praise showered upon them and those who have to praise themselves. Philosophies like "Strong Black Woman" or "Black Girl Magic" do a lot for women like me. I found myself wondering, *Why don't white women tell themselves they are strong?* Perhaps because doing so would undermine the white patriarchy that has successfully convinced them that Jesus wants them to submit to their husbands, the government should control their reproductive rights, and if they were sexually victimized it was most likely their fault?

My white ally, Everly, listened to my theory but noticed a glaring flaw. "Let me throw you a curveball here. Why the hell would they even need to THINK about being 'strong' when the entire system is designed to support them, from white male patriarchy to being considered respected members of society? A white woman doesn't have to do the same deep-digging to find confidence and strength because the messages in society encourage her more than they cut her down. When they speak about leaning in, they're talking about her." Thank God for white allies.

White women didn't need to stop calling themselves "princesses" and start saying and believing they were "'Strong Women" because they'd rather be saved and coveted than held accountable for themselves. What I saw as weakness they saw as their means of survival, far removed from the front lines of battle. The princess paradigm demands that the woman—actually girls, if you've ever watched a Disney film where the princesses are usually less than ten ovulation cycles into womanhood—be abducted, poisoned, cursed, or betrothed for political power in order to be saved by a Prince Charming–type. A knight in shining armor who saved the day with a kiss.

Black women long ago abandoned the thought of Prince Charming coming to save us. Even Disney's only black princess, Tiana, spent the entire movie trying to help a frog get his life back together. Sounds just like a Strong Black Woman. *Frozen*'s Elsa could be considered a strong white woman. Of course they portrayed her as a single ice queen who lacked social skills. Subliminal message received: No one wants a strong white woman. Hope that symbolism wasn't too deep for ya.

Black women yell, tweet, or post various versions of "I'm a Strong Black Woman who don't need a man!" every day. Whether it's to be a mantra or a coping mechanism, the cause for it is complex. During slavery, men and women worked side by side and faced the same brutal punishments. Couples weren't allowed to legally marry and any semblance of a relationship between the two had to be agreed upon by their owner or owners if the couple lived on different plantations. Owners often broke up couples by selling the "husband" off and keeping the woman, who was considered more valuable since the children she bore became the owner's property. Jim Crow led to the reported lynching of 3,959 blacks in America, most of them black men. After segregation, mass incarceration swept millions more into the prison system. All of this stripped black knights of their shining armor. Want to make a person lose hope? Kill their hero.

———

By 1990, Serena and older sister Venus had become sports media's latest discovery. Their brash and unapologetic father boasted that his Compton born-and-raised daughters, who practiced on public courts, were going to dominate the lily-white sport. My mother called me into the living room to watch a news report about the Williams sisters, and instantly I wanted to play tennis. Well, maybe not instantly. I was jealous at first. I'm the same age as Venus. Here she was getting all this attention and I barely went outside. Ironically, for a lazy kid I was secretly competitive. I'd hyped myself up that if Venus and her little sister could do it, so could I. My father dug out an old-school Wilson tennis racket from his college days and gave it to me. "When I see you are serious," he said, "I'll buy you a new one."

Other than being tall, nothing about me read as athletic. I'd never shown any interest in sports. One summer, my dad signed me up for a softball team. We arrived late, so the only position left was in the far outfield. I had my mitt on the wrong hand for most of the game. Hot and bored, my softball career lasted one day. My parents got me to try new things with the skillful omission of details. "Come on, Chloé, we're going for a car ride." We'd pull up to a ballet class, skating rink, soccer field. If I was unenthusiastic by the end of it, we never went back. It was a double-edged sword. Had my parents pushed me a little, I would have learned to push myself instead of being complacent. On the flip side, if my parents pushed me too hard, I would have resented them. Then again, who cares about resentment when you've got millions in the bank?

Another year, another physical activity–focused summer camp. This time my mornings were spent in a modern/hip-hop dance class taught by Rosa, the most beautiful Latina woman I'd ever seen. She had a dancer's body, wore her hair in a slicked-back low ponytail like Sade, and had the patience of a saint. I was always in the last line of the chorus. We danced in whatever clothes we wore to camp and would take our shoes off to help us slide across the dusty classroom floor easier. In my mind, I was doing an admirable job. In reality, I had little coordination and was too uptight to let my body loose. I was always conscious about taking up too much space, intruding on those around me who made it clear I was already an imposing figure.

The only reason I was excited to take dance was because I was told it would help with my movement on the tennis court. I needed to be flexible if I was going to slide and zip while hitting the hell out of an 80 mph serve. Truthfully, I wasn't concerned with emulating the Williams sisters' backhand. Foolishly, my short-lived tennis infatuation was fueled by fashion. What I wouldn't give to prance around in a skirt that ended well above my knee, my thighs not touching, panty shorts to keep my modesty if a gust of wind were to tickle the pleats upward. I didn't own any dress or shirt that wasn't church appropriate. Since I was growing like a weed, I started wearing some of my mother's clothes, mostly around the house. My mother worked in a luxury department store and was a low-level shopaholic. While she was at work, I would dig deep into her walk-in closet and try on outfits, some with tags still on them. I discovered one black skirt that was the closest thing to a tennis skirt I could get my hands on. There was no way my parents were going to buy me clothes for this new fad. This little black skirt was cotton, had a high waist that flared out into the skirt that moved freely as you walked. I'd stand in the mirror and turn from side to side and admire the skirt as it followed my movement with a three-second delay. I felt pretty. However, when your motivation is faulty, there's no way you're going to succeed. For six weeks I struggled through morning choreography, scarfed down a camp-provided white bread sandwich with mystery meat for lunch, then hit the indoor basketball court with a tennis net erected at half-court for three hours of tennis.

There were about twenty kids in the tennis group. The other half were right next to us playing basketball, and from their cheers and smiling faces they were having way more fun. We tennis amateurs convinced ourselves we were the more intelligent group. Tennis is for the refined and dignified. We'd need to start cutting the crust off our Wonder Bread sandwiches and start holding our pinkies up when we drank from the water fountain. Surely anyone could bounce a ball and get it in a hoop. Tennis demanded more. For once, I, the bottom of the totem pole, had someone to look down on. That arrogance left the first time I was called up to serve. We all have a play-by-play in our mind of how we'd execute a physical feat. Even now, I swear I can do some of the fighting choreography from *John Wick*. It's that little voice in our dumb heads that says, "That's easy. No sweat." It's the reason people talk about their sports team and use "we," because in their minds they believe that if given the chance they too could dunk, hit the winning homer, or run for fifty yards with five giants on their heels.

As my foot lined up parallel to the baseline, the motions were fluid in my mind. I saw myself tossing the ball right above my head, so high it'd hit the rafters. Then in slow motion, in a dramatic way, not 'cause I was overweight, I'd elevate feet, not mere inches, off the basketball court and the force from my racket would make the tennis ball combust on impact. That's what I saw in my mind. Well, my mind and my body were on two separate pages in two separate books. I did grunt, but that was because my racket missed the entire ball and all that force with nothing to transfer my energy to led to my first experience with "pulling something." I was ten. My toes never left the floor.

Traveling with my racket was always fun. Adults saw my racket, peeped my height, and would compliment me as if I were a real Williams sister. They had more hope in me than I had in myself. I looked the part, and their adoration was much appreciated. It's funny, because anytime a kid was seen walking around with any sports equipment, the entire hood would raise them up. The church ladies said a prayer, the drug dealers asked if they wanted some money for sneakers. Being athletic was one's Willy Wonka ticket out of the hood. Here I was, close to five nine, carrying a tennis racket. They thought I had made it. On this day, my smile was hiding my pain. It took forever for me to limp my ass home, only to wait hours for my parents to come home from work and draw me a bath with Epsom salt. Dad rubbed me down with Tiger Balm, and my mom wrapped my aches in an ACE bandage.

This dedication thing was hard. I had never committed to anything before in my life. Sure, I was good at things like writing, public speaking, and drawing, but those things came naturally. I didn't have to practice them. When I set my sights on tennis, I just wanted to be good at something, without putting in the work. I hadn't even watched a full Williams sister match. What the hell was "30–LOVE"? Even my parents couldn't really explain the game to me, but they watched every serve, volley, and fault because there was a black person on the court. Growing up, if a black person made it to the mainstream, they had our unwavering support even if we didn't understand what they did. We'd blindly defend their honor, that is until O. J. Simpson ended all that in 1995. Oh, the D.C. Sniper goes on that list too. Even then, not gonna lie, my friends and I were low-key impressed that black men were serial killers or shutting down a city, but there's no way you can root for a killer despite him making inroads in a white-male-dominated field.

An amateur sleuth, I wanted to learn more about other black tennis stars. The Williams sisters weren't the first. I hit up my *Encyclopaedia Britannica*, which my parents loved to say were mine and kept in my bedroom, but I don't recall asking for them. While their eyes followed the tennis ball across our TV screen, I was going cross-eyed trying to absorb as much info as I could on the Williams sisters' most notable predecessors: Althea Gibson and Arthur Ashe.

Althea Gibson—*American tennis player who dominated women's competition in the late 1950s. She was the first black player to win the French Open (1956), Wimbledon (1957–58), and U.S. Open (1957–58) singles championships.*

Arthur Robert Ashe Jr.—*American tennis player, the first black winner of Wimbledon (1975), the U.S. Open (1968), and the Australian Open (1970), the major men's singles championships.*

I memorized their bios from the encyclopedia. That didn't make me a better player, but it did help during Black History Month. My hand shot up first when our teacher asked who they were. They were pioneers whose accomplishments I respected even though I couldn't grasp what it meant for racial equality and civil rights in America. The Williams sisters spoke to me. They were from my generation. We could've been friends if they didn't live three thousand miles away. Full of disillusion, I felt in my heart that if I was skinny, I too would shoot to the top of the USTA rankings. I even begged my mom for beads in my hair as if that was the missing key. I wasn't realistic about my physical shortcomings. I never ran, outside of a short jog to catch the bus or train to school. Even then I'd get winded, stop to catch my breath, miss it, and have to wait for the next one. Then there was the training; the Williams sisters grew up in Compton and utilized free outdoor courts year-round. In New York, indoor tennis centers cost an arm and a leg and there wasn't a single free outdoor tennis court near me. Lots of basketball courts though.

By the end of summer 1990, I was no threat to Venus's and Serena's growing legacy. I sucked at tennis. I had no hop, no skip, no bounce. Amazingly, I did lose weight. My parents' gamble on frugal fat camp worked. It wasn't a brand-new wardrobe difference, but enough to not have eyes burning a hole in the back of my head if I wanted a second helping of dessert. My dream of returning to school looking like a completely different person was within reach. Queen Mother Oprah had done it when she walked out onstage in November 1988 with a wagon full of sixty-seven pounds of fat representing her massive weight lost from a liquid diet. I watched that episode like I watched most shows after school, on the edge of my parents' bed. Their bedroom was the farthest from the front door, giving me enough time to hear their keys and turn the TV off if they came home early. Didn't matter. All they did was touch the back of the TV to see if it was hot.

For twenty-five years, Oprah was the most successful black woman I saw on a daily basis. Every day at four o'clock, she'd greet me after a hard day and broaden my world.

"Chloé, what do you want to be when you grow up?"

"I want to be a mix of Martin Luther King, Oprah Winfrey, and Malcolm X."

That's a direct quote.

During her highest-rated episode of all time, Oprah walked on in a mink coat, then she swung it open and off her now-thin body. There was a huge mirror that hung across from my parents' bed. It led to a weird habit of watching TV, then turning my head to look at myself in the reflection. I'd even look to see how I looked laughing at what I was looking at on TV. When Oprah showed her size 10 success in 1988, I gazed at my seven-year-old self, hunched over, sitting cross-legged, and

imagined the day I would have the same reveal and how all my frenemies would applaud me. Didn't happen. And over the years, like
Oprah, I'd repeatedly gain all my lost weight back.

I didn't pick up my dad's racket again until years later when I
found it tucked away at the top of my closet. I saw my untapped po-
tential in its unraveling wires and tossed it in the trash. Finally, I could
admit I would never dominate on the court like the Williams sisters.
My magic would lie elsewhere.

5

FUCK KATHY IRELAND

Beauty standards in the 1980s were a mindfuck for a brown skin girl such as myself. I'd watch pop singer Robert Palmer on MTV release video after video of über-pale models who looked like lady assassins and wore candy apple–red lipstick and skintight dresses. Their indirect eye contact screamed "there's nothing going on upstairs." On the other side of the pop culture spectrum was the demand for her polar opposite, the wholesome girl next door who loved head-to-toe blue-jean outfits and fluffy bangs. One thing they had in common was their whiteness and lack of curves. Achieving their looks would always be out of my reach. How are you supposed to consider yourself beautiful—hell, cute even—when the ideal is the anti-you? I've had to ponder this at way too early of an age. It was bad enough I rarely received compliments. Mom didn't count. Dad was more honest, assuring me that I would grow into my looks like he did.

There was an abundance of encouragement in the classroom of my fourth-grade teacher, Mrs. Stewart. I knew I wasn't cute, but she confirmed that I was smart. She was my first black teacher and gave off a lot of mother energy, like Oprah. We performed well because we never wanted to disappoint her. Mrs. Stewart was tall, and although she was cool as a cucumber, her appearance was always frazzled. She'd lose a pencil behind her ear, have chalk streaks on her clothes where she'd accidently wipe her hands off. All of that made her more endearing to us.

Halfway through the school year, Mrs. Stewart moved our desks into pods, three pairs that faced each other and a seventh desk at the head. That person was considered the group leader or smartest kid in the group. Mrs. Stewart gave that kid the task of helping the rest. That was not my chair. I was the only girl in my group. Boys are more agreeable than girls, and all six of my male counterparts agreed I was invisible. They weren't mean or bullish, they just overlooked me, all the time. It was a sentiment I'd recognize much later in life when the #TimesUp movement sent shock waves across the country. It's not that some men purposely bulldoze women. They don't even consider that a woman is standing in front of them in the first place. They don't see us as an obstacle, threat, or partner. In the words of the great *Basketball Wives* reality-show star Evelyn Lozada, many men see women as a "non-muthafucking factor." Unless they want to sleep with you—then that aloofness switches to a laser focus.

Whether I spoke up in the group or not, I wasn't heard until another boy supported my voice. Thankfully, I sat next to Marcus, our team leader, who was the smartest of us smart kids and made everything look easy. He was cool, polite, and down-to-earth.

My role at the group's table was to pass things back and forth without being detected. G.I. Joes. Transformers. Baseball cards. Slime. Hot Wheels. Casio watches. Calculators with BOOB typed on it. I was a willing mule. Until one day, the package was larger than normal. The boys had rolled up a magazine so tight you'd think they were going to kill every fly in the building. This haul required a firm grip, which almost blew my cover. The trick to my being a mule was to never take my eyes off the board. I'd get a tap under the table and the next tap would be who I was to pass it to. Well, this day the taps never stopped. Jarrett wanted the package now and Timothy was taking too long. Pissed off, I took my eyes off the chalkboard and looked down. Unrolling the magazine, I see Kathy Ireland. Her hair is slicked-back with a Superman curl on her forehead, and she is rocking a neon-yellow bikini while sitting in the perfect "I'm taking a dump" position. I flip through the inside and see breasts. Naked white breasts. These fools were getting their elementary porn on with the *Sports Illustrated* Swimsuit Issue.

As I shook my head in disgust, Jarrett tried to grab the magazine from my hands. All hell broke loose. I hold on to the magazine with all the strength I have. I was bigger than all of them, so the tug-of-war ended with me pulling Jarrett clean off his chair. Ripping the magazine was my next logical move—Popeye had me thinking I could rip the entire magazine in half. But nope. I was strong but not that strong. My final resort was to rip the pages out one by one, tossing them in the air like confetti.

"STOP! What are you doing?" the boys yelled.

Mrs. Stewart and the entire class turned to me as I destroyed the glossy rag. I'd never been so enraged in all my young life. Calmly, Mrs. Stewart walked over and extended her hand to me. I handed her what was left.

"Mrs. Stewart, that's not even hers. She ruined it!" cried one of the prepubescent voyeurs.

"They're looking at NAKED WOMEN!" I yelled.

Let me start by saying, Kathy Ireland has never done anything to me. I respect her career as a model turned mogul. I'm sure she's a very loyal wife and caring mother. Bet her ambrosia fruit salad is to die for. My dislike of Kathy has everything to do with what she represents: all-American girl-next-door beauty. There wasn't a woman who looked like her living within one hundred doors of me. That church evangelist smile, those big doe eyes, and her wind-blown hair were not my idea of beauty. And let's be real, Kathy Ireland was, at best, slightly above average.

THE PLAIN-JANE PHENOMENON

American models of the 1980s projected the perfect blend of "I'm a good girl" with "I take it from the back." One day they're rocking a white T-shirt and jeans while sitting on a bale of hay, sipping a Coke, and in another they'd be spread eagle on a beach with seashells and rope covering their lady parts. Models Brooke Shields, Christie Brinkley, Carol Alt, and Kathy Ireland all straddled that fence. Women wanted to be their friends, and men wanted to marry them and cum on their breasts because they were too pure for facials. These wholesome epitomes of patriotic Caucasian perfection did nothing for the self-esteem of little girls of color. In my world, the standards of beauty were different.

Phylicia Rashad was beautiful. Jayne Kennedy was stunning. Jackée Harry was sexy. Yet I saw them only on the covers of *Jet* or *Ebony*. I'd interpreted it as black women are classy and should not be reduced to tits and ass. All the black women I encountered were big on respect. Why do you think Aretha sang about it for over fifty years? On the rare occasion that a black woman played the sexpot, it's because she had a plan to take down men, like Pam Grier in the 1970s cult classic *Coffy*. Grier's character is a nurse who goes undercover as a hooker to avenge her little sister's death. She used her intoxicating sex appeal to kill the people who killed her sister. Yet another example of the selfless way black women save the world from evil. What was missing was the woman in the middle. I longed to see a black woman who was pretty, nonthreatening but assertive, down-to-earth yet classy, but looked like she ate fried bologna and cheese grits.

I found great pleasure in ripping Kathy Ireland's face to shreds. I didn't know it then, but Kathy Ireland was just the latest "it" girl on a long list of society's favorite Madonnas. Dr. Sigmund Freud introduced the term "Madonna-whore complex," writing that in public, men wanted a sweet, attractive, respectful woman. In private they wanted a dangerous, sultry siren whose middle name was Bukakke. Women and their right to be loved, pleased, and protected all depended upon how they answered the question: Are you a Madonna/Virgin Mary or a whore? Hera or Aphrodite, Beyoncé or Rihanna?

In the 1980s, Americans wanted their household-name models to be just sexy enough so as to not make them feel dirty or embarrassed. However, Kathy and her fellow Madonnas were going to be pushed aside for a new model of woman. The supermodel. Naomi Campbell, Linda Evangelista, Claudia Schiffer, and Cindy Crawford were far from basic. Their chicness made women envious and men give up. They were ego killers and quite possibly feminist icons influencing culture in a way that allowed beautiful and confident women to be brash and bold. Linda E. was rumored to have said she doesn't wake up for less than $10,000 a day, and as a child, I felt that in my little free-lunch soul. I aspired to be that type of woman. I wanted to be a woman you thanked for coming and not the woman who thanked you.

While Naomi, Linda, Claudia, and Cindy were strutting every run-way around the globe and lip-syncing in George Michael's ground-breaking *Freedom! '90* music video, Ms. Kathy Ireland was selling Bud Light. Basic but not dumb, Kathy packed up her neon-yellow bikini and became a marketing-and-lifestyle mogul, amassing a $350 million fortune selling furniture, jewelry, clothes, and more targeting Middle America mothers and homemakers, a.k.a. all-American girls.

I shouldn't have ripped up that *Sports Illustrated*, but I didn't have the words that I do now. I was angry and hurt. Their infatuation with Kathy made me feel inferior, and I couldn't brush aside my feelings like I normally did, so I felt the need to stand up for the other black girls and women. These boys were surrounded and raised by strong black women and here they were worshipping Kathy damn Ireland. Not. On. My. Watch!

For the boys it was less about Kathy Ireland and more about seeing boobs and butts. It wouldn't have mattered if the woman on the cover was blue, purple, or black. Sadly, it took another seven years for *Sports Illustrated* to put a black woman on the cover, and eight for a black woman to have a solo cover. Both honors go to Tyra Banks.

BOLD-FACED BEAUTY LIES

People magazine's coveted "50 Most Beautiful People in the World" has had only four women of color on its cover since it began in 1990: Halle Berry (1993), Jennifer Lopez (2011), Beyoncé (2012), and Lupita Nyong'o (2014). How is it that only four out of twenty-eight "Most Beautiful of the World" covers featured people of color? The entire continent of Asia makes up nearly 60 percent of the world's population, yet not a single Middle Eastern, Indian, or Asian person has earned the top honor.

People selected Julia Roberts four times. Michelle Pfeiffer and Jennifer Aniston were each crowned twice. First of all, how are you named Most Beautiful more than once? You shouldn't be able to repeat unless you've got an entirely new face. Otherwise it's a one and done, sweetheart. You don't get to come back because you changed your Botox doctor and got a new makeup artist who knows how to contour. Think I'm exaggerating? Aniston's 2016 *People* cover story laid it on thick, calling her "one of the most gorgeous stars in Hollywood." The then-forty-seven-year-old worked out six hours a day, the byproduct of being called chubby in her younger years. The most honest part of the whole article was when she credited her "natural look" to her glam squad who taught her how to contour her round face. So *that's* where your face went, Jen?

I once got into a huge fight with MakeUp Twitter by questioning the irony of "Natural Glam." Ever noticed how we've replaced "Natural Beauty" with "Natural Look"? The former implies, like Lady Gaga, you were born that way. The latter means you've hired a team of fierce painters to optical illusion that face for the world to see.

Just like Kathy Ireland, I'm sure Jennifer Aniston is a nice woman. (Kathy makes the better ambrosia, hands down.) Jennifer is clearly adored. Remember when Brad left America's sweetheart for that dark magic harlot Angelina and the world offered Jennifer its bosom to cry on and sent fruit baskets to console her? You know how many women have been cheated on and left by their significant other? That doesn't mean I start lying and telling them they're the most beautiful woman in the word. I will buy her a round of drinks and fill out her new online dating profile for her. But that's it.

Harsh truth alert: The bar is pretty low for what is considered a beautiful white woman. Yeah, I said it. Watch this be the part of this book that gets cut and pasted and posted without context. Well, here is your context if you so choose to hear me out. White women are up on pedestals for their blond hair, many of whom dye it. (Hi, Marilyn Monroe.) Or their blue eyes and sharp pelvic bones that protrude where hips should be.

White women get to be plain Janes. Women of color have to be exotic in order to be celebrated. Dare I say if Lupita were born in Detroit and didn't speak three languages she probably wouldn't have been on the cover of *People*. Oh, and the fact she was honored the year she played a slave should not be overlooked. The more hardships a black actor/actress deals with in a film, the more revered they are by white award voters.

When Jennifer Lopez crossed over to the mainstream there was so much talk about her ass. Literally, her butt made headlines. She was a spicy Latina who played roles where she was everything but Latina. Remember her being Italian in *The Wedding Planner*? Ciao, bella. JLo's ethnicity was interesting but not overbearing. Plus, once she was engaged to Ben Affleck, that took her white stock up.

White Stock: When a person of color earns credibility and acceptance from America's majority. Often the higher the stock the more their ethnicity is overlooked.

White stock is the opposite of a hood pass.

Hood Pass: When an unproblematic white person is invited to visit the proverbial hood and its cultural activities. They maintain the status of a guest and should not try to change or insult those who control and operate the space.

As for my six classmates whose half chubbs prevented them from standing up in disgust over my Edward Scissorhands swiftness, I was angry that they would defend Kathy Ireland over me. We may have only been fourth graders, but we were living in Brooklyn during the height of hip-hop's Afrocentrism phase. A Tribe Called Quest, Queen Latifah, and Public Enemy were teaching us to love our blackness and African roots.

Folks were walking around with the Pan-African Flag, historically black college sweatshirts, and necklaces with Africa-shaped medallions. We celebrated in the streets when a newly freed Nelson Mandela waved to us through a rolled-down limousine window on Fulton Street. We chanted "Fight the Power" and "I'm Black and I'm Proud." Kathy Ireland was the antithesis of that, and the way those boys valued her made me feel bogus.

It's easy to be mad at folks' choices, but you also have to consider their options. If the country is telling you women like Kathy Ireland are beautiful and that's all you see, a malleable mind is going to start shooting off if/then conditionals.

If you are white, then you are visible.
If you are not white, then you are invisible.
If you are skinny, then you are valued.
If you are fat, then you are worthless.
If you are wholesome, then you are cherished.
If you are loose like a Sloppy Joe sandwich,
    then you are undesirable.

These guidelines would go on to dominate our beauty belief systems until social media opened the floodgates. Overnight, everyone became *someone*. Why wait to see what the latest trend is when you can make it with a selfie shot in your living room? No one needs to give you permission to show your cellulite. For the dozens of commenters who will call you fat, there will be thousands who will cheer you on and ask for more. Body positivity and diversity is now on full display, affirming people like me who needed to see it from day one.

FACE VALUE

Toni Morrison's *The Bluest Eye* tells the story of Pecola, an abused and abandoned black girl who wishes for blue eyes, believing her life would instantly become better. Pecola's fascination with blue eyes isn't fiction.

In 1939, African American psychologists and married couple Dr. Kenneth Clark and Mamie Clark conducted an experiment that asked black children to pick between a black doll and a white one. Most of the kids picked the white doll because they thought it was "nicer." The Clark Doll Experiment was useful in the 1954 Brown v. Board of Education ruling by persuading that "separate but equal" schools were actually not.

I never wanted to be Kathy Ireland. I never wanted to be white or blond or have blue eyes. There were a ton of beautiful women of color I knew and watched in the media who gave me the confidence to love the skin I was in. Mrs. Stewart solidified that, going to great lengths to teach us Black American and African Diaspora history. Seeing the triumphs that people who looked like me achieved for freedom, survival, and love, there was no way I would wish away my pigment and all that comes with it. Not gonna lie, there were times I wished I was lighter like my mom. But most days my daydreams revolved around me waking up skinny with thick pressed hair cascading down my back.

I could be diplomatic and say we're all beautiful in our own way. However, that's a lie. Some of the ugliest spirits I've encountered have come from some of the most beautiful people I've met. I kinda don't blame them. Why work on a personality when the world is too busy bowing down to you? It's the same thing with rich people. Who keeps giving them free shit? They have the money to pay for it!

There are also some very unattractive people in the world. Hopefully they have a sweet disposition; you know, the kind that comes with having to cultivate a personality because you can't coast on your face. I was too lazy to do that work. I got by being "shy," but really, I was an introvert, quietly assessing, absorbing, and judging the same people who were ignoring me. The thought of being the center of attention was exhausting. For one, I didn't have enough confidence needed to command people's attention. Second, I want folks around who liked me for me, not what I looked like. And for many years my strong conviction about "keeping it real" meant I didn't try at all when it came to my appearance. Hair was undone, no makeup, wrinkled shirts, run-over shoes. I refused to subject myself to the superficial games. However, sometimes you need to fix up and look sharp. Presentation is everything, especially when it comes to the things you can control about yourself. So what if your bone structure is janky, throw some highlighter on that bitch and find your angles. Don't ignore what God gave you because a long time ago someone declared what the epitome of beauty is. You know who never made the cover of *People*'s Most Beautiful? Kathy Ireland.

6

WATCH OUT FOR THE BIG GIRLS

Getting pushed out of P.S. 11 and the Caribbean dancehall music explosion of 1992 were two of the best things to happen to adolescent Chloé. I went from being the shunned giant, blamed for everything, to enrolling in a new school and finding a group of like-body girls to call my friends. It was a whole new world, filled with a majority of first-generation, American-born West Indian kids whose cultural norms regarding beauty and sexuality made this late bloomer blush.

Technically, P.S. 11 didn't expel me, but they made it clear that if I stayed I'd be removed from the Gifted and Talented program and mixed in with gen pop because they claimed that I spearheaded a race riot. This implied I had control or influence over my classmates, which I did not. I was targeted for one simple reason: I was the biggest kid in class. If I stomped my foot, they'd say I started an earthquake. If I tapped my neighbor, they'd say I hit them with a right hook/uppercut combo. If I bumped into someone, they'd say I tackled them to the ground. It was always my fault. I was the bigger kid, and big kids should take mercy on others even when they've been repeatedly poked.

Real quick, this is what happened. One of my teachers was a racist bitch who merely tolerated us because she was close to retirement age and NYC school pensions were amazing. She hated her life and us little, smart black kids who called her out on her problematic behavior. One day, two boys got into a physical fight in class. Highly unusual for us, but then again, when your teacher is filled with malevolence, that energy becomes infectious. To stop the boys, the teacher grabbed the yard stick and hit them on their heads. Their fight immediately stopped, and all twenty-eight of us turned to her and lost our minds.

With the civil rights sit-ins and boycotts history lessons we learned the year prior still fresh in our minds, we channeled our ancestors and staged a nonviolent demonstration that would've made them proud. We chanted "No Justice, No Peace." Then we went into singing Kwanzaa songs. So what if it was June, we needed lyrics that uplifted our blackness. In the end, they locked us in the room until we settled down. The next day, a black substitute teacher took over for the last days of school. Our teacher was put on paid leave, and I was thrown so far under the bus you could see tire marks across my forehead.

NEW SCHOOL, WHO DIS?

My mom and grandmother drove me all around Brooklyn in search of a new school with a gifted program. We pulled up to I.S. 383, also known as the Philippa Schuyler School for the Gifted and Talented in Bushwick, Brooklyn.

"Okay, Chloé, you have to go inside and take a test." That's how Mom informed me of most things. There was no days' notice. This tactic robbed me of my chance to panic and ask a million questions. "If you pass the test and get in, you get to wear a uniform." My mom knew how to win me over. Finally, people wouldn't be able to make fun of my clothes, because we'd all be wearing the same thing. Also, I'd get my dream of being Tootie in *The Facts of Life*. It wasn't an all-girls boarding school, but it took forty minutes to get to, so close enough. I hummed the theme song while completing the math, reading comprehension, and essay writing. Weeks later, I received my acceptance packet, and for the first time in years I was genuinely excited for the first day of school.

Philippa Schuyler was a biracial child prodigy and pianist born in 1931 to a black essayist father and a white journalist mother from a former slave-owning family. Her parents believed that interracial unions created extraordinary humans and would catapult society further. By the age of two, Philippa was reading and writing music. She toured the world numerous times performing to sold-out crowds. Her parents practiced unconventional techniques to enhance Philippa's genius, such as restricting her to a raw-food diet. "When we travel," Philippa's mother explained, "Philippa and I amaze waiters. You have to argue with most waiters before they will bring you raw meat. I guess it is rather unusual to see a little girl eating a raw steak." (Here I go being greedy: "Her parents let her eat a whole steak?")

Philippa's parents pushed her to excel, and her namesake school was no different. "To whom much was given, much is required." That motto was drilled into our heads. Every day we were told we were gifted, but under no circumstances were we allowed to coast. Schuyler had high standards, and all eight-hundred-plus of us had to exceed them.

Nadine and Alicia were my first friends at Schuyler; we went to the same church. Alicia knew Candice and Theresa from their elementary school, and we all clicked. With the exception of Nadine, we were BIG girls. Our uniform sweaters were large or extra-large and the backs of our skirts rose up a good two inches higher than the front due to our rumps. There was junk in our trunks. Nadine was average, but we made her look skinny.

We weren't the popular girls or the nerds. We were in the middle and we minded our business. Well, we minded our business as in, we weren't active parties to the junior high drama but we knew all the dirt.

"I heard Harmony is pregnant."

"How she gonna have a baby when she owes me two dollars?"

"Is that why she *stay* wearing hoodies now?"

"Yup! She better be glad we already took school pictures, 'cause they would charge her double for her and her baby."

The girls and I would exchange our latest gossip over french fries and chicken wings with extra ketchup. You know, vegetables are important. Since Schuyler's student body was bursting at the seams, seventh and eighth graders were allowed to leave the building and purchase lunch at a nearby hole-in-the-wall. Our main options were a Chinese restaurant with bulletproof glass, pizzeria with mean-mugging guidos, or Burger King. The Chinese spot had the best deal. Two chicken wings for a dollar. Wings and fries for $2.50. Wings with plain fried rice $2.50. Of course, I could have stayed behind and ate my free lunch in the cafeteria, but I wanted to be with my friends. If I didn't have money for lunch, they would always share. We knew how important food was to us.

My weight wasn't the main topic anymore. There were girls at Schuyler who had me beat by inches, in both height and weight. Folks still found something to pick on me about: I was a Yankee. Located in Bushwick, Schuyler's student body was predominately black and Hispanic. Under the black umbrella, the majority was West Indian.

"What are you?" was a question I was asked often.

I knew the answer they were looking for. "My dad is from Indiana and my mom is from Brooklyn," I'd explain. I always gave them time to try to register where Indiana was. "I'm as American as apple pie" became my go-to line. After three years of having this exchange with my schoolmates, I'd roll my eyes at their confusion and end the conversation with "I'm regular black." No further explanation was needed.

West Indians are not a monolith. Confuse a Trinidadian for a Jamaican and get ready to fight. I had to learn the different countries, dialects, and food in order to navigate my growing social circle. After a year, I came home speaking patois with two lines cut into my eyebrows. All that was missing was gold fronts and spray-painted gold finger waves to complete my transformation from Yankee to rude gal. Mom saw the vertical lines etched into my brow and ordered my father to shave them off. I went to school with eyebrows the size of Hitler's mustache. Mom didn't like my new taste in fashion or dancehall/reggae music, but I think deep down inside she was happy I was exploring my identity. Absent were those sorrowful conversations where I asked with tears in my eyes, "Mom, why am I so ugly?" The first and last time I was called fat at Schuyler, I was in the sixth grade in the schoolyard. A boy and I got into an exchange and he yelled, "Oh yeah"—every juvenile argument started like this—"that's why you're fat." I had no witty comeback. A group of older girls were nearby. One walked over to me and delivered this nugget of advice.

"So what, you're fat. Next time someone calls you that, tell 'em, 'It's more cushion for the pushin'.'"

Ladies and gentlemen, that was my realest and most inappropriate lesson on body acceptance. (For the record, a pre-teen should not have anyone pushing her cushions.)

THE GIRLS DEM SUGAR

Dancehall music gave me a crash course in sex education, specifically the correct attitude to have in order to attract the opposite sex. I became immersed in a culture that didn't care about your size as long as you pulled it off. Confidence outweighed weight. By 1993 artists such as Super Cat, Chaka Demus & Pliers, Patra, and Lady Saw began popping up on Video Music Box, our local version of MTV's TRL except it wasn't live, everyone was black, and all the interviews took place in various NYC nightclubs. In between videos of Run-DMC and Dr. Dre, I soaked in images of shantytowns, rude boys in net tank tops, and gals in poom-poom shorts (American translation: Daisy Dukes). Women wore elaborate hairstyles and plenty of gold jewelry while they whined, boggled, and butterflied on the screen. These women twerked decades before it hit the mainstream. These were not damsels; these were badass women who didn't take shit from men. If my parents understood what was being said, they would have banned dancehall from the house. It wouldn't have mattered much because, by 1993, dancehall was topping the charts. Billboard initially included the genre in the rap charts and "Flex" by Mad Cobra became the #1 rap song of 1993.

R&B love songs were smooth and full of innuendo's like "feel my nature rise," a euphemism for "girl, my dick is hard." Dancehall had smooth beats but crass lyrics that felt like porn to my ears. The repetitive chorus of Mad Cobra's 1993 hit "Flex" left no room for romance. It was a direct and demanding "Girl, flex, time to have sex."

Some of the women were even raunchier. Lady Saw was so X-rated, she makes Cardi B look like the Dixie Chicks. Lady Saw's first hit was "Stab Out Di Meat," a deliciously crafted ditty about a prospective lover penetrating her so good she demands he cause her vaginal harm. American R&B made me a hopeless romantic. Dancehall made me feel like a boss. You couldn't tell me I wasn't West Indian. I'd grill my folks about our family tree just to make sure they didn't forget about any ancestors who stopped through the sugar cane fields of Jamaica before landing in South Carolina.

FEELING MYSELF

Puberty kicked my ass. I stopped growing at twelve, but my awkward phase was thriving. Whatever confidence I had was undercut by a bad home perm. The combination of my big head and thick hair meant Mom had to run back to the store to buy another box perm kit in the middle of my virgin application. I sat in the kitchen with half of my head burning and the other half unaware of its demise. As a result, my last two years at Schuyler were a series of awful haircuts to trim the damage from that fateful day. I made it through disrespectful chin acne that I tried to cover up with Band-Aids that only drew more attention to them. I started to lose my "baby weight." I hated that phrase. It sounded like I was a python and at any minute I would shed a layer of skin. The concept of "baby weight" is a nice way of giving chubby kids a silver lining, just like telling them they have big bones. Honestly, it left me confused. Did people think I had a baby and I'm postpartum at twelve? Teen pregnancy was soaring in the late eighties, early nineties. I watched Tupac's "Brenda's Got a Baby" with disapproval. I was saving myself for marriage. Between my guilt-trip family and church, I knew better than to have my name and "baby" cross paths.

"Mom"—I loved asking her hypotheticals—"what would you do if I got pregnant?"

"You and that baby would be living in your own apartment," she replied with no emotion, no anger, just a matter of fact.

"But I'm a kid!"

"If you are old enough to have sex and have a baby, then you're old enough to live on your own."

She scared my legs shut. I stuck to dirty dancing like Patra taught me.

At age twelve, I wore women's size 12 shoes, stood six foot one, and was regularly being mistaken for an adult. My parents had nothing to worry about. I was awkward and introverted. I was too sedentary to sneak out the house. My rude-gal identity lived only in my imagination. The fear of burning in hell always kept me in check. The girls in my crew had the same fears. We never cut class, took a drink, or smoked.

As close as we were, visits and sleepovers never happened. Our parents didn't want to drive us across town nor would they allow us to take public transit alone. New York was still very dangerous in the early nineties. At the time, the crime du jour was getting sliced in the face with a razor blade. People would walk around with them hidden in their mouths and hit people with a "buck fifty," a gash across the face the required a rumored 150 stitches. When it came time for all the thirteenth birthday parties, the only way I could attend was if Dad drove me and took a nap in the car until I was ready to go.

Nadine's thirteenth birthday was an afternoon affair at her house. The majority of the guests were Nadine's siblings. Spin the bottle was out of the question. My crew had been hyping me up for years to try curry goat; that was going to be the highlight of my day. Well, that and showing off my outfit. I spent days planning my look for Nadine's party. By planning I mean, my mother would start the conversation.

"I was thinking, you could wear that navy shirt with matching skirt. That would be nice."

"Nooooo. That's a church outfit. I'm going to a party, remember?"

Since she bought everything I wore, Mom took my critiques to heart. Shopping for me was a hard job. After my fair share of dressing-room meltdowns I stopped going. Mom would buy things and bring them home so I could try them on in my mirrorless bedroom. The plus-size market we have now was a pipe dream back then. As a teen, big sizes meant grown women's wear—floral prints, separates, elastic-waist pants, full-legged slacks. Instead, my go-to casual look was menswear:

T-shirt and jeans. I looked like a carpenter's apprentice in my shapeless size XL top and 38/32 bottom. Of course, the jeans were high-waters (pants that are so short that if you wore them in water the bottoms wouldn't get wet.). It would be years before my ankles received the full coverage they deserved. On my size 12 feet, Dr. Martens shoes. I asked Mom for the boots, which all the R&B singers and rappers wore. She got me the shoe version because they were cheaper. So close, yet so far.

For Nadine's party, I rocked a purple chiffon long-sleeve button-down, black jeans, and my Dr. Martens, which were also my school shoes. My mom let me curl my hair with her curling iron and wear a pair of her hoop earrings. I felt like a million dollars. Dad drove me to the other side of Brooklyn and agreed to pick me up in four hours after running some errands. I knocked on Nadine's door and waved goodbye to him in the car.

As I stepped inside, I spotted twin sisters Princess and Precious sitting on the couch. The sisters were the prettiest girls at the church Nadine, Alicia, and I attended. They had no idea who I was, but I knew all about them. They were your classic popular mean girls, but I knew their secret. Since I was a foot taller than them, I peeped that they used a roll of masking tape and socks to make their hair buns look fuller. I found joy in their imperfection. My only real interaction with them was creepy as hell. During a church Girls Scouts camping weekend—we didn't actually go camping, the troop slept in the church on cots in an isolated part of the building—the twins claimed they were possessed with a demon. Our night of making s'mores over a hot plate was derailed by an emergency prayer circle to remove whatever evil spirit had taken over the twins. They were lying, but their plan to get all the attention worked. I blame them for missing out on my camping badge and s'mores. I stayed clear of the demon daughters at all cost, but now they were in Nadine's house scanning me from head to toe.

"Hi," I said, smiling at the entire room.

"Hey! This is Chloé." Nadine introduced me to the room with a sweep of her arm and went back to playing a board game.

"Hi, Chloé!" everyone responded.

"Hello," Princess replied.

"Can I sit there?" I asked Her Majesty, pointing to the space between her and the armrest.

"You can't fit." Her words put a stop to all the action in the room. I think the gospel music that was playing skipped. Everyone's eyes turned to me. I looked down and interlaced my hands.

"That's not nice, Princess!" Kelly, Nadine's older sister, spoke up.

"What?" Precious stepped in to defend her. "That space is small. She should sit on the floor."

"Why does Chloé have to sit on the floor? There's room on the couch."

Desperate to get the attention off me, I slowly lowered myself onto the floor and sat with my legs crossed. "It's okay, I'll sit on the floor." The twins smirked at my discomfort. If cell phones were a thing I would have called my dad and told him to come back and get me, but I had hours of partying left. Nadine, sensing my sadness, tried to cheer me up with food.

"Chloé, you want to try some curry goat now?" This was the moment my besties had been waiting for. This Yankee girl was going to earn her stripes. Bets had been placed on whether I would like it or not.

"No, I'm okay." I was sorry to disappoint my friends, but there was no way I was going to eat in front of the sisters. Eating was why I couldn't fit on the couch. Three hours later, I was starving and ate a handful of chips. The demon sisters watched my every bite, shaking their heads in disgust. Their religion was nowhere to be found.

"That's a nice shirt," Precious said.

"You look like Barney." Princess laughed.

How could I have missed that? I spent my life avoiding the color green so kids wouldn't sing "Ho ho ho, Green Giant!" Anything yellow screamed Big Bird. I totally forgot about that damn purple dinosaur.

They started singing, "I love you, you love me . . ." A few others chimed in.

Nadine told them to stop but it was too late. The party was ruined for me.

BIG IT UP

Monday morning the crew and I went back to normal. There was no reason to discuss my feelings. No further apologies necessary. I vowed to never wear that purple shirt again and had some yelling matches with my mom over it. She wasn't aware of the horrific memory now attached to it. Younger me would have cried in that living room, but three years with my Caribbean sisters had toughened me up. The twins caught me slipping because my guard was down. I thought I was among friends, in a safe space, but it was a reminder to always be ready for when people test you. My mouth got slicker after that. You can't be nice to muthafuckas. I learned to walk with my head up and shoot insults down at aspiring bullies.

"Ya mother!" was a personal favorite.

I wasn't seeking out conflict, but I wasn't going to run from it either. My verbal jabs caught people off guard. My delivery was dry and deadpan. "So what, I'm fat. At least I know my dad." Nothing was off-limits. I spent years perfecting people watching, so I had so many notes up my uniform sleeve. When provoked, I released them like ninja stars and left my victims in the hall to pick up their egos before the second class bell rang.

Soon, word got around that I wasn't the one to play with. Kids took my bluntness as humor. They started calling me funny and striking up conversations in class. Eventually my mouth got me in trouble.

"What is Michael Jordan known for?" Mr. Harrison, my eighth-grade math teacher, was trying to give us an example of "if/then."

"Gambling," I blurted out.

"Chloé, get out." But I could see he wanted to laugh. Some kids already were.

This was a pivotal time in my life set to the bombastic soundtrack of dancehall. I could tell someone to kiss my big black ass then break into the salt and pepper, butterfly, or spider to accentuate the diss. (All three were very popular dances of the day that required loose joints.) When I hear a song from back then I have only fond memories of becoming a young woman, forming and expressing my thoughts, and chopping a fool down because my inner rude gal said so.

7

WHAT WOULD JANET JACKSON DO?

For some reason, I'd convinced myself that once I became a "woman" (a.k.a. started my period) I'd instantly transform from an ugly duckling to a swan. That swan looked an awful lot like Janet Jackson. I wanted her shape, her abs, and her 4B auburn hair that probably cost thousands per bundle. Don't get me started on her faded ripped jeans and chokers. 1993 was a big year for both of us. Janet released her fifth studio album, *Janet*, and I discovered boys.

Years before, my parents had no choice but to have "the talk" with me. During summers, my aunt Evelyn babysat me while my parents worked. Barely thirty, she was the cool aunt who smoked cigarettes, watched soap operas, and taught me how to knit. Aunt Ev was also a schoolteacher, and in her stack of educational books was *Where Did I Come From? The Facts of Life without Any Nonsense and with Illustrations*. I was six at the time. I couldn't read all the words, but the images were self-explanatory. A naked man and woman took a bath together.

There was a page full of semen charging toward a smiling egg. Anatomically correct male and female genitalia were in full view. Since then, I'd been clear on the science of sex. Now, as a budding teen, I wanted to learn about the chemistry of attraction, flirting, love. For that, I turned to Miss Jackson.

After the rape case of Desiree Washington v. Mike Tyson and the sexual harassment case of Anita Hill v. Judge Clarence Thomas, Janet made it acceptable for black women to be sexy and respected again. Ironically, the 1992 trial of Mike Tyson for the rape of the nineteen-year-old beauty queen was how I learned about oral sex. You couldn't walk past adults without hearing that phrase or "consensual sex," "date rape," and "gold digger." To help us get a grasp of this new national dialogue, my junior high school sent us home with a printout of sex terms and acts to discuss with our parents.

"Dad, what's oral sex?" I handed him the list. He did that thing when you hold a piece of paper and give it a quick shake like that would change what's on it.

"What do you think it is?" He's a master at deflection.

"Well, oral is mouth and sex is sex." Like all kids, I took things very literally.

"Yes."

"I don't understand."

"Go ask your mother," he said, handing me back the paper. Mom was in the kitchen making dinner. I stood in the narrow doorway, which is right next to the stove.

"Mom, what is oral sex?"

"Ask your father."

"He told me to ask you." With a sigh, she wiped her hands dry and took the paper.

"I know oral is your mouth." I wanted her to know I wasn't a total idiot.

"O-kay." If I listened closely I probably could've heard her cussing my father. "If oral is your mouth, then that means you're having sex with the mouth.

"So when they said Mike Tyson had oral sex with Desiree Washington, he put his thing in her mouth?"

"Yes."

Both parents would have saved time if they said, "Chloé, oral sex is sucking dick." I would have known exactly what they meant because the boys at school would yell "suck my dick" to us girls or each other at least once a day. Any girl who was accused of being a whore was rumored to have sucked some boy off in school. In that case, I knew what oral sex was. It was nasty. No way Janet was doing oral.

BE THE FLAME, NOT THE MOTH

Sex was out of the question. I wasn't trying to go to hell or bring shame to my family name. But a kiss? I was ready for a kiss. A kiss was innocent. I wasn't going to be satisfied until I made first contact with a boy. I enlisted the help of my downstairs neighbor, Indigo. Indigo was two years older than me and everything I was not—petite, slim, assertive, savvy. She taught me how to shave my legs, pluck my eyebrows, and tongue kiss on my hand. The trick was to tickle the roof of their mouth with the tip of your tongue. (It still works to this day. ☺)

We'd stare at pics of Janet and deconstruct her look so we knew what things to shoplift once we made it to the city. Janet's video for "That's the Way Love Goes" sent us on a quest for the perfect jean vest and choker. Our favorite store to steal from was Joyce Leslie. Imagine Forever 21 but smaller and with more clothes thrown on the floor. Indigo would rack up with her five-finger discount. I had to settle for lots of accessories. Most of the tops couldn't get over my chest, the bottoms stopped at my knees.

When we walked around the West Village, I looked like Indi's bodyguard. Only the courteous dudes addressed me as I stood next to her. They didn't have to talk to me to understand that I had the power to shut them down. I exploited their lust for Indigo by accepting food and drinks. The longer you kept me satisfied, the more time you had to talk Indi's ear off. She would get annoyed with my requests for McDonald's or Mango Madness Snapple, but she also knew once I got bored I would complain about wanting to go home, and if I went she had to follow, because I was only twelve after all and, at the advanced age of fourteen, she was responsible for my safety.

This was "the good old days" when flirting was hands-on. Men initiated everything. Walking down the street meant navigating packs of men every couple feet. Indi would glide, while I stomped, through the jackal herds. If they saw something they liked they would say, "Hello," extending a hand for her to take. Most times, being the savages they were, they'd grab at her belt loop or wrist as she walked by. We'd go through several of these interactions in a day. Today it's known as catcalling or street harassment; back then it was *the game*.

The game elevated once we (really she) started attracting suitors in luxury cars. If a guy driving a Range Rover pulled up to holler out his window at us (really her), it was game on. Back then, the Range Rover was at the top of the foreign-car craze. Girls threw all caution to the wind to ride shotgun with a stranger. If he was pushing a Range, I knew he had Mango Madness money. The reality of the situation always escaped us. These were grown-ass men flashing their (often illegally procured) money in order to prey on young girls. If you've seen one drug dealer, you've seen them all. You pick up a lot while sitting in the back seat.

OPERATION: K.I.S.S.

On my morning walks to the train, I found myself crossing paths with a boy from my apartment complex. The half-mile trek gave us time to chat. His name was Delano. He lived in the neighborhood, but I had never seen him before. Remember, I was lazy and never went outside. He was a year older, and when he talked to me he always had a smile in the corner of his lips. It's the look every man has when he's sizing up fresh meat. Morning flirts quickly turned into an after-school invitation. Both latchkey kids, we figured out that if I went to his house straight from school, we'd have an hour to ourselves. Extra precautions were taken to sneak into his building. I'd walk up the stairs, catch my breath for ten minutes, walk across the floor to his apartment, and knock lightly on the door.

"Hey." Smiling, Delano opened the door in a T-shirt and sweats. It was barely 4:00 p.m., but it was so dark in his apartment. He led me to the couch, and I sat on the edge. "You can take your bookbag off, ya know," he said, laughing at my innocence. I slid my bookbag off and placed it on the floor in between us. I kept my jacket on and my knees closed. None of his smooth small talk registered. All I could hear in my head was the disappointment of my family if they knew I was over here being a harlot. My first visit was cut short by guilt.

The following week, encouraged by Indi, I went back. "He clearly likes you," she said. "You talk on the phone every day. This could be your first boyfriend." Determined not to be deflowered, I wore a pair of jean shorts over my white tights and under my uniform skirt. This time I sat back on the couch, close enough for Delano to put his arm around my shoulders. He placed his other hand on my thigh and I jumped like it was a jolt of electricity.

"You okay?" He didn't move his hand.

"Ahh, yeah, I'm okay," I lied. My invisible chastity belt was going into lockdown mode. I was praying to Jesus for forgiveness. My lady parts were throbbing. Delano lifted his hand off my thigh and relocated it to my double chin, gently pulling my face toward his. His lips touched mine and I froze. He puckered up again and I could hear Indi in my corner like a coach. *Tilt your head, good, good. Okay now, open your lips a little more. Yes! Move in closer and hit him with the tongue on the roof. There ya go!*

He sat back with a Cheshire cat smile. Speechless, I grabbed my bookbag and blurted out, "I got to go."

"You sure?"

"Yes. I have a lot of homework."

"Oh, okay, maybe you can come by tomorrow."

"Yeah—" I was already out the door and down the long corridor.

Once I hit the corner and was out of his sight, I felt faint, bracing my-self on the wall. *I'm a whore. I kissed a boy and I'm going to hell.* During the ten-minute walk from his building to mine, I promised God I was going to read the word every day, be happy about going to church, do all my chores, and listen to anything my parents said. I was *shooketh*. I avoided Delano for a week. Finally, I took his call.

"I've been looking for you!"

"Huh, oh. Really?" Did he still want me after all this time?

"I wanted to tell you something. I really like someone."

Oh, this is it. He's going to confess his love to me like one of those R&B songs. I perked up. "Well, you should tell her." I smiled. I was the mouse and he was calling me to remind me he was the cat. I finally was getting this thing down.

"I am, when I see her in school tomorrow." We did not go to the same school. "She's a pretty Puerto Rican girl."

There's no rejection like your first one. I hung up the phone, melted into my bed, and played Janet's "If," a promising of all the things she'd do if she was a girlfriend, on repeat for a week. Heartbreak is much better when there's a soundtrack.

Listening to Janet made me feel like I was a woman, but I was still very much a child. No song, music video, or poster could prepare me for the complexities of sexuality, gender identity, and social expecta-tions for a girl. I made a deal with my libido to wait a while. When the time was right and, preferably, I had a flat stomach like Janet's, I would be ready for an intense sexual experience with the man of my dreams. However, I wouldn't let him feel up my skirt in public like Janet did on "Anytime, Anyplace." I was still trying to go to heaven.

YOUNG AND NOT READY

Summer of 1995, Mom gave birth to my little brother and I became a mom by proxy. I made bottles, changed diapers, and babysat when needed, which was often once Mom returned to work. All the above was a surefire way to make sure your fourteen-and-a-half-year-old, hot-in-the-pants daughter didn't end up pregnant. My brother's arrival co-incided with the shedding of my "baby weight." I was starting to feel good about my changing body but any attention I should've gotten was directed to the cockblocking kid I was pushing around in a stroller. The worst was running into people and seeing them mask their shock with a lukewarm "Congratulations!" Is anyone ever really happy to see a young teen mother? Once I told them the little bundle of joy was my brother they let out a sigh of relief and unclenched their teeth. Meanwhile, I'm pissed. *You really thought I was pregnant? These past nine months I was losing weight!*

The responsibility of caring for my brother (although he refuses to acknowledge my hand in his upbringing) is a large part of the reason why I don't have children now. Babies are the best birth control.

———

The following year, my babysitting duties took a back seat to my sum-mer job at the U.S. Open tennis tournament. (Hey, Serena!) Almost six-teen, I was finally allowed to work this one time. "Your focus is school," they'd say whenever I asked to get a part-time job at a food-swamp fast-food joint so I could hang out with friends, eat fries on the clock, and flirt with boys at the register. "You have the rest of your life to work."

The U.S. Open was an exception; it was three weeks of work and ended before I started eleventh grade. I took the hour-and-a-half train ride to Flushing, Queens, where I slaved away as a cashier at a pizza hut. No, not *the* Pizza Hut. This was a temporary hut with two hotter-than-hell pizza ovens placed three feet from my back in the dead of summer. We had cash boxes. I was horrible in math, but I couldn't keep the rich people who were willing to pay $5.50 in 1996 for a pita-size pizza covered with three slices of tomato, four pieces of pepperoni, and a sprinkling of mozzarella cheese waiting while I counted on my fingers. A lot of wrong change was made, but they brushed it off because Serena or Agassi were about to take center court. I never caught a match, but don't worry, I had my own action going on.

His name was Joey, and he passed by my booth every day as part of the cleaning crew. I was his favorite stop along his route. On sweltering days he'd walk up and ask for a courtesy cup of water.

"It's hot today." Joey lifted up his navy-blue polo uniform shirt, showing off his six-pack abs and Ken doll cuts. Lord, I prayed he had more than Ken in the penis department. Joey and I started taking lunch together. Once the tournament ended, we kept things going. I'd make the hour-long trek to the Bronx, where he lived with his cousin. My first time there I was surprised to hear him speak fluent Spanish.

"Wait, you're Spanish?"

"I'm from the Dominican Republic."

No idea where that is. "Oh, cool." That was the most revealing conversation we had. We'd fake our way through small talk and start making out. After a few more visits, I let him go further. He wasn't my boyfriend; we never went on a date. He was sexy. I thought I was ready.

Joey told me I was beautiful. I believed him. He even said it in Spanish, so it had to be true.

Joey's older cousin and his girlfriend were in the living room watching TV. We had nothing on in the room. No TV, no music. Nothing to mask the sounds of my losing my virginity. I watched as he rolled on the condom. I kept my bra on, wishing the room was dark, but it was the early afternoon. He got on top of me and I felt this immense pressure. I had never seen a dick in person before, so this felt like the biggest one ever.

"Owwwww," I whispered.

Joey stopped, looked me dead in the eye, and with no sympathy said, "Look, it's gonna hurt." How romantic. Afterward, I went to the bathroom, shaking as my innocence left my body. When I came back into the room, he was lying naked on the bed, basking in the glory of soiling me. *Of course, I'm being a drama queen right now. When else does one get to write about their shitty first time other than in their own book? If you are a virgin reading this, do better than Joey. If you had better, share your story with me so I can live vicariously through your tender, loving experience.*

I told him I was bleeding. The last thing I could do is go home with spotty panties. I couldn't chance Mom seeing them in the hamper. She knew my cycle by heart. Anything out of whack would be a red flag, pun intended. Annoyed, he put on some sweats, went into the living room, and asked his cousin's girlfriend in Spanish if she had any pads. Joey came back and tossed me a huge pad. The entire train ride home I sat on the edge of my seat, arms wrapped about my stomach, my legs shaking.

The next day in school, my bestie, Monica, laid eyes on me and instantly knew. Dressing in all black could have tipped her off.

"Oh my GOD! Nooooooooo." She started crying. Between the two of us, I was the good girl, the voice of logic and reason. Monica was devastated. She wasn't able to save me from a bad decision. "Why? Chloé, you don't even know him!" She was wrong! It had been five weeks.

The next time I went to see Joey, I took heed of Monica's concerns. *Let me learn more about the guy who popped my cherry.* I laid my head on his chest.

"Where were you born?"

"Texas."

"Really, you're American?"

Joey pulled his arm from under my head. "Yeah. What, do you think I'm with you for a green card?"

"Ahh, I'm fifteen." *Bruh, slow your roll.* You think I'd be down with a green card marriage? Being a child bride was not in my cards. I saw how Janet Jackson's teenage secret marriage ended. She canceled James DeBarge and hid their alleged secret baby quicker than an album interlude. Joey's overreaction was a cue. We stopped seeing each other after that. I made a vow that the next guy I slept with would be my boyfriend and we'd be madly in love, even consummating our relationship to a playlist of Janet slow jams filled with deep cuts.

IS THIS THE WAY LOVE GOES?

His name was LaJarvis. Smitten would be an understatement. The neurons in my brain created new pathways to better accommodate my nonstop thoughts about him. My accelerated class schedule put me in several of his AP classes. Whenever there was a group project, I'd suggest we pair up. On weekends, we spent hours in the library or museum. I'd soak in his tall, dark, and handsome frame, pretending not to understand the assignment so he'd take extra time explaining it to me. When my Janet giggles and cutesy body language didn't work, I resorted to being his best friend. I'd drop everything when he so much as sniffed in my direction. I was going to wear him down. Janet taught me resilience.

After failing miserably with Delano and Joey, I'd get a "do-over" with LaJarvis. My bestie, Monica, and I did some calculations and devised a "Get LaJarvis" plan.

1. Start dressing cuter (e.g., wearing miniskirts).

2. Get my hair done more often. (Perms were the law of the land. Afros were not an aphrodisiac.)

3. Lose more weight.

Freshman year, I joined the basketball team (more on that later) and barely ate (I'll get to this as well), which helped me lose a lot of weight, but I still didn't have an hourglass figure. In school, girls shared their body tips and almost all the suggestions were off the wall. Things like having sex to make your hips spread, preferably via doggy style. I wasn't up for rekindling with Joey to find out if it was true. No one ever had suggestions for stubborn belly fat. I had a muffin top that could only be camouflaged with men's relaxed fit jeans, size 36.

"I got this for us." One day in between classes, Monica handed me a bottle of diet pills she saw on TV. "I took one this morning but it says three pills a day." Big bold letters on the side read "#1 ingredient Ephedra." It was even touted as the secret weight-loss drug to the stars. We walked around the triangle-shaped school in search of a working water fountain. We each took a pill, and I stuffed a couple in my pocket for later. I couldn't afford to have a rib removed or liposuction, but these pills weren't going to break my piggy bank. If Janet cheated, I could too.

———

America has long been fixated on quick weight-loss trends. In the 1920s, cigarettes were prescribed by doctors for having appetite-suppressant superpowers (not to be confused with its cancer-causing powers). The 1930s brought on the "grapefruit diet," also known as the Hollywood diet. Dieters were encouraged to eat foods high in fat, which would be eliminated by the grapefruit's purported fat-burning enzyme. Carbohydrates—sugar, sweet fruits and vegetables, grains, and cereals—were off-limits. Now we know why classic golden-era Hollywood films showed starlets eating grapefruit at breakfast.

The fifties brought about the "cabbage diet," which claimed a 10–15 pound weight loss in a week from consuming the bland and nutritionless soups two to three times a day. My personal favorite, for holistic points but not for levels of creepiness, is the "tapeworm diet." Someone used their knack for science and designed a pill that contained the parasite that would then grow inside of you and do its work. Feels dumb admitting this, but I seriously contemplated joining

Habitat for Humanity so I could live in a remote third-world village, contract a parasite, and come home waist snatched.

In 1963, housewife Jean Nidetch launched Weight Watchers, which started as a small support group of fat friends who felt stuck. Queen mother Oprah is now the company's most influential spokesperson, all while being thicker than a bowl of oatmeal. (Boss life.) Nidetch's brainchild is available in over thirty countries and has proven to be one of the more successful diet programs. Clearly it worked for Nidetch, who passed away at age ninety-one. No word on if she counted points to the end.

By the eighties, the fad recipes and practices were dwarfed by largely unapproved products like Dexatrim, Ayds (not to be confused with AIDS), and Ephedra. Common side effects of the now banned Ephedra include trouble sleeping, anxiety, headache, hallucinations, high blood pressure, fast heart rate, loss of appetite, and inability to urinate.

To be young is to live free because you're too stupid to know limitations and are fearless as a result of that. Monica and I, with our youthful arrogance, popped diet pills at lunch and went window shopping for new, cute, and noticeably smaller clothes for skinny Chloé at shops in the World Trade Center.

———

"Hey, LaJarvis, maybe you could come over to my house on Saturday. My parents won't be home. I'll be babysitting my little brother." Two weeks on diet pills, I was feeling confident about my tiny weight loss. I had enough energy to keep up with a toddler and get some action on the side. LaJarvis was picking up what I was putting down but wanted to make sure there was no gray.

"If I come over, you gonna wear something sexy?"

Baby brother was not with the shits. He refused to go down for his nap. I opened the door in my button-down with my baby brother on my hip. LaJarvis's and my romantic afternoon was over before it started. "Touch Me Tease Me" by Case featuring Foxy Brown and Mary J. Blige was my foreplay song of choice but was drowned out by the screams of my brother, who wanted out of his crib. Choosing family over dick, I asked LaJarvis to leave. My brother fell asleep minutes after the door shut. We didn't have cell phones, so I couldn't call LaJarvis to come back. Like Jesse Jackson, I was determined to keep hope alive. This cat-and-mouse game continued for months. My bestie, Monica, reached her breaking point.

"Chloé, I have to tell you something." We were in between classes and she pulled me over to our favorite talking corner. "LaJarvis is dating someone." After several blue ball debacles, LaJarvis began pursuing another girl at our school. I couldn't believe it. Tears. Real tears streamed down my face. Shortness of breath followed, and a sharp pain in my chest. Was it the Ephedra or, worse, my actual heart breaking?

I am far from emotional. Even today, I cry maybe two times a year and one of those times almost always involves PMS and watching little kids do cute stuff in viral videos. A baby in a diaper dancing on the kitchen table to Bruno Mars when my period is coming? Pass the Kleenex. Don't let there be a dog in the mix, or I'm a puddle on the floor.

"Oh my God! Are you crying?!" Monica panicked. "Don't cry, Chloé. I'm sorry. Please don't cry." We missed our next class. "Want some cookies? I can go down to the cafeteria and get you a candy bar from the vending machine." Food was of no comfort. With no appetite, taking the pills was pointless. Monica threw out the rest of the bottle when she began having what felt like panic attacks.

LaJarvis flaunted his new girl in front of me. He portrayed me not as his friend but as a lovesick puppy. I mean, I definitely was, but she didn't need to know that. The melodrama came to a climax when his girlfriend called my house. "LaJarvis don't want you! You jealous and ugly and fat." I had no choice but to believe she was right. She won the boy of my dreams. She had to be right.

———

The worst thing you can do is give power to a person who doesn't want you. Whatever LaJarvis was willing to give I was willing to take, even if it was brutal. I was setting myself up for failure and didn't even know it. He was in a relationship, so I lied to myself about the value of our "friendship." I'd play around with him. A hug here, a push there, play fights; perhaps those touches could lead to affection. What I didn't account for was his frustration.

On one occasion, LaJarvis reacted by gripping and twisting a handful of my inner arm so tight, it left a massive bruise from my armpit to my elbow. I wore long sleeves for weeks to cover up the purple black-and-blues.

———

It was easy to hide from my parents. My teammates noticed and vowed to punch whoever did it in the face, but I would never give LaJarvis up. Monica knew, but I downplayed it so she wouldn't make a big deal about it or, worse, confront him. To me, our roughhousing was harmless. In reality, LaJarvis would get aggressive during our play fights because he didn't have the maturity or the words to reject me and leave me alone. He enjoyed the adulation. I fed his juvenile ego. You don't fire the president of your fan club. At a group dinner, I finally got the hint. He leaned over and whispered in my ear, "I wish my girlfriend was here." That hurt more than my bruises ever did.

College provided some much needed space from LaJarvis. Two years passed. Then, in the

WOMEN AND INTIMATE PARTNER VIOLENCE

* 1 in 4 women have experienced IPV.

* 1 in 10 high school students have experienced physical teen-dating violence.

* More than 4 out of 10 black women will experience physical violence from a partner.

* Black women experience higher rates of psychological abuse, including: humiliation, insults, name-calling, and coercive control.

* More than 20 percent of black women will be raped during their lifetimes. A higher percentage than women overall.

* Black women are 2.5 times more likely to be murdered by men they've been involved with or know than white women.

* Black women are less likely to report IPV.

summer of 2000, LaJarvis reached out. He'd moved to California, near my homegirl Ella, who was in school out there. I booked a student standby plane ticket to California to visit Ella, and if by chance I crossed paths with LaJarvis, even better. What follows is a pure, grade A shit show.

LaJarvis was bumming it. All the fly clothes were gone. He had a little gut where there used to be washboard abs. No idea what he did for a living, but his car had seen better days. Its broken AC left the entire back half of my body soaked in sweat. He picked me up from Ella's dorm room and drove to a shitty motel. Yes, a charge-by-the-hour MO-FUCKING-TEL. The room was so disgusting, I refused to sit on the bed and used the sandpaper towels as a germ barrier. We had sex on a chair. I straddled him like I'd seen Janet Jackson do countless times. This was not the fantasy I had in mind.

But wait, there's more. I'm sharing the next part of this story because I want any person who finds themselves excusing dysfunction to learn from this.

My last night in Cali, LaJarvis and I were on the phone.

"I'll come get you at eight." He'd agreed to drive me to the airport in the morning.

"Thanks," I said. This was going to be my farewell. I finally consummated this toxic relationship and could now leave it miles behind as I soared into the sky.

"Don't thank me. I want to see you before you go."

"WHO DO YOU WANT TO SEE?" A woman began yelling in LaJarvis's background.

"LaJarvis, who is that?" I asked.

"Yo, chill . . ."

"WHO 👏 DO 👏 YOU 👏 WANT 👏 TO 👏 SEE? Is that the bitch you was with yesterday? Oh, you thought I didn't know. I'm at work, pregnant with your child, and you out here with someone else?"

"LaJarvis, what is going on?" I couldn't believe what I was hearing.

"This is my friend from New York," LaJarvis explained. "I don't like her like that."

"YOU'RE A FUCKING LIAR!"

"Baby, she means nothing to me," he said, then switched from damage control to gaslighting. "You are tripping."

My ear was pressed so close to the phone, it started to get hot. I needed to hear every single word. The worst was not knowing if he was lying to her or if those were his real feelings toward me. All this coming from a man whose car AC didn't work in *California*. Bum-ass dudes are the worst.

"Get out! Get the fuck out. I'm tired of all your shit." I heard a commotion, then a dial tone. I was shaking, too stunned to cry.

———

Eight months later.

My dorm room phone rings.

"Hey!" It was LaJarvis.

"How did you get my number?"

"I called your house and your mother gave it to me." *I really should update Mom on who's on my shit list.*

"Okay. What do you want?" I hated him, but I also wanted to know what happened back in Cali. The student journalist in me needed answers.

"I'm back!"

"Okay." There were no more hopes to get up.

"I moved back to Brooklyn. Things ended with my wife."

"YOUR WIFE!"

"Yeah, it was a whole mess. Let me take you to dinner."

Dinner was at Dallas BBQ near my dorm. I was twenty years old, jumbo sticky honey wings, corn bread, and a virgin piña colada was a nice dinner in my book. As I licked honey off my fingers, LaJarvis told me his version of events. After leaving college, he moved to Cali, where he met a young woman at church.

"There was a lot of pressure from her family for us to get married, so we did." They were married for about a year and expecting their first child the night she found him on the phone with me. According to him, soon after that, she lost the baby.

"You got me," LaJarvis said with a smile. "You wanted me; you got me. I'm yours."

This didn't feel like a prize; this was a punishment—but I subjected myself to it because I was convinced our affair played a hand in him losing his family. His psychological games made me feel worse. He started popping up to my NYU dorm at random times of the day. He learned my schedule and would wait for me after class. I was suffocating. Whenever I tried to cut him loose, he'd hit me with some version of "I don't have anyone but you."

"He's crazy and you need to stop messing with him." Lynn, my roommate, was furious. She didn't understand why this guy popped up, and I lost my mind. After weeks of unannounced visits and the destruction of my self-esteem, Lynn had had enough. LaJarvis called and rudely asked to speak to me.

"Don't call here anymore." Lynn yelled into the receiver. "Chloé doesn't want to see you anymore, and if I catch you creeping around here, I'm going to call the cops." I was so relieved. Why couldn't I have done that? LaJarvis never called again.

———

Ten years later.

I'm sitting in the emergency room with a cousin who broke her arm. Out the corner of my eye, I see an EMT pushing a stretcher into the ER. *LaJarvis?* I quickly looked away, but I was too slow. LaJarvis saw me and started walking over. He still didn't respect my boundaries.

"Hey!" I said, faking excitement. "I thought that was you."

"Yup, it's me," he said proudly. "It's been a long time."

"It has. How's your mom?" I didn't want to know anything about him.

"She's good. She's a grandma now. Yeah, my lady and I had a son six months ago. He was thirteen pounds." *Did this man say he had a thirteen-pound baby? Girl, he would've destroyed your life and your womb.*

"Wow! Well, good seeing you," I lied. Hearing about his son did make me feel glad that he was able to move on from his loss. He got his family.

"You too!" As he turned to walk away, I could see he was going bald. The luster had faded.

———

I was well into my thirties before I realized that I was projecting door-mat vibes. Yes, I was strong and determined in every department except dating. When it came to men, I gladly accepted bullshit in hopes of love. As a result, my entire dating roster was a variation of Delano, Joey, or LaJarvis. I'd been chasing a fantasy that started when I was twelve, listening to Janet's "Love Will Never Do," dancing around my bedroom with my imaginary boyfriend who worshipped the ground I walked on. When that miracle man didn't materialize, I was ready, willing, and able to turn a toad into a prince. Love songs are not measuring sticks for real life, and folks don't tell young girls that. They're too busy telling us to keep our legs closed and our skirts long or risk being Desiree or Anita, when all you were trying to be was Janet.

P.S. You'll be happy to know Joey did apologize to me. In 2007, he hit me on Facebook messenger and told me he was sorry for the way we ended things. It was the first sincere apology I'd ever gotten from a beau.

8

HOOP DREAMS

After my failed attempt at dominating the world of tennis, I had no desire to be an athlete. Yet here I was, a freshman at Murry Bergtraum High School for Business Careers, signing up for team tryouts. I decided on volleyball for all the wrong reasons. The players were slim and girly. They giggled a lot and wore ribbons in their hair. The uniform of skintight tops and bright yellow panty shorts got all the boys' attention. I wanted all of that. But before I could sign my name on the tryout sheet, I was interrupted.

"Hi, I'm Mr. Jay. I coach the girls' basketball team. You're a big girl! Gotta be, what, six feet? Have you ever played? You should try out for the team. What's your name?" He crossed my name out under Volleyball and wrote it under Basketball. Thus began the start of my basketball career.

This isn't a Cinderella story, like Michael Jordan being cut from the team then turning around and changing the game. I never loved ball or even dreamt about it. I stuck with it because it could immediately get me in with the cool kids at school and, if I worked hard enough, a college scholarship. I'd never win a championship, become MVP, or land endorsement deals. That doesn't mean I wasn't put through the fire. Ball set me on a crash course with diet, exercise, and discipline.

Making the team was easy. I was six one and bigger than everyone else. So big, in fact, the uniform shorts didn't fit. (And I thought I could dart around in panty shorts, ha!)

Mom loaned me a pair of purple knee-length aerobic leggings to wear under 2XL men's mesh shorts that I had to buy. Whenever I ran, I'd stop after two paces to pull the mesh shorts down from my crotch. Dad bought me a mouth guard, knee and elbow pads. I looked more like a defensive lineman than a power forward. This power forward/center was ready for war.

———

Murry Bergtraum High School for Business Careers was a white nationalist's nightmare. Throughout the halls you'd hear Chinese, Russian, Puerto Rican Spanish, Dominican Spanish, patois, and Ebonics. For the most part, each group stuck with their own, but I wanted to move across all borders. Why pay for a buffet if you're only going to eat orange chicken? (*Yes, I can relate anything to a food experience.*)

My track was computer science, but I knew I wasn't going to get popular from knowing how to code. This was the midnineties; C++ and Lotus 123 were not poppin' in the streets.

"Shhh, the teacher is here." My first day at Bergtraum, I walked into class and all the students fell silent. I looked around for the teacher. "Ain't you our teacher?"

"No, I'm a freshman," I said.

"Damn, you big as shit!" They laughed.

This wasn't bullying as much as it was natural amazement. I could handle this, but I was not equipped for the attention to fashion and trends. I was coming off three years in a uniform. My teammates showed mercy and got me together real quick. Seniors Gina and Farrah took me under their wing. They were both A students, fashionistas, and beautiful. Gina spent extra time with me after practice, going over the drop step and left-hand layups. Farrah spearheaded my makeover, inviting me to her house, where I sat on the toilet seat while she flat ironed my hair and taught me how to wrap it at night. They gave me tips on where to buy pants that weren't high-waters and shoes for my size 12 feet. Most important, they'd yell "Hey, Clo!" when they saw me in the halls.

My off-court transformation was light-years ahead of my on-court game. As Charles Barkley says, I was *turrrible*. My job, during the few minutes that I played, was to stand in the lane and scare my opponents. On the rare occasion I'd catch the ball and score, the entire team would jump up from the bench and cheer. I was their Rudy, averaging three minutes and .8 points per game. Whatever I lacked in natural ability I'd make up for by studying the mechanics. I started watching college ball with Dad and sat glued to the couch during March Madness, crushing on Chris Webber, Antawn Jamison, and Corliss Williamson. I devoured the acclaimed documentary *Hoop Dreams* about two

Chicago high schoolers who traveled to a privileged white prep school with the hopes of making it big in the NBA. Shot over five years, William Gates and Arthur Agee were a cautionary tale of what happens when you put all your eggs in the "finna be rich" basket.

Unlike guys, girls didn't turn to basketball for a life-changing money grab. Sports agents and sneaker companies weren't throwing money into our laps or buying us exotic cars. Going pro was never an option. The WNBA didn't launch until my senior year, and by then I knew I didn't love basketball. I tolerated it because it gave me access to the things I wanted: friends and a good education. Once I realized I could get a college scholarship, I put my head down and dug my toes into every sprint. My mission was to be a solid role player and land at a school with a good journalism program.

Getting looks from college coaches was going to be hard. I joined several teams outside of school to work on my game. During the summer, I'd leave the house at 9:00 a.m. and come back at 9:00 p.m. Between games and practices, it was normal for me to touch down in all five boroughs in a single day. My bookbag was packed with two bottles of semifrozen water to battle the summer heat, a hand towel, change of shirt, my playing sneakers, and maybe five dollars to buy a hero, juice, and chips.

Sophomore year, I was down twenty pounds. In retrospect, I'd also developed an eating disorder. I was starving myself. Breakfast was a bowl of Honey Nut Cheerios. At lunch, with a budding reputation to protect, I'd forego cafeteria food and slide a crumpled one dollar bill into the vending machine, selecting cookies, chips, or a candy bar. Basketball practice was two hours long and I'd power through, running off pure sugar. Dinner was whatever my parents cooked, or a sandwich. Anything I ate had to fit on a salad plate. I told myself portion control was more important than the quality of the food. Countless times I would be so "over hungry," as my parents called it, that I'd go to bed nauseated, unable to eat.

Family dinners were when we'd catch up. My hectic basketball schedule left little room for quality time. My parents would take turns cooking and, if they were feeling nostalgic, watch out! Mom's family was Southern, so her jog down memory lane involved frying and smothering. Yum. Being from Indiana, Dad's blast from the past was white rice, lima beans, and smoked sausage. I hated all three but was never able to decline, thanks to Mom's guilt trips.

"Chloé, your father made this for us. It won't kill you to eat it." I didn't see her licking her plate. *Fine, I'll play along.* Biting into the sausage link, I braced for the casing snap followed by a burst of liquified fat. Then I felt it. It was the size of a unpopped corn kernel and almost cracked my molar.

"Ow!" I was disgusted, but hammed it up to get out of finishing dinner. "Something is in my sausage."

"Well, spit it out," Mom said calmly. Into my napkin, I spat out a chunk of gristle. Gristle is like the crappy toy in the cereal box. It's the cartilage that keeps on giving; an animal's last little "fuck you" protest from the big farm in the sky.

"Eww, that's nasty!"

"No need to make a scene." Dad was very defensive. "You've eaten this before and it was never a problem. Just eat it."

Saying "I don't like it" wasn't going to work. I had to make a statement that hopefully they would respect, even if they didn't agree. Here is where them allowing me to be an independent thinker came in handy. "I'm done with meat," I said, pushing the plate away from me. "I'm going to be a vegetarian."

"You, stop eating meat?" Dad laughed. His Midwest was showing. "We'll see how long that lasts."

After our SlimFast era, Mom handled any discussion about me and food with kid gloves. She supported my decision and gave me some old cookbooks she had from her short-lived vegetarian stint during college. Stubbornness wouldn't let me reveal my ruse, so I stuck with it but had to clarify that I was only giving up red meat. I was still eating fish, chicken, and turkey. They didn't have a term for it, so I said vegetarian and few people corrected me. My will was tested several times. Soon after I denounced meat, Mom made what felt like five pounds of bacon. She rarely cooked big breakfasts anymore, so her frying up that much swine felt suspicious. I turned the corner, spotted the crispy bacon, and my mouth watered. *How dare she!*

"Good morning." My mom smiled, removing the last piece of bacon from the frying pan.

"Morning." I squeezed past her to the fridge, grabbing milk for my bowl of cereal. As soon as she left me alone, I stared at that mound of bacon and lost it. I stuffed my mouth.

"Umm-hmm! Some vegetarian you are." She caught me pig-handed.

"This is it! I promise. Please don't tell Dad." I would never hear the end of it. It could be my wedding day and Dad would make a toast and joke, "I hope this marriage lasts longer than the time Chloé claimed she was giving up meat, then ate bacon two days later." When it comes to food, I get my lack of willpower from him. We once had a yelling match when he ate my last brownie, then declared that, as my father, he shouldn't have to explain why he ate my brownie. I didn't talk to him for a few days.

———

Becoming an athlete is more than picking up a ball and running fast. One must learn their body and how to nurture it for optimal performance. There's weight training, stretching, cardio, and, most important, diet. None of this became apparent to me until I started playing AAU ball. The Amateur Athletic Union was founded in the 1880s by James Sullivan to create uniformity and regulation to amateur sports. It was also the governing body and breeding ground for the U.S. Olympic program. Today it's a gatekeeping empire that charges parents anywhere from $400 to $4,000 a single summer season so their kid can join a team. Parents buy into the AAU system, which gets you seen by college coaches and recruiters. But the reality is, only about 1 percent of the nearly 430,400 student athletes who play high school girls' basketball will play at the Division I level.

I joined the Five Boro Falcons with some of the best players from across the city. Practice was Coach embracing their natural ability and drawing up Xs and Os for me to compute since I was the "smart" player. That's just a nice way of saying I wasn't good. Dubbed a nerd by my peers, I found my way back to the bottom of the social ladder. They clowned me because I did my homework before practice and read books on road trips while they listened to music. There was one other girl who did the same. They didn't crack on her as hard because she was really good. Ella and I became fast friends. Ella was six two, lean, and ambidextrous. She went to a private prep school in the city and lived in a beautiful Harlem brownstone with her mom, who would come to games wearing a business suit and carrying a briefcase. We came from two different economic backgrounds, but we shared the same temperament and laser focus.

She ended up in California, I stayed local at NYU. When I went to visit her—and to see LaJarvis 😒—we rehashed how our friendship started but realized what really brought us together was our teammates' big secret. Except for Ella, myself, and one or two others on the team, the rest were gay. Ella and I only connected the rainbow dots once folks were in college and came home for the summer out of the closet. Understandably, high school in the nineties was not the place to live in your sexual identity truth. So they hid behind closed doors, holding hands under team jackets on their lap during van trips, covering up hickies with flipped collars on their Polo shirts. It's amazing how Ella and I missed all of that.

Stupid people believe that playing basketball turns you gay. As many boobs and butts as I've seen in the locker room, I can assure you, that's not the case. If anything, sports and the community around them will help you embrace who you naturally are, making you more confident overall.

———

The Women's Sports Foundation lays out the benefits of girls participating in sports:

* High school girls who play sports are less likely to be involved in an unintended pregnancy; more likely to get better grades in school; and more likely to graduate than girls who do not play sports.

* Girls and women who play sports have higher levels of confidence and self-esteem, and lower levels of depression.

* Girls and women who play sports have a more positive body image and experience higher states of psychological well-being than girls and women who do not play sports.

Even though I wasn't a natural, I did appreciate the benefits of playing. For starters, there was no idle time to do teenage stuff. I liked boys, but basketball kept me from being boy crazy. Half joking, I say "basketball stopped me from being a ho." No telling where I would be if I had all that free time on my hands and two working parents out of the house. In a parallel universe there's a Chloé who didn't play basketball and now has a twenty-three-year-old kid because that Chloé would sneak LaJarvis in every day after school and trusted him to not finish inside her because they didn't have money for condoms. (Don't act like I'm the only one who thinks about their other selves out there in the universe.)

Becoming aware of my physical strength was an awakening. Rarely do I need the physical help from others to lift, carry, or grab stuff. Its freeing to be a woman and not be a damsel in distress. Society loves to equate a self-aware and independent woman with being lesbian when her purpose for performing life isn't based on the adulation of a man. It was a critique that started early in my life. I would often be called a lesbian or a bitch. Now I identify as bi-curious at best, but depending on the day, I can *definitely* be a bitch.

My first AAU tournament, we piled into a fifteen-seater van and drove to Connecticut. We entered the gym with our New York swag and were drowned out by ten courts of simultaneous games, bleachers filled with middle- and upper-class parents who wanted a quick return on their investment, and the shouts of white girls with ponytails and Nike headbands communicating every move on the court.

"Katie, go left. LEFT!"

"Becky, pick right. SCREEN!"

"Jill, SHOT!"

Some teams had a trainer who was taping up the girls before the game. There was a water person who handed each girl her own water bottle when they subbed out. Our arrogance made us think that since we were black we were going to be the better athletes, but once that whistle was blown and we were running up and down the court with these tough-ass white girls, our DNA failed us. They were faster and stronger because they were better prepared. They'd been training for years, like Russian gymnasts. After taking the loss, we drowned our sorrows in McDonald's, while our competitors unzipped their home-packed lunches—whole-wheat sandwiches, veggie sticks, water, fresh fruit. Their access to better resources made all the difference, and while we were scrappy kids from the inner city, we would never measure up, given what our community offered.

———

Brooklyn is the most populated New York City borough, with an estimated 2.5 million inhabitants. It is also home to several food deserts, which means that, depending on where you live, you may not have a supermarket within a mile or more of your home and limited transportation to get there. Williamsburg qualified as such. If I wanted a hero sandwich or a slice of pizza, I had to walk half a mile to Broadway, the main strip that split my Hasidic neighborhood on the south with the Hispanic neighborhood on the north. Within my apartment complex there was the "Jewish store." I'm sure my neighbors just called it the store. It had the basics, but all the products were from their own kosher brands. It was Trader Joe's before Trader Joe's. Adhering to kosher law, the store didn't carry meat products in it. When my parents wanted a steak, that meant a four-mile trek to Western Beef or Waldbaum's. We didn't have a car for most of my childhood, so food shopping meant carpooling with Grandma in her Jesus-mobile to Metropolitan Avenue in Queens, where "the supermarkets were better 'cause white people lived there."

Food deserts impact low-income communities three times more often than affluent neighborhoods in Brooklyn. This inconsistency exists around the world, but in a first-world country it feels ludicrous. The powers that be think those who make less than $30,000 don't need fresh fruits, veggies, and meat without brown spots. As an adult, I tried making excuses for it. Maybe NYC's competitive real estate market was the reason. Or perhaps the order is gentrification to bring up the median household income, then you get rewarded with Whole

Foods, Trader Joe's, Fairway, and artisanal markets. Turning "blighted" neighborhoods into flourishing communities with bike lanes, green spaces, and stroller parking lots shouldn't be that hard of a process if you truly give a damn about all people—despite their income—having access to good and healthy foods. (Look at me thinking like a decent human being. The nerve.)

Several studies have shown that diets with high levels of saturated fats actually impair learning and memory. The choices made on the plate can alter one's quality of education, employment, and long-term health. "You are what you eat" takes on a sinister meaning. The biggest lie we tell ourselves is that cancer, diabetes, and high cholesterol are hereditary, when really they are by-products of what's available near us. Major fast-food corporations thrive in lower-class neighborhoods because those communities are food deserts that make them perfect for transforming into food swamps.

Food Swamp: Areas with a high-density of establishments selling high-calorie fast food and junk food, relative to healthier food options.

Growing up, whenever I visited the posh parts of Manhattan, I didn't understand how there was a market or fancy restaurants on damn near every block. Where was McDonald's, Subway, Crown Fried Chicken, the Chinese restaurant with the bulletproof glass? Is it because they knew value meals have no value?

My junior year of high school, AP classes and basketball were sucking the life out of me. I had to earn high marks in both to make myself more attractive to a prospective college coach. I was a latecomer. Many of the girls I would be competing against for scholarships had been on the scene since they were in seventh grade. There was no way my parents could afford to send me to college. As the pressure mounted, I ate less. I wasn't purposefully not eating, I just had repressed my desire for food so far to the back of my head I would legit forget to eat. On one such day, I rode the train home from school after practice. As we came across the Williamsburg Bridge, I held on to the overhead grab hold as my stomach growled loud enough for the entire car to hear. I was so hungry I started talking to myself using motivational basketball energy to give me strength. "You got this, girl. One more stop. You're almost home. You can eat when you get home." Depleted, I rested my forehead in the bend of my elbow. "If I close my eyes, maybe the hunger will go away." I fainted.

The only time I knew black women to faint was at funerals and when the Holy Ghost hit them. Otherwise, fainting was reserved for petite white women in movies when they got bad news. They'd place the back of their hand on their forehead and declare, "Oh no!," and melt down to the floor. Someone would catch them before their silk gown touched the ground. And yet here I was, no silk gown, no captivating suitor, and very much having just fainted. I opened my eyes, looked up from the filthy subway floor to shocked commuters. A man offered me his seat. A mother with a stroller pulled out a banana and pushed it in my face.

"No, it's okay," I said. I hate bananas. "I'm okay." Embarrassed, I kept my head down until we pulled into the station. I used twenty cents in my pocket and begged the Asian fruit grocer to sell me an apple. On the walk home I devoured it. After that, I started packing a granola bar in my bookbag as a fail-safe. I considered my fainting a fluke and not a sign that my young body needed more to survive. I didn't know anything about vitamins or supplements, how to measure protein, or that my body could not refuel off a slice of pizza.

———

Fast-forward three years. I'm a lower classman at NYU and a benchwarmer on the women's basketball team. Even though the program is Divison III, our coach was hard-core. I was in the best shape of my life, but nagging injuries slowed me down, preventing me from reaching my weight goal of 195 pounds. (Note: I've haven't been under 200 pounds since junior high school, so this was a big ask of Coach.)

On the first day of preseason, my teammates and I nervously walked onto the court, where a scale stood in the center. Seeing that gave me a flashback to Mrs. Hirsch's class. *Please don't let them weigh us out in the open.*

"211," Coach read it out loud. "We got to get that down." I love the "we" in that statement. That was the beautiful thing about team sports, the idea of "we." My teammates were going to help by making sure I ate one bowl of Captain Crunch instead of three when we went to dinner. They would cheer me on when I'd hit the treadmill, even pushing the speed up and daring me to sprint out the last minute. Moments like these were what I loved about basketball, the sisterhood.

Not wanting to let the team down, I went to the gym every day during summer break. I was benching 150, squatting 300. I'd play a couple games of pickup with the fellas. My muscles had muscles, but I still had a FUPA. It kept me humble. After a week at the gym, I took a well-earned day off. Mom and my little brother, now in kindergarten, were sitting at the dining room table eating lunch. Home for the summer, I came out of my bedroom after hearing them talk about how delicious their food was. *I'm going to get something to eat too.* As I walked to the kitchen, I got dizzy. *I'm just gonna lean against the wall.* Next thing I feel is the cold, hard linoleum floor. I push myself up. Blood is everywhere. Dad ran from my parents' bedroom; my mom started praying.

By the time Dad got me to the emergency room, I was feeling back to normal except the gash over my eyebrow was still bleeding profusely. When Dad saw how crowded the waiting room was, he turned to me and whispered, "Act like you're still dizzy." I slumped my weight onto him, holding the bloody rag over my face.

"My daughter needs a wheelchair," Dad said, sounding panicked. Nurses sprang into action. If you thought my sausage scene at the dinner table was Oscar-worthy, Dad playing "desperate father of a fainter" would've earned him best actor. Dad made sure to tell them I played for the NYU team and any further injury would be bad for my Division III career. I felt guilty for being rushed to the top of the list all because my injury could have been prevented.

"Are you pregnant?" The West Indian nurse didn't look up from her clipboard.

"Huh?" It was just her and me in the small ER room. The curtain was closed, but my paranoia still wasn't comfortable talking about my inactive sex life.

"Are. You. Pregnant? You having sex?" So much for bedside manner.

"No!"

"Why you faint for? You could be pregnant and don't know. See it all the time." She popped her gum while scribbling something on my file. "Let me see."

I lowered the rag from my wound.

"Oh, that's nothing. You sure you don't want to take a pregnancy test?"

"I'm sure." I hadn't had sex in over a year. After LaJarvis there had been two others, but the guilt of sinning, plus my wanting to keep my number of partners to one hand and the panic I felt after a foolish pregnancy scare had led me to become a born-again virgin. Months before my fall I was seeing someone. My period was four days late; I spent the entire time in my dorm room playing "Zion" by Lauryn Hill on repeat. I called Mom and confessed. She didn't even know I was dating.

"Mom, my period is late."

"You've been having sex?"

"Yes."

"Did you use protection?"

"Yes, of course."

"Did it break?"

"No." Silence. Mom could tell I was freaking out and now was not the time to poke fun at my naïveté.

"*Oohhh-kay*, well, go to the drugstore and get a pregnancy test." Mom was so calm. "Take it and call me back." Knowing her, she wasn't going to spring into action until things were confirmed.

Scared out of my mind, I asked my team captain, YaYa, to go with me to the drugstore. YaYa was a senior and the highest scorer in our conference. Of course she'd know what to do. We added some chips, a magazine, and some other goofy shit to make the purchase less suspicious, which just made it more suspicious. Do cashiers judge you more when they see condoms, Plan B, or a pregnancy test in your items? I would argue that condoms suggest you are living your best life and being smart about it. Plan B means you slipped up but as a woman are taking care of business before things get way too complicated. A pregnancy test means you fucked up the first two preventative measures. However, if the test is on the counter by itself and you don't stuff it in your purse on the way out of the door, congrats, you are part of the one out of five women who actually planned a pregnancy. Turns out, I wasn't pregnant then, and I damn sure wasn't pregnant now when Ms. Rude Nurse was taking my vitals.

In the end, I received six stitches that day and would tell everyone I was going up for a rebound and a girl on the other team elbowed me. My only basketball injury wasn't basketball-related at all, unless you count passing out from not eating because I was trying to make weight. Eating disorder notwithstanding, basketball changed my life.

9

FAT AS SHIT

Shortly after busting my head open to the white meat, I quit basket-ball. With two years left, I survived the threat of Y2K and figured life was too short to be in the gym six hours a day doing something I didn't love. It wasn't like I was going to the WNBA or playing overseas. I'd gotten everything that I wanted out of ball—friends and into a good school. My deal with the hard-court devil was done. I had songs on Napster to download, *Sex and the City* episodes to catch up on, and thanks to *The Matrix*, conspiracy theories to investigate. On late nights I'd meet my former teammates for postpractice dinner. Looking at my tray, you'd think I, too, just burned 1,500 calories and needed to refuel. Chicken sandwiches, fries, bowls of Captain Crunch, an apple 'cause I was trying to be healthy. The girls didn't police me anymore. I was a free agent, free to get fat.

The only reason people like the Rock's cheat meal photos on Insta-gram is because you know that six days out of the week he's busting his ass, squatting dump trucks, and eating lean. Back then, every one of my meals looked like a cheat meal. Chicken sandwich, curly fries, two bowls of cereal, a slice of pizza, and cherry Coke—my version of a tasting menu sponsored by sweatpants and an unlimited meal plan. I was working up to my own episode of *My 600-lb Life*. (Check your local listing for air times.) All I know is, that show always finds me when I'm contemplating a bad food decision. Try eating a cookie when you're watching a woman who can't reach her own ass to wash it. Also, where are these morbidly obese women finding loving and dedicated husbands and boyfriends? One such devotee woke up early every morning to cook his woman a dozen eggs and two pounds of bacon before he went to work. Meanwhile, I'm single and can see my feet. No, I'm not body shaming. I'm a fatty at heart and have the stretch marks to prove it. I'm just in awe of these dudes' support, especially when their woman has the audacity to be verbally abusive when she can't eat what she wants. *Lady, if you don't roll over on your good knee and thank God for bringing you this man who picked melted M&M's out of your belly button* . . . Needless to say, I am a fan of *My 600-lb Life* and watch whenever I can.

By senior year of college, I had gained fifty pounds and no one told me. All my mirrors stopped below my chest. I didn't buy my first full-length mirror until 2009 because, subconsciously, I didn't want to see the truth. I'd blame it on not having enough space in my place. Pictures were a good document of my various sizes, but back then we only took pictures when the crew looked super cute for a night out. We'd pose in the narrow hallways of our dorm and say, "That's gonna be a good one," after taking a few snaps of the camera and wait weeks if not months before we had the money to get them developed. Picture taking was a faith-based process before digital cameras allowed instant image approval. By the time I'd get my pictures back, I'd go around asking my friends, "Do I really look like this?" Always kind, they would point out something cute about me to draw attention away from the obvious.

"I love your hair like that!"

"That was a fun night."

"Oh, can I borrow those earrings?" Real friends know how to divert.

My entire social circle was still on the basketball team, which meant I had no one to hang out with during the season. Under no circumstances was I going to be the solo girl in the club dancing by herself. That woman reeks of desperation. The more she tries to blend in, the more she sticks out. She goes to the bar and orders herself a drink. It gives her something to fiddle with since she has no one to talk to. She holds the glass in one hand, the straw in the other, taking a tiny sip. This drink has to last until a man offers to pick up the next one. There's still no one to talk to, so she bounces her eyes around the room and smiles at whoever catches her glance. She looks down at her outfit, occasionally checking to see just how much her boobs are showing. When you're a woman in the club without friends, you got to have them bait boobies on display. Men are easily seduced by titty meat. Once the night comes to an end, she puts on a brave face and electric smile, still hoping to snag whatever is left in the barrel. There's a sexy emphasis on the way she says "Have a *good* night" to the bartenders and bouncers, her last options. She gathers her things and slowly walks out, down the block to the twenty-four-hour deli where she buys a little snack for the ride home and wonders if she should pick up some batteries for her vibrator as well.

———

Before I quit the team and blew the hell up, going to the club with my girls were some of the best nights of my young adult life. We didn't do keg parties or stay on the quad. New York City was our campus. We went to the city's hottest spot and hustled our way into VIP. We called ourselves The B.E.L.L.s—Beautiful, Educated, Lovely Ladies. Jazz had a long-term boyfriend but loved being our hype woman when we went out. Daphne was from Georgia, hands down the quiet one, but would call a guy ugly right to his face. YaYa was our team captain, had six-pack abs and would lose her mind anytime an Aaliyah song came on. I was the self-designated guardian of the group. While on the dance floor, I'd be checking for emergency exits, rapey men, and fights. We didn't smoke and barely drank, which is why our go-to drink order was either Amaretto or Midori sours with extra maraschino cherries. In the spring, we'd go out every week to make up for the hours under Coach's watchful eye. The skirts were tight, the spaghetti straps loose, and the lip gloss greasy. Four black Amazons rolling up to the club, within minutes we'd be escorted inside and comped. Always in athlete mode, we'd strategize the night's game plan:

1. Point out tall, cute guys.

2. Dare someone in the group to go up to one of them.

3. No dare can be turned down.

4. If you find a guy who wants to buy you a drink, order one for the rest of us. We'll met you at the bar once we see you headed there.

5. Lock in a guy who, at the end of the night, will treat all of us to breakfast.

There were hand signals for when you were dancing with someone. If you liked him, you'd wipe your forehead with your hand, like, "Whew, I'm good." If you wanted us to get you away from dude, you'd place the palm of your hand on the back of your neck, holding it like it hurt. Whoever was close would dance their way in between you and the gremlin and float you away to safety.

Daphne and I tied for least outgoing. After five minutes on the dance floor and one lap around the perimeter, I'd park it in a corner where I'd watch the rest of the B.E.L.L.s' purses and jackets. Being a true introvert, I could muster up only spurts of energy. Big shocker, my nonchalant attitude attracted more guys. They saw me as wholesome and easygoing. I became the group's bait. While they danced and flirted on the floor, I sat in the corner like a black widow waiting for my web to shake. Men mistook my disinterest as my being shy. Soon, they'd leave and come back with a drink, usually champagne—which I detested—so each time they'd turn away I'd pour some into the flower-pot, vase, or empty glass next to me. At 4:00 a.m. the music faded, the lights came up, and my suitor would ask the million-dollar question, "Would you like to get something to eat?"

Even in the best shape of my life, something about me gave off a "feed me, Seymour" vibe.

"I would love to but I'm with my friends."

"That's cool. They can fit in my car."

Walking to his car, the B.E.L.L.s would play "guess the make and model." Ford Expeditions and Cadillac Escalades were the cars du jour. This was the start of the "Cash Money taking over the 1999 and 2000s" bling-bling era. The flashier the car, the more expensive our restaurant suggestion was. A good night ended with a trip to Chelsea's Cafeteria or the Coffee Shop in Union Square. An even better night included walking away with extra orders of food for the next day.

Jazz and I would split french toast and buffalo wings. YaYa was into egg white omelets before it became trendy. Daphne could eat a man out of house and home and not gain a pound. Once our food sponsor heard our generous orders, it was clear sex was not going to be for dessert. None of us were fucking, especially on a full stomach. Instead, he'd settle for lively conversation from his leeches. Phone numbers were scribbled down on the back of receipts, but I'd never see or hear from him again. I should have milked it more. I wouldn't be this hot again for a while.

———

First, my skirts became too tight, then they couldn't go above my thighs. Slinky tops didn't make it over my inflated boobs. Pants with elastic waistbands and hoodies became the uniform. My ugly-girl sweatpants were my most prized article of clothing. Every woman owns a pair that we age like fine wine. They comfort us on good days and especially bad ones. Men won't see them until it's too far into the relationship. Your love must be solidified before you unveil those grease-spot-speckled sweats that look like the Exxon Valdez oil spill happened in your lap. There's no elastic left in the waist, and the drawstring popped, so you're left with a flaccid shoestring penis that hits your leg with every step. You're constantly hoisting them up to keep them from falling down. If it's movie night, no need for a blanket. Just pull up your ugly-girl sweats, tucking your boobs in and even your shoulders, creating a dingy tent around your body. The bottom of the pants are gross from being dragged around the ground since the inseam is three to thirty inches too long. One of the pockets has a hole in it that we always forget is there and get a surprise when our keys end up by our ankle. *(I write this after having just ripped the inner thigh of my jeans squatting into a Lyft pool. I wish I had a pair of ugly-girl pants handy to change into.)*

The B.E.L.L.s dragged me out for old times' sake. During one such reunion, we stepped out of a cab, trotted across the street toward the hottest bar my fake ID could get me into, and CRACK!

"Oh no!" I whimpered. "I think my heel broke clean off."

"What? Girl, stop playing." Daphne laughed.

"No, I'm not. Look, but don't look." We were standing in the middle of the street. It felt like everyone was watching.

"Yeah, it's off." YaYa bent down to pick it up.

———

Did you know a fourteen-year-old is credited with being one of the first women to wear high heels? During the sixteenth century, Catherine de' Medici, of the power-hungry Italian dynasty that shaped modern banking, the Catholic Church, and politics, was engaged to be married to the taller King Henry II, and in a quest to keep his attention, had high-heeled shoes constructed. Prior to that, heels were said to originate with members of the Persian cavalry as far back as the tenth century, who wore them because it was easier for them to stand up on a galloping horse while shooting arrows. During the Middle Ages, men and women wore chopines, the original platform shoe. Records show pairs reaching up to thirty-inches high. The height protected the wealthy from dirtying up their hemlines with the raw sewage that filled the cobblestone streets of Europe. Heels were a status symbol for the privileged. If someone not among the elite was caught wearing them, they could be punished.

Fast-forward a couple hundred years and my heel was now in my pocketbook because my fat ass was too heavy for my Steve Madden boots.

"Excuse me, sir, do you have Krazy Glue?" We went to a nearby deli in hopes of a quick remedy. "My friend's heel broke off but we're trying to keep the party going." The glue didn't work. Letting it set would cut into our party time, plus they charged a cover after midnight, and we did not have the money to pay. The MacGyver in me kicked in.

"Do you have a hammer we can borrow?" I asked the clerk. He found great joy in watching four sexily dressed women pry a nail from the wall with said hammer and attempt to cobble my broken heel back on. Five minutes later, the heel was back in my purse and I went the rest of the night balancing on one three-inch heel. The B.E.L.L.s made sure to get me drunk so I didn't lament and secured me a seat so I didn't cramp up. Most would see this as a breaking point, but being in denial, I made it about the quality of the shoes, not my weight.

The next time my fatness was front and center was while working a home basketball game. My student employee job was in the gym offices. I'd walk past my friends on the court every day during their workout and never once lifted a finger to exercise myself. Rejecting all things fitness came to bite me in the ass when I ran into a former high school teammate there to play against NYU. She took one look at me in the hallway and yelled, "DAMN, Chloé, you got FAT!" You could hear a pin drop.

"Yeah, I know. I can't even zip my pants." Self-deprecation was my second language. Plus, there was no way to refute her claims when the proof was in my unbuckled pants. I'd blown up like Violet Beauregarde. Sure, I was embarrassed, but I couldn't let it show. My days of being bullied taught me better.

"I didn't even realize you gained that much weight." Jazz tried to soften the blow. "I guess it's because I see you every day; I don't see it. Don't worry, you're still cute though." I denied all B.E.L.L. requests to hang out after that.

Senior year, I picked up a minor in sociology and enrolled in a course on Public Self vs. Private Self and Conspicuous Consumption. In essence, we wear a mask when presenting ourselves in the world, and one way to execute the facade is through materialism. People wear gaudy, logo-laced brands and post curated Instagram spreads to declare their social status. History shows, folks have used clothing and jewels to stunt on these hoes since the dawn of time. One assumes a lot about a person by the car they drive, shoes they wear or, hell, mobile phone they use. I'm sure there's a cave drawing somewhere with a man flexing with the first-ever leopard-skin loincloth.

———

American economist and sociologist Thorstein Veblen originated the concept of "conspicuous consumption" in his 1899 book, *The Theory of the Leisure Class*, which refers to those who would rather buy expensive items to showcase their bank accounts than address their own real needs, often with the hopes of easily navigating the social ladder. Fake it 'til you make it, if you will. Once I understood this, I stopped turning my nose up at the Jordan sneaker obsession. When a person of color makes buying a pair of Jordans a priority, they get slammed. Carrie Bradshaw didn't eat so she could buy Manolo Blahniks, and she was revered. Both parties wanted the same thing, to walk in the shoes of and be seen as an elite. It's like the time I saved up all my student job money and bought the super-exclusive Chloé sunglasses with the diamond-encrusted heart on the lens. Showing off was never my thing, but there was something about these $250 sunglasses that pulled me in like Gollum. They literally had my name on it. I wore them around campus while in my ugly-girl sweatpants. Had to let the world know, *Yes, I'm a mess, but not that much of a mess. I can afford these shades.* It's like putting a bow on the hood of a hooptie. Yes, it drives, but it's in terrible shape.

Whatever the opposite of performing "conspicuous consumption" is, that was and to a lesser degree still is me. *Why conform to one-sided social expectations of how I should look as a woman? You are going to welcome and respect me for who I am and not what is on my back.* Translation: Years of being too wide and tall for commercial clothing left me resentful, so I saw clothes as nothing more than functional and buried my disappointment in not being able to fit the trends of the day. And in the early 2000s there were a lot of them. Juicy Couture's pastel-colored velour tracksuits stopped at my knees; not the hem, the waist. I couldn't get them up. Cargo pants were great for keeping snacks on hand but very unflattering for my lower silhouette, especially when there were snacks in the pockets. Full dresses worn over jeans were a big look at the time. Thankfully, I sat that one out. Pointy-toed boots that came below the knee didn't work for me either. Being tall, my calf never lined up with the calf cut into the boot sleeve. Low-waist jeans and lace tops—out of the question. I did get to experience pashmina scarves. Those fit. Since I was tall, ponchos hit me right above the waist, like a lobster bib.

For the class final, our professors, a very eclectic and stylish man and woman, told us to dress up as the member of another social class and document a night out and the responses. My love/hate relationship with *Sex and the City*—*I mean come on, a freelance journalist who writes one column every few weeks does not have the lifestyle of Carrie and, economically, she was the weakest link in the group*—was my inspiration. Chic fashionista it was. Armed with a pair of scissors, a sewing kit, and elastic size 20 jeans, I pieced together what I felt was a sexy, sophisticated current look. I wore a black Kangol newsboy hat because I had just done the big chop and my teeny weeny Afro was not my friend. I put makeup on my entire face, not just lip gloss, which was kinda pointless because my hat came over my forehead and I wore my Chloé glasses all night. I found a cheap sleeveless black lace top, well, it was lace from the high neck collar to above the breast, the rest was a forgiving cotton/polyester blend that cased my stomachs like a second skin.

Yes, stomachs plural. For as long as I can remember, my stomach has been partitioned into the north belly and the south belly divided by the belly button border. North Belly a.k.a. N. Beezy is the most tyrannical of the two. Depending on her mood, it will ruin any clean-line look I'm going for. On bad days, N. Beezy sticks her head over the balcony of my waistband, soaking in the good weather, chatting with passersby, waving to onlookers like "What the hell you looking at? This is my balcony and I can come and go as I damn well please." If you haven't noticed, N. Beezy can be seen on the back cover of this book. This is the smallest she's been in a long time. It took a great deal of negotiating for her not to show her ass. South Belly a.k.a. S. Beezy is shy. Depending on the tightness of what I'm wearing she can fade away, but her imprint is always there. Most would refer to her as a FUPA. When I sit, she lays her head on the top of my lap. She peeks out the sides of hipster, bikini, thong, G-string, and high-cut brief underwear, like a kitten playing behind a curtain. I've seen S. Beezy get on the smaller side a few times, but I'm pretty sure defectors from the north smuggle their way past the border to infiltrate, bringing her back to her full status. These two are my oldest and dearest frenemies.

Why wasn't I born during a time when women wore rib-crushing corsets and hoop skirts to accentuate their manufactured waist? North and South Belly would have assimilated swimmingly behind rigid boning and fabric cinched together by my strong basketball grip.

The North would be taken in by the breasts of the north, while the South would join the southern hip region. And who was the first to popularize the corset across Europe? Catherine de' Medici, the same woman to appropriate the heels of military horsemen for her own personal gain. Not to undermine the shrewd business and political mind of de' Medici; after all, the woman puppeteered the French kingships of her three sons after the death of their father, King Henry II. However, one could make a strong correlation to her success ruling Europe in the 1600s to her having a snatched waist while strutting around the castle in heels. Come on, you know the world bends to a woman with 36-24-36 body measurements.

If I ever were to achieve a 24-inch waist, just know something terrible is going on in my life. Most women could never achieve that small of a waist naturally, which is why corsets have survived for centuries. In the 1500s, early corsets were made of hardened fabric and restricted a woman's feminine curves. They were also worn outside the clothes as an accessory like a belt. Then the shape shifted to the highly marketed and popular "S shape," which had women looking like they were about to tip over at any moment. The popular "S shape" style of the 1800s left many women with deformed spines, broken bones, and rearranged intestines. Corsets were so effective in helping women achieve the perfect "hourglass" shape, that the 1881 Rational Dress Society formed out of concern for women's health and comfort. The group protested any women's fashion that impeded movement and caused physical harm, and their specifications for the perfect dress included:

1. Freedom of movement.

2. Absence of pressure over any part of the body.

3. No more weight than is necessary for warmth, and both weight and warmth evenly distributed.

4. Grace and beauty combined with comfort and convenience.

5. Not departing too conspicuously from the ordinary dress of the time.

I rounded out my senior sociology fashion project outfit with "high-water" slacks. I cuffed them up and threw on some black knock-off Diesel men's "Wish" sneakers. Heels were dead to me. Final pièce de résistance, a single camouflage shirt cuff sewn from fabric scraps my roommate gave me, similar to those tacky Chippendale male dancer white cuffs. Again, I was wearing a sleeveless top.

Jazz, YaYa, and Daphne were excited to help with my social experiment. The four of us took a picture together in the dorm lobby. It was the first time I smiled and appeared in front of the camera in months. After gaining the weight in college, my twenties and some of my thirties were filled with moments that I avoided capturing on camera because I knew my double chin would show, or my chubby cheeks, and of course every region of my gut. Moments that were filled with love, laughter, and accomplishment—a birthday, new job, cover story, house party—went largely undocumented due to low self-esteem.

Of the pictures I did take, most never found their way into a frame, showcased for public view. They are tucked away in a box, discovered once a year when I searched for something and would come across them, genuinely surprised that snapshots of me from then existed. I'd pick up younger Chloé and hold her in my hands. Now I can look past the weight and focus on her face, the eyes, smile. Was she happy then? Often, the answer is yes.

Now, traveling as a comedian, I've met hundreds of young women on college campuses who come up to me after a show, beaming from ear to ear. When I ask if they want to take a picture with me, they wave their hand no, nervously tuck their hair behind their ear, and give a mumbling explanation of why they hate taking pictures.

"Don't be silly, you're beautiful!" I say. I scan their body to find something specific to compliment. "I love that T-shirt; Steven Universe is my shit!" They giggle some more and most times will walk away without taking a picture. I want them to take it so bad. Not for my ego, but so they will have more keepsakes of them being happy. It's a regret I have. I would have taken more pictures because, with flaws and all, that version of me in that moment is part of the reason why I'm a better woman today.

CHLOÉ, YOU HAVE A VERY PRETTY FACE

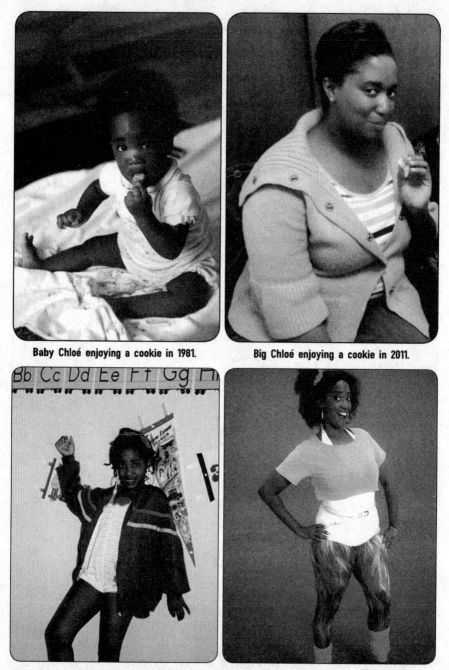

Baby Chloé enjoying a cookie in 1981.   Big Chloé enjoying a cookie in 2011.

I was four and obsessed with looking like Madonna. In 2015, I would re-create the eighties retro look for a short-lived sketch TV show. I was vegan at the time and amazed I could fit into this American Apparel bodysuit.

Easter Sunday at Grandma's house with Dad and Mom. We were probably waiting to eat.

Age thirteen, heavy into my Janet phase. You see the cowrie shell choker.

Junior high school graduation versus high school prom. Four years of basketball helped me lose my "baby weight."

My fifth-grade photo features what was left of my hair after my first perm fiasco. Fast forward twenty years, everything is covered up except my smile.

NYU: 1998, freshman year, and the smallest I've ever been, versus 2002, senior year, when I gained fifty-plus pounds because the only thing I was lifting was my fork.

Beached-whaling it while on a couples' vacation in 2011; I was pushing three hundred pounds.

Carefree in a two-piece in 2019.

10

REAL WOMEN, YEAH RIGHT!

Trigger Warning: The following chapter deals with race, class, and working with white women.

T his is Chloé!" My editor-in-chief, Connie, was giving a tour of our offices. The year was 2002. I was five months out of college. That's how long it took to land a job because the dot-com bubble went bust and a shit ton of new graduates flooded a market that didn't want them. I was lucky enough to land a job, more than likely because I brought diversity and a big college name to the table. "She interned at *The Source*. My son loves hip-hop." My blackness gave her cool points. I was the second hire for the newest Hearst magazine, *Lifetime*. Why would a cable network launch a print magazine, you ask? Old-fashioned, shortsighted, technophobe companies were terrified of losing more money on the uncharted internet. At the time, Lifetime was the number one cable network in prime time and had an unparalleled hold of the coveted women age 30–45 demographic. The success of Oprah's O *Magazine* sent publishers scrambling for celebrity and brand-specific titles. Anyone remember *Rosie*?

Graduating with a B.A. in journalism during a recession was humbling. I was twenty-one, stressed out, living at home, and shared a room with my seven-year-old brother. I kept my Lane Bryant interview suit, size 20, hanging on the closet door. Eventually I landed a few interviews, no doubt because of my ethnically ambiguous name. "Oh, *you're* Chloé." My size and blackness was a surprise to whoever retrieved me from the lobby. Their embarrassed faces said, *I did not see that coming.*

Between 1998 and 2008, America was participating in what I call "The Diversity Decade." Corporations and colleges spent time and a boatload of money to recruit and appeal to people of color, specifically African Americans and Latinx. The country was hell-bent on appearing to support equal opportunity initiatives especially since they'd run the risk of class-action lawsuits or losing funding. Being a proud product of Affirmative Action, I used to tell this joke onstage:

> *When applying for college, the push for diversity was so strong that the only thing on the application I filled in was race: African American.*
>
> *If they needed more info I added, "100 percent black, family former slaves who built this country, African American."*
>
> *I got into every college I applied to. The acceptance letters read: "Dear African American, come on down!"*

You may be able to tell why I retired this. Most audiences heard "Affirmative Action" and their racial bias overshadowed the sarcasm. I could hear their mental contortions: *See, she got a free ride 'cause she's black. That's bullshit!* Let me say this for the thickheaded folks in the back. Affirmative Action wasn't run like a soup kitchen. I busted my ass for top marks. The academic bar wasn't lowered for students of color such as myself; AA programs simply took into account economic and social disparities and balanced the playing field a tiny bit.

It especially became difficult telling that joke with President Obama in office. His historic win stopped the diversity train in its tracks. How do you justify the need for diversity training and inclusion when a black man was occupying the most powerful office in the world? America was so busy patting itself on the back to realize this was a superficial fix. If only I had a Harriet Tubman $20 bill for every time I heard, "America: We're postracial."

When Connie offered me the position, our conversation ended with her saying, "We think you'd be a great addition to our diverse staff." Of the forty-plus staff, I was the youngest and one of four women of color. Sitting in my cubicle with my back to the floor, I'd hear Connie's heels from around the corner, "Wait until you meet our editorial assistant; she's from Brooklyn . . ." She showed me off like a rescue. "She went to NYU . . . She's is so great . . . Kinda quiet . . . Gets along well with others . . ." My blackness came in handy. Whether it was properly identifying black celebs in photo captions or pointing out appropriation, stereotypes, and racial insensitivity to mostly deaf ears. Our cultural differences amused them and over time annoyed me. If I had a Sacagawea dollar for every time they opened their mouths and said some white nonsense to me, I could have bankrolled my own Lifetime movie, *Token: The Chloé Hilliard Story.*

"Chloé, where can I find black-eyed peas?" *Bitch, do I look like Fergie to you?*

"Hey, Chloé, are my elbows, like you say, ashy?" *Sweetie, that's eczema.*

"OMG, Chloé, I love your hair." Their hand itching to reach up to touch my Afro. "I wish mine stood up like that." *Boo, you've flat-ironed to death any sign of life in those strands. Now put your hands in your dress pockets before I get arrested.*

They assumed they knew my story because, according to TV and movies, the only way a person or color gains entry into a white space is with the help of a savior à la *Dangerous Minds, Finding Forrester, The Blind Side, The Help, 12 Years a Slave, Green Book.* I had to remind them I wasn't a down-and-out ghetto child who escaped the streets, my parents were married and I'd never lost a friend to drugs or gangs.

Lifetime catered to the budget-conscious, middle-American wife and mother who loved stories about women overcoming obstacles—"My Mother Is Carrying My Baby"—and enjoyed fancy recipes for foods they've already been making for years. So many bland and unnecessary takes on potato salad made it to print. Ironically, the simple, wholesome life we were putting on the page was a far cry from the designer clothes, personal trainers, nannies, Wall Street husbands, and trust funds some of my coworkers enjoyed. Our staff had very little in common with the women they were selling dreams and fake solutions to.

———

The first women-focused publication, *The Ladies Mercury* newsletter, debuted in 1693 London, giving advice to reader-submitted questions. It lasted four weeks. Almost forty years later, Englishman Edward Cave invented the word "magazine," which was inspired by the Arabic word for "storehouse," *makhazin*. Early publications were so expensive, only the well-to-do could afford them. *The Atlantic, Harper's,* and *Scientific American* sought the educated and elite. As resources became cheaper, lower-grade magazines skipped the smarty-arty stuff and concentrated on amusement and entertainment. Early women's magazines were all about that domestic life. Readers were treated to embroidery patterns, sheet music, literary pieces, and fashion notes. By 1898, *Ladies' Home Journal* became the first American magazine to reach one million subscribers. In 2018, the top women magazines—in order of biggest circulation—were *Good Housekeeping, Family Circle, People,* and *Women's Day*. Clearly the average American woman is not so interested in Dior's new runway collection or philosophical columns on the current state of humanity.

Lifetime's slogan was "Real Life. Real Women." Shania Twain graced the debut issue with cover lines sure to make us stand out from the crowd.

* INDULGE WITH NO BULGE

* Eat Your Way THIN This Season

* Stress-Free Ways to Stay Healthy

* How to Make Your Own Luck!

* 250 JOY Celebration Ideas

In the early 2000s, magazine editors went overboard, using huge letters on their covers to attract readers. Apparently, women are hypnotized by 100-point type announcing 738 new fall fuschia fashion trends for left-handed women, or 482 ways to host a silent dinner party. Ridiculous lists, unfounded life and career advice, bland recipes, fashion makeovers, sex tips, and horoscopes aren't as empowering as women's magazines would like you to believe. The industry feeds off women's insecurities and the desire to reinvent ourselves according to the latest trend. Each month, I'd wonder, who was this American woman we were writing for?

The American woman is not a monolith, so how were we supposed to depict "Real Life. Real Women" if we all weren't on the same page? Depending on the region, women vary in how we vote, our level of education, earning power, and access to health care. That's a wide net to cast. Baking cakes and sex tips won't bring all women together. And speaking of cakes, a lot of women are too damn busy to make a cake from scratch. Looking at women's magazines even now you'd think we were still in the 1950s, where once a woman got married their duty was to bake every day. That's probably why men used to die of heart attacks at thirty-two. After lunch, they'd pass out on the factory floor. Don't believe me, go check your grandmother's china cabinet and I'll bet you there's a nice crystal cake dish that may one day be yours. I plan on storing gluten-free edibles in mine.

Being a modern woman who kissed her kids goodbye then slugged it out in corporate America was a stark contrast to the women of yesteryear. Inside our cubicle maze and corner offices, we dealt with this existential crisis; constantly defining and redefining who we were versus who society expected us to be because we carried the XX chromosomes. The office was comprised of three types:

The Perfectionists

The editor-in-chief and her senior-most staff set the tone for the rest of the team. The power suits were black, the button-down shirts cocaine white, and shoes stiletto or kitten, which is why they expensed cab rides as short as four blocks. They'd walk up, and like Pavlov's dogs, we underlings salivated, hoping to be picked to run an errand, grab coffee, or help unfreeze her computer or PalmPilot. The Perfectionists appeared to have it all—the six-figure job, husband, kids, small waist. Secretly, they were stressed-out by the pressure to maintain it. The ones who had small children at home had it the worst. Morning recitals, sick nannies, apple-picking trips, sleep training, these moms had to negotiate every minute of the day and who took priority. The kids didn't always land on top.

You could tell how their day was going by how they closed their office doors. A walk in and light push of the door meant, "I'm working, but knock if you need me." If a Perfectionist briskly walked to her office, entered, turned to face the door, slowly pushed it shut, and clicked the door handle lock, she was about to pitch a fit about something. Meltdowns only occurred in front of a Perfectionist's assistant, who knew way too much. They saw the tears when a husband canceled dinner plans for the third time that month or when an arch-nemesis stole her nanny or a vajazzler fell ill, forcing the Perfectionist to go without Swarovski crystals on her vagina runway for another week. They vacationed in the Hamptons; some came from big money. Their engagement rings were huge, which made them toss their hands around during conversations for emphasis. One woman liked to remind us that her husband told her she didn't have to work, but she didn't want to be stuck with "those annoying housewives who did yoga all day."

The Understudies

Power-hungry assistant editors treasure troved any information they could find, hoping it would come in handy when they were ready to climb the ladder. Information was traded between them in the kitchenette. They whispered over mugs of K-Cup coffee. Understudies decorated their cubicles with vision-board clippings, had guilt-trip phone conversations with their boyfriend who hadn't proposed yet, and kept a pair of cute comfortable heels under their desk that they changed into from the sneakers they wore to work on the train.

Each time they passed you on the floor, they'd give a chipper "Hey ya!" whether it was the first or 101st time that day. In front of the Perfectionists they'd wear a charming smile and agreed with everything. If an Understudy's direct boss hated chocolate, she suddenly hated chocolate. If a Perfectionist's favorite perfume was Stella McCartney, then the Understudy would show up smelling of it. Among themselves they were superficially close friends but prayed for the downfall of another if they surpassed them in the ranks. Understudies seldom took responsibility for their screwups; going out of their way to set up a fall person, usually an unwitting delivery guy or intern. Work, to them, was 30 percent skill and 70 percent charm.

The Outsiders

This mixed-bag group set themselves apart by believing that their work would speak for itself. Operating from a place of efficiency and not ego, their words were direct. However, when everyone else speaks fluent "passive-aggressive," an Outsider's directness is seen as disrespect, labeling them "difficult to work with." Once that happens, hallway "hellos" from the higher-ups were replaced with awkward silence. Dead woman walking. Every Outsider must decide to either dig her sensible clearance rack shoes into the ground and stand firm or slowly morph into an Understudy and perhaps, if the stars aligned and enough backs were stabbed, a Perfectionist.

I was an Outsider determined to establish myself as a great asset without having to kiss ass or compromise my integrity. It didn't matter how much money was on the table, I would always tell the emperor he wasn't wearing any clothes. Well, if there was a good amount of money, I would maybe whisper it instead of yell it, but the words would definitely come out of my mouth. That's what being a child of the hip-hop generation gets you. I kept it real! During my college internship at the #1 hip-hop magazine, *The Source*, it was strongly encouraged. Interning under the senior music editor, I was asked to give my opinion and, get this, he listened. Editorial brainstorms were lively. I'd sit in a chair along the back wall and listen to editors and writers verbally duke it out. Someone would have their idea shot down, "Nah, that shit wack." No harm, no foul, and no tears.

Some of the most talented and professional journalists I've ever worked with were during my internship and later full-time employment at *The Source*. That experience taught me to speak up and fight for what I believed in, but this mindset was not celebrated at *Lifetime*, where the unspoken opinion was that I should assimilate. I was the poster child for "When keeping it real goes wrong." Eyes would roll when I'd tell the truth. *This is a women's magazine, why is Matt Damon on the cover?* My editors grew tired of my questions and suggestions. Several times they shot me down with "that isn't your place." *But you said you wanted diversity. Does that not include "of thought"?*

What does assimilation look like for a woman of color in a white space? Granted, it's been over a decade since I last worked in corporate, but I'm confident these points aren't too far off from what's currently being taught at the Token Black/Brown support groups that meet every third Thursday of the month.

Fix Your Face

Smile. Resting bitch face is only tolerated from a woman whose physicality is never seen as a threat. When you're my height, size, and let's not forget race, a face devoid of emotion, often misinterpreted as attitude, is seen as a red flag.

"What's wrong?"

"Nothing, why? What's up?"

"You just look like something is wrong."

"Nothing is wrong. This is just how I look. I'm working."

"Yeah but, I've seen you look happier. You don't right now, so I figured something is wrong."

Well, thanks to your unwanted observation, now something is wrong.

My annoying coworker would then make it a point to tell the next person, "I'm not sure but I think something is wrong with Chloé." The next day my boss would call me into her office and tell me to close the door.

"*Heeeey*, Chloé! Just wanted to take a minute to check in with ya, see how you're doing. How's work?" She leaned in like every white savior in a movie waiting to hear their black costar's gut-wrenching, tragic life story.

"Uh, I'm fine." Still no smile or happiness conveyed in my voice. "Work is fine."

"Fine?"

"Great, work is great!" *Shit, "fine" means something totally different to white women. "Fine" is like saying, "I want to kill myself." I really need to work on my code switching.*

After my new token smell wore off, I had to put in work. In addition to performing my job at the highest quality, I also needed to learn to act my ass off. Every face-to-face contact, even a passing glance in the hallway, had to include a smile. Anything less would be marked as my being unhappy, or even worse, angry. Once I became really good at smiling, I added a chipper, soulless "Hey!" Next, the expert-level combo: A smile, "HEY!," and a quick compliment about something they're wearing, "Loooooove that top!" It was like a video game cheat code.

Dump the Bass

Business was still heavily conducted via phone, and I, being the editorial assistant, fielded a lot of general calls. After hearing me answer the phone with a simple and direct "*Lifetime*," my cubicle neighbor and constant ear hustler, Ruthie, peaked her head over the wall.

"Hey, Chloé?"

"Hey!" *See, I was getting the hang of it.*

"I don't mean to pry but I heard you on the phone. You mind if I give you a little tip?"

"No, of course not." *Ugh*.

"When you answer the phone, try smiling and, like, make your voice *lighter*."

Sound happy and less black, got it.

After Ruthie's unrequested coaching, my phone greeting expanded to "Good morning/afternoon, *Lifetime* magazine, Chloé speaking. How can I help you?" Spoken in the key of Alicia Silverstone.

Bass has long been a trigger for them. Why do you think they hate rap music so much? Vocal bass has the same effect. You want to go for light, whiney, and even vocal fry, which has been perfected by the Kardashians. A baseless voice leaves a sense that the woman attached to it will need help or a boost of confidence at some point and the world would be ready to oblige. Damsels in distress never have bass in their voice. If Britney Spears spoke with more bass, we'd all expect her to have her life more together. But alas, she talks like she's still in the Mickey Mouse Club and we wish her the best, praying she is protected from hurt, harm, or danger because clearly she's fragile. How about Michael Jackson? None of us would have tolerated his nonsense—the high-water pants, nose jobs, dangling his kids over balconies—if he spoke like James Earl Jones.

Perfect the "Food Meltdown"

These women rarely ate lunch and when they did it was preceded by a declaration of how they were suddenly *starving*.

"OhMyGod, I'm starving!"

"Me too, my stomach is growling."

"Uh, I'm literally about to pass out."

The Perfectionists had lunch meetings damn near every day, and if they didn't, their assistants would grab them a mixed salad with a selective mix of toppings and a half ounce of low-fat dressing. You could hear them chewing on their dry-ass salads across the floor.

Understudies hated lunch because they didn't want to be away from their desks too long and risk looking like a slacker. They'd stampede in with their meals and seltzer swinging in a plastic bag, eat at their desk, then for the next thirty minutes walk around and visit each other while trading stories about how stuffed they are and couldn't finish their food. On a bad day, they'd follow up with "I'm trying to lose five pounds." It's always five pounds. I've never been five pounds away from my goal, and if I was, I'd be so happy to be that close that I'd settle for keeping the five pounds.

Living vicariously through me, the dieting divas would ask what I planned on getting, moaning in satisfaction and envy when I'd fearlessly say, "Mexican," or "Italian."

"That sounds delicious. I'm so jealous. I wish I could eat like that." *You hear that? She just called me fat and judged my poor food choices.* The other women of color and I started going together, communing over a prix fixe lunch special with real tablecloths. We had to stop once the others took notice and started speculating as to whether we were a sleeper cell.

———

Warding off fat was a huge issue both under our roof and on the pages of the magazine. Editors projected their food insecurities to readers in big, bold letter on the covers. These are actual cover lines that hit newsstands.

WHAT MOM FORGOT TO TEACH YOU

BURN 1,000 CALORIES FAST

THE LAZY WOMAN'S WORKOUT

THE ONLY DIET THAT WORKS

SANDWICHES. QUICK LUNCH OR DIET BUSTER?

ARE ENERGY BARS RUINING YOUR DIET?

Nothing about the *Lifetime* audience screamed, "I want to be a size two." Because American women were getting bigger. In 2004, SizeUSA, a survey sponsored by clothing and textile companies and the army, navy, and several universities, delivered some eye-opening news about the state of women's bodies. The average American woman was not a size 8 or 12, she was a 14, thereby plus-size. How the hell is the average size considered plus when it's the norm? That means the women size 2–10 are the exception, not the rule. *Today, the average American women is even bigger, size 16–18. It feels so weird to say, I'm below average.*

Honey, when the SizeUSA report came out, so many women lost it. They were disgusted that women were accepting of their full figures and willingly walked around with their thighs rubbing together. The only other time I saw them collectively have a fit was when someone left cake on the giveaway table. Each publication has a desk, table, or file cabinet that serves as a "freebie" table. Its where staff place gifts, samples, and promotional items they received from marketing and public relation firms who want to be featured in an issue. Around the holidays, we were sent cookies, pies, or cake. An anonymous staffer would take the gifted baked goods and place them on the table. No announcement was made, no emails sent out, we'd just hear a coworker say out loud, "Oh my God, there's cake!"

"Who brought the cake?"

"I can't eat any of it but it looks ah-maze-ing." Cut to the same woman asking aloud, "Anyone want to share a slice with me, there's no way I can eat the whole thing."

They'd stand and stare at the sweets from two feet away, any closer and they'd be sucked into its gravitational pull. Then here I come, walking up, looking more like the average American woman than they'd ever be, with a knife from the kitchen. I needed to get a piece before they started picking at it like vultures, some even pinching off crumbs with their fingers like savages. I'd slice the cake the way my grandfather taught me: cut a circle in the middle of the cake, then cut rectangular slices from the edge of the cake to the circumference of the circle. This technique yields more pieces of cake, which we needed, since all forty-plus women were going to sneak a taste when no one was looking. Do yourself a favor and google comedian Janeane Garofalo's joke "cake in the house."

Compliment, Compliment, Compliment

Coming from a world where verbal compliments were taken with a grain of salt—strong black women don't need confirmation about what they already know to be true, so our response tends to be a dry-ass "Thank you." *Duh, I know my hair is cute!*—I was floored by just how much value was placed on showering your friends and, more so, foes with empty, superficial compliments from their bangs, nail color, phone cases, umbrellas, lip color, water bottle, to even their stapler. A good quid-pro-quo compliment session could go on for minutes, especially if a passerby joined. The highest-ranking woman present is often the first to leave the circle jerk, and without the top dog, the underlings find no purpose to continue the charade. The trick is to hold a purposeful, work-related conversation and at the end toss out a compliment while you are already taking a step away. This way they get the attention but not your valuable time.

Reflect Who They Are

By the grace of God, I survived my first year with the company, which was marked with a gift of Tiffany & Co. champagne flutes—magazine companies had big money back then. Our holiday party was at Tavern on the Green and the cocktail shrimp were as big as my hand. Expensive perks aside, work wasn't working for me. I came in early, left late; my assignments were well reported and written, my filing was organized but it wasn't clicking. I wanted more responsibility. How was I going to make it to editor-in-chief if I couldn't climb the ladder?

Atoosa Rubenstein was the shining example of a young editor making history at Hearst. In 1998 she designed a mock-up of *CosmoGIRL!* in forty-eight hours and presented it to the company president, who decided to launch the title, making Atoosa, twenty-six, the youngest EIC in the company. Every recent college grad who walked through Hearst's door knew this tale, and it gave us motivation. I wanted that kind of success, and I knew in my heart, given the opportunity, I had the vision and drive for a big role like that. I started small and bribed an art assistant with McDonald's to help me design a single music review page that I would write. So proud of myself, I scheduled a meeting with my boss to show her. Unenthused, she told me I needed to focus on the tasks she had for me.

Next, I set my eyes on a lateral move, one that would allow for more creativity and writing versus the administrative work I was doing. Don't you know, my boss denied my request. I think she knew it wouldn't look great if I left her and shined bright like a diamond. Determined to succeed, I sought the expertise of a shadowy figure within the company. Ms. Shadow was a highly respected and decorated journalist, called in to help whip into shape cover stories and special packages. She didn't have an office or even a desk in the building. I begged my mentors, who knew her from their veteran black journalist circles, to get me in touch with her. She agreed to go to lunch.

"I don't know what to do." I sat across from Ms. Shadow. If I was the type to cry, I would've. Not having my work speak for itself felt foreign. Now I had to master personalities and politics. Ms. Shadow listened to my gripes and sat in silence for a moment. Her brain was working.

"You have to be a mirror. Reflect who they are back to them."

"Why can't I be myself?"

"You can, but to them who you are makes them uncomfortable. They can't identify with you, and once they think you aren't on the same team, they will shut you out."

The shutout was already happening. A new editorial assistant was hired, and I watched as she slipped right into their social conversations and got assignments I'd been hinting at for months. I was more experienced and a better writer, but she looked the part and knew their language. Ms. Shadow broke it down. "If your boss watches *The Bachelor*, you watch it too, and the next morning you pop into her office and chat about her favorite show. Learn her favorite Starbucks drink and grab her one on the way back from lunch. Compliment her outfit. These are the things that we have to do in order to be seen and accepted. You have to get them to trust you."

I hated *The Bachelor*, didn't drink coffee, and my boss's fashion sense was wack, but I had to decide how badly I wanted to make it in the mainstream media world. It's a decision that most POC operating in largely white spaces asks themselves. Am I going to sell out? Young and eager, I took Ms. Shadow's advice and buttered up my boss. After about a week, she invited me out to a fancy lunch. Small talk was cordial, and my face hurt from smiling throughout the entire convo. Just when I felt like we were turning a corner, she hit me with a haymaker.

"Chloé, I see you are a smart young woman with a lot of drive, but that's not what I need from you. I need someone who is going to make my job easier. Look, you were hired before me. I didn't pick you, so let's just make the best of it."

Hear that sound? That was my ladder falling.

I shake my head when articles about the lack of diversity spring up every year. Yes, diversity is important, but so is retention. It's not enough to hire a token POC or LGBTQIA person when you don't have the sensitivity, language, and guidelines to make sure they are given the space and protection to bring who they are to the table at all times. Yes, there is such a thing as an office culture, but far too many times it means having to erase one's own if you are in the minority.

Rejection didn't faze me. Years of bullying had made my skin thicker than a whale shark's. Hell-bent on using my coveted position at a major white women's magazine to launch my Pulitzer Prize–winning journalism career, I convinced human resources to send me to the biggest convention for journalists of color, UNITY: Journalists for Diversity. The UNITY convention was a joint venture between the National Association of Black Journalists, National Association of Hispanic Journalists, the Asian American Journalists Association, and the Native American Journalists Association. Every four years they formed like Voltron for a multiday conference that empowered TV, radio, newspaper, and magazine journalists. In exchange for Hearst covering my expenses, they asked that I submit a report of the event, gathered résumés, and appeared on panels. They made me feel like I, an editorial assistant, the lowest person on the totem pole, had a say in the hiring practice, investment in, and promotion of people of color at the 100-plus-year-old media conglomerate.

Excited to finally make a difference in spite of my bitter boss, I rushed home from the Unity Convention in Washington, D.C., and worked on my report till the wee hours. On Monday morning I slid my color-print report, complete with graphics and charts, across HR's desk. She was also black; in fact, most of HR was people of color. *So, this where y'all been hiding.* I was optimistic that sis was gonna make something happen.

"Thank you for this, Chloé. I'll be sure to reach out." The next time I heard from HR was three weeks later. The entire *Lifetime* magazine staff was called into a conference room. In walks the new president of the company. *This is not good.* She said all the things one says when you're being let go.

"We really wanted to make this work . . . unfortunately the readers didn't respond the way we anticipated . . . You're all great and we are going to work really hard to place you at other magazines within the company."

By the time we got back to our desks, folks from other magazines had already started leaving Post-it notes on our furniture and computers. Talk about some ghetto-ass shit. My chair wasn't even cold yet. I walked into the HR office of the woman who had yet to reply to my diversity presentation for my exit interview and watched her blow smoke up my skirt. She knew all the right things to say, like how much a young talented woman such as myself means to Hearst. Even if she believed her words to be true, I knew firsthand that HR had no influence on who actually got hired on these lily-white staffs. Sure, they posted the jobs online because legally they had to, but that job was already earmarked for the next Perfectionist or Understudy. Meanwhile, this Outsider never worked for a mainstream publication again.

11

THE $1,500 MISTAKE

Whoever decided it was okay to give a twenty-three-year-old a credit card should have stipulated that said young adult not max it out with one swipe on, of all things, a treadmill. Like millions of Americans I put my faith in state-of-the-art gym equipment to change my life. This was part of my twentysomething crisis. I was out of my parents' house, building up a social life, and finally going to tackle the thing that was holding me back—my weight. This was going to be the start of Chloé 2.0. Operation: Cute Face and Slim Waist was in effect. Once again, I told myself this was the last straw. *I'm going to change my life.* My life was changing. I was working at *Lifetime* and moved into a massive rent-stabilized apartment in West Bumblefuck Queens with my cousin Dawn. I got my hands on an American Express card and the rest, as they say, is a ruined credit report.

Ancient civilizations developed the treadwheel crane to move heavy objects during construction. Shaped like a hamster wheel, the early treadwheel was either man- or animal-powered. As they walked inside, the wheel triggered gears and pulleys. Then in 1818, an enterprising sadist thought a version of the treadwheel would give idle inmates something to do while simultaneously using their manpower for profit. Sir William Cubitt's invention featured a hollow cylinder of wood on an iron frame. Grooves, or steps, on the circumference of the cylinder allowed inmates to climb up, similar to the StairMaster. It was dubbed the "treadmill" probably because the rotating inner wheel powered an attached mill that ground up grain, pumped water, et cetera. In alternating groups, inmates walked the new treadmill for a total of six hours a day. Wildly popular and productive, treadmills were installed across Europe and became one of the main components to a "hard labor" sentence.

By the turn of the century, the treadmill hit the uber-rich mass market. Refitted for in-home use, the indoor treadmill had a horizontal belt of wooden slats, handrails for stability, and an incline, and was manually powered by the user. The Industrial Revolution transformed everyone's lifestyles. Gone were the days of tending to the land and walking miles to fetch a pail of bubonic water. Factory jobs and office work meant standing or sitting in one place for hours. Which brings us to the present day. In 2017, treadmill sales in the United States were roughly $800 million and are expected to reach over $900 million by 2024. That same year, fitness equipment sales are projected to bring in $14 billion worldwide. As I write this, there is a new Peloton home treadmill on the market for $3,995. That price does not include its monthly fee for streamed workouts and tips. *For damn near $4k, I better orgasm after every run.*

DADDY'S LITTLE JEZEBEL

My transformation was sparked by vengeance. I abruptly moved out of my parents' house because my cockblocking father didn't want me borrowing his Chevy Tahoe to go Netflix and chill with my fuck buddy (we'll call him Mr. Friday Night). Please note: These were the days when Netflix meant actual DVDs that you had to order a week in advance. The early 2000s were special.

Friday evenings I'd rush home from work, freshen up, borrow Dad's truck, and head over to my *friend's*. Mr. Friday Night often selected a foreign film with subtitles, which I'd thought made him so smart, artistic, and sexy. Shut up, I was twenty-three. We'd get through one and a half movies, eat vegetarian takeout, get sleepy, retreat to his bedroom, and smash to blaring neo soul and conscious rap music so his roommates couldn't hear the squeaks of his cheap IKEA bed. To this day I can't listen to Common's *Electric Circus* without having eye-rolling flashbacks.

Usually, I'd get back home by 3:00 a.m., but this particular morning I pushed the limit and the snooze button on my "take your ass home" cell phone alarm. The difference between walking into your parents' house at 3:00 a.m. versus 7:00 a.m. is more than four hours. In my father's eyes, those four hours made me a loose woman, a harlot, common. He wouldn't come straight out and call me a whore, so instead he'd bitch about me keeping his car out. Ahh, the classic double standard. If I were his son, I might get a pat on the back. But I was a young woman, raised in the church. Where was my dignity? *Around my ankles, clearly.*

I don't know why Dad was tripping. As far as I was concerned, I was grown. Correction, I was a grown-ass woman. Unfortunately, if you are a twentysomething dependent reading this; I hate to break it to you but the only way you're considered grown is if you pay *all* the bills. Family hierarchy is easily upended by cash. Dad didn't like the idea of his little girl being a hussy. *Who was this man I was with? Were we in a relationship or was I just letting him get the milk for free?*

My parents married when Mom was nineteen and Dad twenty-four. He had to know I wasn't going to save myself for marriage, and if he was bugging about me having sex at twenty-three, he would've died if he knew when I actually lost my virginity. Mom already knew. I had told her when I was eighteen while we wrapped Christmas presents. She asked me if I had deep feelings for him, you know, that made the moment special. I lied and said, "Yeah." Dad didn't know any of this, which is probably why my new social life did not sit well with him. There's no way to tell your dad you've *been* fucking.

"If you can't respect this house, then you need to think about finding your own place where you can walk in at seven a.m." The last of his parental control was slipping through his fingers. Mom was caught in the middle; of course she would prefer that I wasn't out all night, but she knew that I would never put myself in a situation where I was unsafe. Also, she married young and made it clear that I should live life before settling down.

"Fine, I'm moving out." I had no plan, but the way the universe works, my cousin Dawn just kicked her weirdo roommate out because the chick was stealing Dawn's underwear. Four days later, I took off from work, rented a U-Haul, went to IKEA, and bought my own squeaky bed for all the loud sex I was about to have. Only downside was, instead of living fifteen minutes away from Mr. Friday Night, I was now an hour away in Southside Jamaica, Queens, and carless. The upside, my new apartment was huge and only $654 a month—sit-in kitchen, two real bedrooms with closets, living room with a balcony. It's a sprawling black middle-class apartment complex filled with judges, cops, teachers, and their entitled kids who wanted to be stick-up kids turned drug dealers turned rappers like 50 Cent.

BLACK LAVERNE & SHIRLEY

Dawn was older by nine months; I was taller by nearly a foot. As children, our parents dressed us in matching outfits, like Arnold Schwarzenegger and Danny DeVito in *Twins*, except we fought like sworn enemies. Our parents would force us to play and sent us to sleepaway camp, where we'd deny being related. Dawn and I finally started to hang out during high school, mainly since we went to the same one. Now, as blossoming adults, we were developing into real friends and nicknamed ourselves Laverne and Shirley.

Ten p.m. was the "kitchen hour"; we'd bump into each other on our way to raid the fridge for a snack and end up discussing our day. "I was on my way to work today and everyone was saying 'Hello' and 'Have a good day' to me." I had never lived around so many black people before, not being ignored was foreign to me.

"Yes, silly, this isn't Williamsburg," Dawn explained. "These are black people. We talk to each other. Do we have chocolate syrup?"

Dawn and I stood at the kitchen counter, taking turns scooping a tablespoon of ice cream out of a shared carton. This was a Fat Girl Moment.

RULES FOR FAT-GIRL-MOMENT ENGAGEMENT

1. ANNOUNCE YOUR MOMENT

When someone stumbles upon you dusting off a row of Oreos, inform them that it is not just a case of the munchies but a cathartic experience that must be respected. Simply respond to their stare or shaking head with "I'm having a Fat Girl Moment."

FAT GIRL MOMENT: An unhealthy food binge triggered by one's inner fat consciousness struggling to deal with stress, boredom, anger, sadness, or lackadickaphobia.

LACKADICKAPHOBIA: Long-term absence of penis in one's life, which leads to depression, poor food choices, and the fear you'll never feel the warmth of a man again.

ORGASMS: Things you don't have due to the aforementioned.

2. CREATE A SPACE FREE OF JUDGMENT TO INDULGE

When supporting the afflicted, remember not to critique their comfort food of choice or ask for any. Any conversations about what they're eating should be avoided. The food is an innocent party.

3. DON'T PRY

Let the moment taker eat in peace. Anything other than a generic "What's up?" is going to be received as intrusive and judgy. Allow them the space to come to you once their ice cream is finished, and share what caused their moment. Next-day analysis is better, giving the person time to recover from their sugar rush.

4. RESCUE WHEN NEEDED

Moments shouldn't last longer than one sitting. An experienced moment taker will procure all of their comfort foods at once, spread them on the coffee table in front of the couch, cue up a movie, slip into their ugly-girl sweatpants, and commence with the chow down. That's a good two-hour window. Past that is cause for concern and one should push the abort button while yelling, "All right, that's enough!" Allow them one last bite and toss everything in the trash, going as far as pouring dish detergent over it. The chances of said fat girl getting dressed to go get more snacks is slim to none by this point.

———

Ever since we were kids, Dawn was skinny, which made for some interesting pictures when our parents dressed us as twins. As a teen, she ranged from size 2 to 4. In high school, she took the birth control shot Depo-Provera and actually lost weight, shrinking to a size 0. I wanted to strangle her. By the time I moved in, Dawn, twenty-three, switched to the pill. That's when her weight issues began. There's no rhyme or reason to the side effects of birth control pills. Some types made your skin glow, others caused deadly blood clots, and in Dawn's case, they made her gain weight faster than a baby elephant.

"Before the pill I didn't have a relationship with food at all," Dawn remembers. "Then I had to keep returning my DKNY jeans every two weeks to Bloomingdales for a bigger size." The plus-size movement was about to gain a new member, Dawn was now a size 10/12, barely cooked, and ate fast food for most of her meals. I introduced her to food shopping and cooking healthy meals, which turned into me cooking and her eating and critiquing. I have this weird competitiveness—when alone I'll allow myself to eat like trash and wallow, but if there is someone present, I kick into "I have to do better" mode. They become my motivation, and, in turn, I become theirs. The more fat girl moments Dawn had, the more I ate clean and exercised out of pompousness. It worked; I lost weight. After work, I bummed my way into NYU's gym. I bought a car, got a social life; early-twenties Chloé was doing great. Then *Lifetime* magazine folded. There was talk that the parent company, Hearst, would find jobs for us. I was confident I'd get scooped up by another magazine. Surely they needed a good diversity hire. Weeks turned into months. The spacious apartment now felt cramped. Other than checking the mail for my unemployment check or food shopping, I barely went out. Life was a mystery. What was the point of going to college if I couldn't get a job?

To make ends meet and hold off insanity, I took a freelance editor gig for the biggest urban fiction book publisher. The stories were raw and mainly involved a drug dealer, the woman who loved him, his side chick, a double crossing, a murder, and a strong message pertaining to "snitches get stitches." I was given, at most, one month to make them make sense. My authors were teenagers, single mothers, truck drivers, one writer was in prison. His book came to me on five legal pads, written in pencil. Hey, you do what you got to do. I edited all night until sunrise, retreating to bed as Dawn went to work. Days were lonely, nights long, and the catalyst for my move—sex—was nonexistent. Want to know the status of your relationship? If they travel by bus and two trains to see you, they are the one. Otherwise, fuck buddies will tell you to hit them up when you're in their neighborhood. I was in a deep bout of lackadickaphobia.

"Are you going to take a shower today?" Dawn asked.

"I took one two days ago," I replied, shuffling around the house.

"Look Quita Mae, stop acting like your life is over." Quita Mae is Dawn's nickname for me when I'm being ridiculous, which I was. "Get dressed, you need some fresh air. Let's go to the mall." This was a trick. Yes, I could have used some sun, but Dawn also wanted me to drive to the mall. We could stunt in my truck, a 1998 Eddie Bauer edition two-door Ford Explorer with a tricked-out subwoofer sound system, six-CD changer, and color interior LED that the Puerto Rican guy I bought it from installed. Before getting the axe at *Lifetime*, I took out a $3,000 loan to buy it and prayed each month I'd have the money to keep up payments. I loved that truck. You could hear me coming down the street a block away, and I attracted men who loved seeing a woman behind the wheel of a fly whip.

Mall trips were for stuffing our faces with free samples of bourbon chicken, making fun of ugly babies, Cinnabon, and window shopping.

After six months of this, I'd hit my wall. "I'm going to get my shit together!" I yelled to the heavens.

"Okay, Quita Mae," Dawn piped from her bedroom. She'd witnessed this breakdown before.

"No, I'm serious this time," I yelled back. "First, I'm going to wash my ass, then I'm going to clean this place from top to bottom. After that, we're going to the mall and I'm buying a treadmill."

"Since when you got treadmill money?"

"I don't, but I have a new credit card."

I received my first credit card in college and had a max of $500. The interest was sky high, but I didn't care because it came with a free Frisbee when you signed up for it on campus. Always the entrepreneur, some friends and I launched a gaudy T-shirt business. I'm talking tie-dye, bedazzle, and spray paints. Sometimes all three on the same shirt. My card became the company card. Profits were small, but the IRS didn't care. I had to shut it down or risk losing my financial aid. Since then, I had stayed away from credit cards until the height of my post-*Lifetime* unemployment, where the preapproved notices flooded my mailbox. Mom convinced me it was smart to have one in case of emergencies. This was an emergency. I was fat and miserable.

Dawn came along for moral support. Macy's home fitness department was empty, the salesman was surprised to see us checking out machines.

"Can I help you ladies?"

"She wants to get skinny." Dawn was such a supportive hater.

"Look, you don't have to sell me on anything, I'm definitely walking out of here with a treadmill. I just need you to show me which one is the best."

Seeing a commission, he put on a show. "This is the Moonwalker 8000, 47-horsepower engine, with a CD player, mini AC unit, and stock exchange ticker. For two hundred dollars more it will fold your clothes and do your taxes."

"I'll take it!" One swipe and I maxed out my $1,500 Amex. This was going to be the answer. In celebration, Dawn and I splurged on lunch. "Say goodbye to fat Chloé," I said. We toasted with Red Lobster cheddar biscuits and ordered the ultimate shrimp feast.

WHO RUN THE WORLD?

Tank tops and low-waist jeans. Those were the first things I was going to buy once I got ripped from running. "I just want to lose my stomach," was all I would tell anyone about my weight-loss goals. I've been prohibited from wearing fitted tops since childhood because my stomach would protrude, so I wore baggy shirts like a teenage girl hiding her pregnancy. The treadmill was going to change all that. Never mind changing my diet or stretching. I would step on one weight and step off another. It was going to be magical and easy, or so I dreamt.

Once delivered, my $1,500 treadmill shined like a trophy in the corner of the living room. Its conveyor belt could be lifted, condensing it or remain flat on the floor, ready for use. Since I was possessed with the fitness spirit, I left it down for whenever the mood struck. Before ever turning the thing on, Dawn and I had a photo shoot. I wore basketball shorts, a tank top, and new running sneakers that I bought for my new treadmill, of course.

"Stand next to it," Dawn prompted. She was both photographer and creative director.

"Like this?" I posed like a man standing next to his dream car. I may have even had my thumb up.

"Don't smile; this is you getting serious and losing weight. Good. Now get on it." Dawn was really getting into it. I stood on the sides of the conveyor belt, with my back to the console, my hands were on my hips like Superman. "Okay, time for some actions shots."

"Wait, is the camera on the 'Sports' feature? I want to make sure I don't look like a blur." I had never used the sports feature on my camera before. No time like the present.

"Girl, please, you are not going to be running that fast." Dawn was right. I did a light trot until I started to feel sweat beads. I wasn't ready to work out right this minute, plus I didn't want to look moist for the crucial "before" photo. I removed my tank, leaving my sports bra; all angles of my gut had to be archived.

"Turn. Turn. Turn. Turn." Dawn got it all.

On my calendar, I wrote in forty-five minutes of cardio, six times a week. By my guesstimate, I'd be on track to lose thirty pounds in three months. I never achieved that. At best, I stepped on it three times a week for forty-five minutes total. I'd get bored, hungry, had to pee, took a call, needed to get off to get a new CD because the one that was playing in the console was skipping. Playing music was the most use the treadmill received, followed by being a hanger for wet clothes. When Dawn and I moved to a three-story walk-up in Woodside, Queens, the floor was too thin for me to get a good stride on, so it stood closed in the corner of our now tiny living room, covered by Kente cloth to match the decor.

———

Unemployed nearly a year, I received a call from the new editor-in-chief of *The Source* magazine, offering me an assistant editor position. He and I had shared a workstation during my college internship. Three years later, he was running things. Ironically, I was window shopping in the mall with Dawn and had just finished telling her my unemployment checks were about to end, when my phone rang. God threw me a lifeline. I was a contributing member of society again. Work was demanding, fun, and frustrating. My paychecks went toward new clothes—couldn't possibly wear my fat girl sweats to work—paying outstanding bills, and a personal trainer at Crunch gym.

Why step on the good-as-new treadmill at home when I could get one-on-one instruction from a fine-ass, muscle-neck man with an accent, who stretched me out after for the low price of $75 an hour? Big pimpin' spendin' cheese, I dropped $700 on my first round of sessions. Didn't think to pay down that Amex bill though. It went into collections and they snatched all $1,500 plus interest. There's nothing worse than fighting with a bill collector over debt you accrued for something you don't even want anymore. Why didn't I just buy a jump rope? For seven years I had to look at that debt collection judgment on my credit report. Could have bought a house, but nope. I wanted to be Flo Jo in my living room instead.

Treadmill and I had a conscious uncoupling, well, at least on my part. I moved into my own place, a sweet brownstone apartment. When the moving truck got to my front door, we learned that good old treadmill wouldn't fit up the narrow stairs. They twisted it, turned it, tried to unscrew it. Nothing. Dear treadmill sat abandoned on the curb.

It rained that night.

12

THE TIME I ALMOST DIED

We're obsessed with death. It makes us feel alive. That's the reason why people get excited to share an "I almost died" story.

"The doctor said if the knitting needle had been two inches to the left, they would've been knitting me a casket cover."

"Last thing I remember was asking for extra cheese for my mozzarella sticks, then waking up in the ICU. Just my luck, it was a bad batch of cheese."

"I wasn't even supposed to be working, so imagine my surprise when I took my coffee break and the pot exploded all over me. It was a black-on-black crime."

The traumatic tales wrap up with "I know, right, crazy!" which is a cue for you to chime in with disbelief and/or fake concern. Then what do we do? We take that person's story and share it. "I knew this guy who almost died . . ." Humans are experts at the transference of tragedy. We're subjected to these stories at weddings, funerals, water coolers, even on dates. Ladies, don't lie, if you were on a date with a fine specimen and they told you their survival story, you would be turned on by it. *They're so brave and strong. Ohh, we may have to get married.* Not sure if men have the same reaction. A man may hear an "almost died" story and think, *I bet they're ready for a commitment. That sucks.*

I don't tell my story for sympathy or cool points. It will never be optioned for a movie. It's not sexy, or dramatic. There was no missing heartbeat or coma. No ambulance or last rights. My story starts at the gym.

I survived three years at *The Source* magazine, which included one hostile takeover, occasional office visits from the police, and a huge beef with damn near the entire hip-hop industry. At twenty-six, I was burnt-out and excited to launch my own website, Journalisticks.com, an online community for journalists to break news, share sources, find jobs, and promote their work. Funded with my own money, over three hundred members joined the first month. You couldn't tell me I wasn't about to be the next Myspace Tom. Only difference was my site wasn't generating any money. To supplement, I returned to freelancing, pitching a cover story to the iconic alt-weekly newspaper *The Village Voice.*

In spring 2007 my debut article, "Girls to Men," profiled a group of black AGs (aggressives) raised on hip-hop's misogynistic culture and overlooked by the larger LGBTQIA community. I was motivated to write about young lesbians of color after the death of fifteen-year-old Sakia Gunn. In 2003, Gunn had been stabbed to death by a man for rejecting his sexual advances toward her and her girlfriend. I became so enthralled by her story that over the next four years, I reached out to her family, met with her friends, and traveled to New Jersey to attend community memorials and town halls. My goal was to publish her story where it mattered most, black media. Stories like Sakia's were ignored by the hip-hop industry that often perpetuated anti-gay rhetoric. Every black publication I pitched it to declined. "Hip-hop don't care about gay shit." I had put the story on the back burner while I worked at *The Source* and on my website, then one night on my way home from work, I spotted two black teenage lesbians in love, giggling and kissing on the train and thought, "That should be Sakia." It was time to tell her story again, and I wasn't going to take no for an answer. Within hours of *The Village Voice* cover story hitting the street, my in-box and phone were flooded.

"Hello, Chloé speaking?" Unknown numbers could be work, so I always answered.

One conversation went like this: *Hello, Chloé, we're calling from GLAAD and wanted to ask you a couple questions about your recent article. Do you hate gay people? If you don't mind us asking, what is your race?* (Go ahead, Mom, for the racially ambiguous name win!) *Who put you up to this? How do you sleep at night?* Those weren't the real questions, but the interrogation was real. I understood GLAAD's concern, and assured them I wasn't trying to profit off or bash their community.

In the weeks that followed, a group of older black lesbians held a town hall, upset that a straight woman was airing their community's dirty laundry. My article depicted the normal amount of drama and beef within any subculture, but they felt that by including a quarrel between lovers or a subject talking about being sexually abused and kicked out that I was only focusing on the negative, whereas I saw it as my focusing on the whole.

Since the dawn of time, black people—all people of color, for that matter—have been the target of bad press. The few images and stories about POC that make it into the mainstream are negative, unbalanced, and inflammatory. We were shown as pimps never philanthropists, hookers not housewives, thugs not teachers, struggling single mothers not scientists. Many felt that I, a black woman working at a white publication, was selling my people out by reporting on this marginalized group of young women. I'd come to work anticipating Al Sharpton yelling through a bullhorn, calling for a boycott.

My article did more than attract some detractors, it landed me a three-month "diversity" fellowship at the *Voice*. They could have hired me outright, but since I was black and they needed to make good on their union-demanded diversity initiative, I got the slot, hence the scare quotes around diversity. Ugh. Good ol' diversity decade was still poppin'. *The Village Voice* was home to gold-standard investigative, local, and counterculture journalism. Never in my most ambitious dreams did I think I'd get a job there, so when the door opened, I leapt through and walked the same halls as the great Nat Hentoff, Lynn Yaeger, Nelson George, Wayne Barrett, Greg Tate, and countless other literary legends. At the end of my fellowship, the *Voice* offered me a staff writer position with free, let me say this again, free health care thanks to their kickass union. I never understood how the working class bought into the anti-union agenda, shooting themselves in the foot to the pleasure of the corporate office occupiers, but I digress. I was a real notepad-, pencil-, quarter-in-my-pocket-for-the-payphone-carrying reporter. I pounded the pavement and covered education, crime, conspiracy theories, and social injustice. Pulitzer Prize, I was on the way.

With the journalism career back on track, it was time to focus on the personal life, which meant taking care of the body I neglected since returning to the freelance life. Rebecca, an old coworker, was a gym rat, so instead of catching up over dinner, she suggested I be her guest at her swanky city gym, excuse me, Health Club & Spa. Marble floors, heated towels, free soap in the showers, slippers, I could've sworn the barbells were dipped in gold. The clientele were the type to walk around the locker rooms butt naked with a towel over the shoulder. *Ma'am, you're too old to not know how a towel works. Now pick up your boobs and wrap them up in that towel. No! Do not sit on the bench with your bare ass. Now I gotta wipe it down with my Purell.*

Rebecca led us through one of her "easy" workouts and nearly killed me. I started to believe my old trainer was bullshit, 'cause he wasn't working none of the muscle groups Rebecca had me using. Then again, most male gym trainers are mainly there to rack up sugar mamas and teach them how to bench-press dick. Rebecca pushed me on the treadmill. "Come on, girl, I know you want to look sexy come summertime." The weight room brought out her competitive side—"How am I lifting more than you?" We ended our session stretching on floor mats. "Spread those legs, your man just walked in the house." I melted into the mat, feeling the parts of my body that were going to be out of commission the next few days and debating how much worse my life would be if I gave up and became morbidly obese. *It couldn't hurt much more than what I'm feeling now.*

———

For centuries, exercise—especially lifting weights—was considered unladylike. The few women who did turned their physiques into carnival acts and freak shows. In the late 1800s, Minerva stood six feet, 230 pounds, and held the Guinness Book World Record for lifting 3,564 pounds in a hip-and-harness lift. Thomas Edison's 1901 film "Trapeze Disrobing Act" featured Charmion, another strongwoman. Charmion was famous for her vaudeville trapeze artistry and jacked arms. Dressed in Victorian attire, she'd ascend to the air and disrobe down to her leotard. Pretty risky for the time, it's considered the first striptease caught on film.

Women stayed clear of the gym, scared by doctors who preached lifting weight was too dangerous, making women too masculine. Walking, horseback riding, and calisthenics were low-impact exercises recommended to women until the women's gym craze of the 1960s through 1990s pushed the "bikini body." Even then, women stuck to Jazzercise, step aerobics, stationary bikes, and other nonbulking exercises. Women didn't want to be strong, they wanted to be svelte. Chains like Elaine Powers, Lucille Roberts, Living Well Lady, Spa Lady, and Curves popped up all around the country and advertised as safe spaces for women to work out. They indulged women's fitness naïveté and treated them like delicate flowers they pacified with "Sweatin' to the Oldies" classes. Even when I started playing basketball, some of the older women in my family would tell me not to lift too many weights. "You don't want to get man arms." They said this as they power-walked with weights on their ankles and chewed on fat-free SnackWell's devil food cookies. They wondered why they never lost weight. I viewed myself as a strong woman, to this day, not as strong as Rebecca, but I could deal with the pain knowing the results were going to be beneficial to my mind and body.

"I'll see you tomorrow?" Rebecca's radiant smile made it hard for me to say no.

"No."

Days later, I stood in the storefront business of a renowned vegan holistic healer in Brooklyn. She had agreed to be featured in the pilot of my video web series. Working at the *Voice* was a dream, but I knew in order to reach *my* people, I needed to make my stories visual. People don't read; it's one of the reasons I retired from journalism. I'd spend weeks, if not months, on an article, only for my own circle to say, "The pictures were nice." Forget the photos, what about the six thousand words I slaved over? *Let's not overlook the fact that you are reading this book. You are the real MVP, and if you can get your friends and family who "don't like reading like that" to buy a copy or borrow yours I'd be forever indebted to you.*

All afternoon, as the Healer broke down the importance of a vegan diet, herbs, and meditation, I was bothered by a throbbing pain in my inner left thigh. It felt like a spider bite but worse. When I got home, I ripped my pants off and saw a tiny whitehead on the area. Nasty confession: I love popping pimples. My eyes danced at the sight. Euphoria swept over my body as I squeezed my pointer fingers together and ended its short-lived life. So satisfying; if I smoked cigarettes, I would've sparked one up. But the next morning, the tiny whitehead had turned into an open hole the size of a pencil eraser. *What the hell is that?* I squeezed it again and nothing worthwhile came out. I flushed it with some witch hazel, bandaged it, and headed to work. A week goes by, the sore is healing but now there's a tennis ball–size mass in my upper thigh that's emitting heat, and I had flulike symptoms. Over-the-counter medicine made me feel worse. In the emergency room, the doctor saw me, took one look at my inflamed thigh, and scribbled a prescription for antibiotics. I took the horse pills for two days and on the third, something was definitely wrong. I went back to the ER.

"Ms. Hilliard, your tests results are inconclusive, but it's clear there is some sort of infection your body is fighting." *No shit, Sherlock.* "We're going to keep you here a couple days, switch you to a stronger antibiotic, and see how that goes." First two days, I was cool. My parents came by, Shelly, my bestie from elementary school, stopped by with sticky wings from Dallas BBQ. Yep, I'd fallen off my self-righteous "vegetarian-but-I-eat-chicken" horse a few years prior. It's hard to eat clean when your pockets are empty, and the city didn't consider me poor enough for food stamps. I'd been eating everything from the rooter to the tooter, which may have been a contributing factor in this mystery illness. Conspiracy Chloé will explain later on.

"Oh my God, this girl is burning up." Three nights later, things took a turn. I had chills and sweated through my bedsheets. Earlier, the night nurses brushed off my complaints to them about the room being too hot—to them, I was the young girl who didn't look sick. "What you doing here?" they'd ask as if I enjoyed laying up in a place that smelled like mothballs and bleach. There was no Munchausen syndrome over here, and now I had the physical evidence to prove it. "One hundred and five degrees." The head nurse stared at the thermometer in shock, "Quick, go grab some ice packs." *Oh, now you want to spring into action. Y'all lucky I'm too weak to cuss y'all out.*

The 2016 study "Racial bias in pain assessment and treatment recommendations, and false beliefs about biological differences between blacks and whites" by Kelly M. Hoffman et al. found that whites (both everyday people and medical students) had some very interesting and asinine beliefs about the physical differences between themselves and blacks such as:

* Blacks age more slowly than whites.

* Blacks' nerve endings are less sensitive than whites'.

* Black people's blood coagulates more quickly than whites'.

* Whites have larger brains than blacks.

* Whites have a better sense of hearing compared with blacks.

* Blacks' skin is thicker than whites'.

* Blacks have a more sensitive sense of smell than whites.

* Whites have a more efficient respiratory systems than blacks.

* Black couples are significantly more fertile than white couples.

* Blacks are better at detecting movement than whites.

* Blacks have stronger immune systems than whites.

All of the above are false, but that doesn't stop racial bias from impacting how black people are medically treated. No wonder black women in America are by far the most likely to die during pregnancy and childbirth.

My now-attentive nurses scrambled to bring my fever down; they changed my sheets with me still in bed, packed me like a fish in ice, and offered me Tylenol. I should have pitched a fit earlier, but fatigue and fear had me giving the medical professionals the benefit of the doubt. Sure I know my body, but I naively believed that they knew my body better. I wouldn't have known to factor in racial bias. Big mistake. I drifted off with a mission fueled by rage: Wake up in time for morning rounds. If not, I'd miss my one opportunity to talk to the doctor whose care I was under and demand answers.

Watching doctors do their "rounds" on TV, the patients are up and alert—talking, smiling, joking—when the truth is they do that shit at 7:00 a.m. They really expected me to be up, like my old-lady roommate didn't keep me up all night audibly farting and harassing the nurses for apple juice and ice. If you are asleep, the doctor breezes in with a posse of residents, talking about you like you aren't even there.

"The patient came in five days ago complaining of inflammation in her upper thigh; we don't know what the bitch got but we know she got insurance, so she stays." Exit scene.

Well, not today, Satan. I set my cell phone alarm to 6:15 a.m. Tossed all the melted ice packs in the trash and elevated the back of my bed so I'd be sitting erect, ready to stare the white coats in their mutha-fucking faces. I was tired, hot, frustrated, helpless, and on the brink of an emotional breakdown.

"Oh, you're awake." Doctor knew what was up.

"Why yes I am, Doctor." It took all the energy I had left to use my "proper" customer service voice. I needed her to know I was educated and could articulate my concerns and was good for any threats to go above her head. "I'm hoping you can help me understand what is going on here. You and the peanut gallery come in here every day without answers. I'm confused."

Saying "I'm confused" is the best information tactic I learned from my passive-aggressive white colleagues at *Lifetime*. My time on the other side provided some life hacks, but how to make potato salad is still not one of them. When used during a tense exchange, "I'm con-fused" puts the responsibility on the other party to explain themselves, thus giving you the ammo to hold them accountable for their words. The more Doc talked, the more I had to use against her. She blabbed on for a few minutes about the inconclusive tests and upping my IV antibiotics, then turned to exit.

"Fatima!" I yelled her first name out so disrespectfully, my old-lady neighbor turned the volume down on her TV, a first. "We're not done."

"I'm sorry, I have other patients to see." The residents chewed on their bottom lips and looked at their ugly Skechers.

"I'm sure they're not going anywhere." Fatima was a brown sister, and for a minute all her prestigious medical training went out the window. We were two annoyed hoes staring each other down until the first one jumped. She caught herself because she knew at this point I had nothing to lose. With whatever was in me, I would've gladly patient zeroed them if I could. *Don't try me, Fatima. I'll kiss everyone in here.* "Since you're unable to help me, perhaps we can find another doctor who can. I've been here almost a week, this knot in my thigh is now the size of a grapefruit—"

"Oh, you have a knot?" *Bitch, you serious?* She was serious. See, this is why they need to stop with the crack-of-dawn morning rounds. How you gonna check on me if I'm sleep?

"Also, something is wrong with my vagina." No point in being coy. A fever I can deal with, but a broken pussy? I'd sue this entire hospital.

"Okay, Ms. Hilliard, we'll send you for a CT scan and we'll have a GYN come by to see what's going on."

"Thank you! Have a blessed day."

Be careful what you ask for. The level of attention I received went up tenfold after I came to life on Fatima. Also, the several eloquently worded emails I sent to the patient advocate and social work department helped. The CT scan showed nothing irregular. A man came by with a huge needle trying to drain the mass in my thigh to no avail. The gynecologist diagnosed my fire crotch as a bad yeast infection caused by, surprise, the antibiotics. Of course, I had to take more medicine for that. On the ninth day of uncertainty, a social worker stopped by with her clipboard. "Ms. Hilliard, unfortunately, your health insurance is no longer willing to cover your stay here. Your doctor has informed me that although the cause of your illness is unknown, you have been without a fever for the past two nights, making it okay for us to send you home and monitor you from there." The cost just for my half of the hospital room was $1,500 a day. That didn't include the cost of medical treatment and being ignored. However, my free *Village Voice* union insurance covered at-home care. I was discharged with a PICC line implanted in my upper right arm. A semipermanent IV, the PICC line allowed me to administer vancomycin, then the strongest antibiotic, four times a day—6:00 a.m., noon, 6:00 p.m., and midnight. Again, no idea what I was taking it for, but the only other option was scrapping my meds, possibly dying alone in my apartment, undiscovered for years like Joyce Vincent. Dying unnoticed is one of my biggest fears—that, and having someone walk in on me while using a public bathroom. The latter I've avoided by using my long arms to push the door closed while peeing.

At 5:50 a.m. the alarm rang for my first dose of the day. Normally I'd hit the snooze button and roll over, but this was an actual matter of life and death. The IV pole stood next to my most comfortable living room chair. It took a couple of tries screwing the IV into the PICC line in my right arm, using only my left hand. As the medicine dripped into my vein, I'd drift off to sleep wishing I had a boyfriend who would help me in the mornings, call from work to check on me, and turn down his coworker's invite for after-work drinks because he'd rather rush home to bring me soup. Then I'd awaken, alone, to the sight of an empty IV bag, my blood traveling up the plastic tube. *Even my blood doesn't want to be bothered with me.*

After a week the symptoms disappeared. The grapefruit-size knot in my thigh reduced to a stress ball. Fever- and ache-free, I declared myself healed and ready for normal life again. Normal lasted two weeks. I woke up to sunshine warming the back of my head, but a crazy heat spread all over my body that felt like needle pricks. The pain kept my eyes closed until I sat up in the bed and threw the covers back. Overnight, blisters and boils had erupted all over my body. There were so many, you could play connect the dots.

Jaded by my medical mistreatment at the hospital—which has since been shut down—I spent my time at home soliciting referrals and researching doctors. It was clear I had to save my own life. So when I woke up, in pain and terrified, I reached out to a specialist who'd been kind enough to review my file days prior. Not an inch of my body was exposed as I rode the train to the hospital. I kept my eyes down and my hopes up. Once in the examination room, samples from my sores were collected. Days later, I returned for the results.

"Ms. Hilliard, you have MRSA." Took three months to get this diagnosis. Methicillin-resistant staphylococcus aureus is a bacterium that causes infections in different parts of the body. It's tougher to treat than most strains of staphylococcus aureus—or staph—because it's resistant to most commonly used antibiotics. It can cause blindness; skin, bone, and blood infections; heart failure; and more. I was one of the hundreds caught up in New York's 2007 MRSA outbreak. Newscasts aired specials on MRSA precautions. It was transferable via bodily fluids and contaminated surfaces. *That fucking gym mat.* I lay on that mat before wiping it down. That had to be it. There were no other times I had my skin exposed. It was winter, and my sex life went into hibernation a year prior. It was definitely that fancy gym with their free coffee station and hot rock massages. I'd played in street parks, sat on the train with my thigh meat touching the surface, I've drank after friends and even took a piss in a McDonald's bathroom, yet I get a life-threatening infection from the fucking $500-a-month gym.

If the gym wasn't ground zero, maybe it was my plate. Remember when I mentioned Conspiracy Chloé would explain the connection between food and this now-confirmed illness? Put on your tinfoil hats, kids.

Science researchers have made a connection between the way animals are raised for slaughter and antibiotic-resistant bacteria being transferred to humans via meat consumption or air breathed in from nearby slaughterhouses and animal farms. Formal data is hard to find. Farm lobbyists won't allow the tracking of antibiotic-resistant MRSA in the food chain. In true *X-Files* fashion, reports of antibiotic-resistant meats making it to supermarket shelves have been deleted from the U.S. Food and Drug Administration website. So of course this all sounds nuts. Yet headlines like "Pig MRSA carried by workers from North Carolina intensive hog farms" and "Prevalence of Livestock-Associated Methicillin-Resistant Staphylococcus Aureus (LA-MRSA) Among Farm and Slaughterhouse Workers in Italy" show the major contribution and effects of one of the world's strongest superbugs are worldwide.

America's high meat demands force farmers to inject their animals with antibiotics that help the animal survive the farm's harsh conditions. The farmer's only goal is to keep them healthy enough to kill. However, the antibiotics, when introduced in low doses, don't kill bacteria but instead makes them resistant, similar to getting the flu shot.

We then eat the animal's meat and, along with it, deadly microorganisms that are now immune to lifesaving antibiotics. Okay, I'll simplify. Animals get antibiotics. The bacteria in the animal becomes resistant. We eat them and we ingest the antibiotic-resistant bacteria, along with traces of antibiotics, and the resistant gene. Now I'm no scientist, but that surely sounds like a pork chop I ate left the back door open for MRSA. Again, that's just one possibility.

All the medicines I received up until that point were useless, suppressing the bacteria instead of killing it. Once we all *thought* it was out of my system, MRSA was like, "Hold my beer, we're breaking through to the epidermis." The boils were my body's attempt at flushing out the infection. I was prescribed a stronger oral medication for a few days and when those ran out, my only recourse for boil treatment was a trip to the ER. I'd walk in like Norm in *Cheers*. Everyone at the front desk knew my name and why I came. I'd run down the entire backstory with whatever doctor got stuck with me, and answered their dumb, condescending questions while stressing my level of discomfort so they wouldn't send me home with something goofy like Tylenol. Again, POCs threshold for pain is perceived to be greater than whites. I could walk in with a hole in my head and they'd offer me a lollipop for my troubles if I'd let them.

This time, a boil the size of a dime decided to camp out on the nape of my neck. The skin was so inflamed it hurt to laugh or turn my head. Before it could be drained and cleaned, it had to be numbed. That was the absolute worst part.

"Doctor, is it going to hurt?" I lay facedown on an examination table.

"Yes." Dr. Coldhearted administered a four-inch needle into the center boil. *Why is he pushing so hard? Is this what a spinal tap feels like? Shit, no one knows where I am. What if he puts too much pressure on that needle and I'm paralyzed? Is he a doctor doctor, or a physician assistant? I don't remember him clarifying that. Oh my God, I can hear the needle going down. Lord, why hast thou forsaken me? I know I'm strong but damn, I've reached my limit. I'm so tired of being sick. Can't we wrap this up already?* The tears from my eyes dripped onto the exam table paper. It was the first time throughout this whole ordeal that I cried.

I never took pity on myself, seeing every obstacle as a life lesson. However, that four-inch spike drilling toward my spine snapped the last strand of strength I had. I withdrew from physical touch for months, afraid of spreading the superbug to others. My immune system was wrecked, and for the second time in my life, I swore off the gym. I went back to the Healer, this time as a patient, and began the steps of learning detoxification, meditation, and a clean diet. Overall this experience taught me:

1. Never have your bare skin on disease-infested gym mats.

2. Doctors are not gods.

3. Speak up for yourself in medical situations.

4. Second opinions are a right, not a luxury.

5. Holistic medicine isn't fringe science.

6. What is on your plate may be trying to kill you.

I don't like to dwell on hypothetical worse-case scenarios. In fact, this is the first time I've retold this story in its entirety. I wish my almost but not really near-death experience was sexier, like being bit by a lion or being electrocuted by a vibrator. My tale is a small reminder of how life is precious and can slip through your fingers. One thing you'll never hear me say for clout is "I almost died." I'm too focused on living.

13

THE POWER OF LOVE

Every attempt to write this chapter has been met with procrastination, emotional eating, and naps, because love is hard, frustrating, and exhausting. I debated whether to start with the story of my first—and to date, my only—boyfriend. I'll get to him, but first I need to set the stage. It was a time marked with immense vulnerability, trust, maturity, and a forty-pound weight gain because we spent the first several months unemployed, eating Chinese takeout on his couch. I was twenty-eight and yes, that is pretty late in the game to have your first serious relationship, but hey, we can't all be child brides.

Also, do you know how hard it is to date as a black woman?

Just some facts.

Forty-eight percent of black women in America have never been married, compared to the national average of 34 percent. Black women—along with Asian men—are the least likely to get picked on dating apps. The dating pool is smaller for sistas, with an estimated 1.5 million brothers "missing" due to high incarceration and death rates of black men in this country. Then there's the economic and education disparity that has black women among the most college-educated minority groups. However, we're also in debt, thanks to being one of the lowest-paid groups in America. You can't win for losing; black women who earn more than $100,000 a year are also less likely to get married. Can you blame them? You can buy a lot of vibrators with that kind of money.

———

Pose the question "What is love?" and no two people will have the same answer. Is it a feeling in your head, heart, stomach? Is it an action or philosophy? If you asked the ancient Greeks, there were several types of love. Yup, the same people who considered orgies to be part of a religious rite, same-sex relationships the norm, and heterosexual partnerships the result of moon people being split in half, had to have known a thing or two about love.

THE ANCIENT GREEKS' 8 TYPES OF LOVE

EROS: PASSIONATE LOVE

Source of our modern and overarching concept of love. Fueled by lust, passion, and infatuation, it often ends in disaster once the facade fades and the real person shows up, flaws and all.

PHILA: FRIENDSHIP LOVE

We call this platonic love, or, let's be honest, love for the people who you don't want to sleep with.

STORGE: FAMILY LOVE

For family and friends who might as well be family. It's unconditional because you know you can't change the person but must accept them because you're trying to get into heaven.

AGAPE: UNIVERSAL LOVE

Love for people, nature, and things. Often the basis for religious "love thy neighbor" edict.

LUDUS: PLAYFUL/UNCOMMITTED LOVE

Flirty, no-strings-attached one-night stands and fuck buddies.

PRAGMA: ENDURING/PRACTICAL LOVE

When you've been together so long, sex isn't a factor and you don't have any interest in leaving because this person records all your favorite shows and knows the way you like your eggs.

PHILAUTIA: SELF-LOVE

Finding the balance between the healthy and unhealthy version of this type of love is crucial. It is the difference between meditating and finding divine purpose from within and being the jerk who thinks they are God's gift to the world and their shit doesn't stink.

MANIA: OBSESSIVE LOVE

Stalking, jealousy, codependency, violence, otherwise known as any storyline on Love & Hip Hop.

Boys—and later men—didn't court me. I was like a nickel you'd picked up off the street and tossed in your pocket to only find weeks later, say, "Who the hell still uses nickels?" and chuck it. Yes, this self-assessment is harsh and not the way I view myself today, but for a large portion of my life I felt disposable—hoping every hug, kiss, fondle, or sex act would lead to love. I repeatedly set my sights on guys I thought would be perfect for me, making ample excuses for their imperfections and practicing the patience of a saint, hoping they would wake up one morning with me lying next to them after an early morning "no strings attached" session and, as the sun rays hit my pillow, angels would sing into their ear, "This is the woman for you." Instead, I became the quintessential homie, lover, friend providing a girlfriend experience for guys who would never claim me in public. If I received eHarmony stock for every time I heard, "I love you, but I'm not *in* love with you" . . .

Rejection dried my heart up like a raisin in the sun. Love became a liability, a sign of weakness. I became critical of my friends who fell in love, losing themselves. I couldn't fathom their reasons for working through issues, taking back a cheater, or stalking social media pages. *Dear Lord, if you ever find me staking out a man's house 'cause he hasn't returned my text in a couple of hours, beam me up ASAP.* I had no time for the feels. I redirected my love energy into my career, pulling all-nighters while my homegirls played with their man's chest hairs. The few men who crossed my paths were, without fail, broken and unavailable, making the choice to stay single a no-brainer.

Some of them were nice guys, like the one who spent our first date talking about what drew him to being a social worker but forgot to mention he had several kids. There was the guy who begged to come see me, then showed up with a duffel bag 'cause he was newly home-less. Oh, how could I forget the guy who told me to always text before I called and when I pushed the issue admitted that his wife gets mad if his phone rings after a certain time. All of this was my fault. By law-of-attraction rules, I appealed to men who couldn't give 100 per-cent because I wasn't willing to give 100 percent. I was booked and busy. This big heart of mine was being protected from any further dis-appointment. Can you blame me?

After twenty-eight years, someone claimed me.

———

Quentin and I first crossed paths via New York's black media commu-nity in 2004, which was so small it was dubbed "Main Street." Urban media was buzzing with launch parties, album releases, tastemaker din-ners, press trips to exotic islands. Every week there was a party and I'd attend for the expensive gift bag, free drinks and food, air traffic controlling the passed hors d'oeuvre servers to my section. A benefit of being tall. Once, I slipped a huge bottle of Hennessy from the table decorations into my purse. I don't drink Hennessy, but it added to my already well-stocked "man trap." You know how doomsday preppers stockpile a pantry for the end of the world? I stocked my apartment with snacks and beverages a guy would appreciate once I've lured them over. I hate to use "lured," but that's how my interactions with men felt until Quentin. Since we started as friends, there was no need to leave cookie crumbs leading to my heart. If I did, he would have laughed it off, "What are you doing? I know where I'm walking. Stop wasting cookies."

I don't recall meeting Quentin, he was just around. However, I vividly remember when things shifted. As usual, we were at a party. We smiled at each other and made our way across the floor, holding our open-bar drinks. This time the conversation was different. Everyone else in the room melted away. Whenever we got pulled apart, we'd return to each other like magnets. A photographer asked to take our picture together and we obliged, standing awkwardly near each other because industry friends didn't embrace. A level of professionalism had to be maintained.

Weeks later, I sat on my couch scrolling through my BlackBerry Bold and stopped at his name.

Call him.

What would I call him for? This isn't work-related.

So what, you're home alone bored. Call him.

There are no parties going on. Do you call someone you small-talk with to have more small talk?

He's a DJ in his spare time, right?

Yeah.

Tell him you want lessons. Call him.

Damn, I've always wanted to DJ. I already got my name picked out.

DJ Bunzy. Great name. Call him.

Lesson one was at his place, the turntables were in the bedroom. Admittedly, he was not a good teacher, skipping over the little things and growing slightly frustrated with remedial questions. Thirty minutes of attempting to DJ was followed by hours of conversation. Soon the lessons were out the window. We just enjoyed hanging. The tricky part was deciding if and how to let Main Street know. Hooking up was expected, but dating was a scandal. The few couples who made it official were talked about in whispers. Who would choose meaningful companionship in a world filled with open bars and free merch?

Worried about people's opinions, Quentin and I attended a screening of *Notorious* and watched the entire movie holding hands, which were covered by my scarf. Childish yet adorable. Part of me was ecstatic to potentially have a boyfriend, the other part of me placed a bet that this was just a phase and I'd be back to my lonely existence in no time.

In the wee hours of a winter morning, Quentin and I sat on his living room floor, illuminated by Yankee Candle light. The status of us wasn't defined, but for my own sanity I needed reassurance, although it had been only a couple of weeks. When you've *almost* died, you tend not to waste time.

"So"—my voice was shaking with nerves—"do you want to do this?" I was giving him a way out before I got my heart broken.

"Yes." He stared me in the eyes like Prince looking at purple rain. I felt naked, yet oddly safe.

"Yes?" Maybe I was hearing things.

"Yes, will you be my girlfriend?"

———

On January 20, 2009, history was made. The country swore in its first black president, and Quentin and I became exclusive. America, I had a boyfriend!

Quentin was the yin to my yang. I was direct and assertive. He was warm and patient. The first time I spent the night at his place, he gave me the bed and took the couch, and in the morning bought me a brand-new toothbrush and breakfast. He anticipated my needs and to some degree spoiled me. If I sneezed he would get up, without saying a word, bring me a blanket and put on a pot of tea. He indulged my fat-girl moments, which were plentiful since being laid off during the Great Recession. The nearby Chinese restaurant knew our takeout order by name. I gained forty pounds our first year together. He never passed judgment, laughing as I once took leftover brunch bacon out of

VIDEO VIXEN: An ample, often augmented, bodied woman of black or mixed-race descent, who was featured in black men's magazines or rap music videos as the principle love interest between 2002–2012. *See Amber Rose, Karrine "Superhead" Steffans, Melyssa Ford, Buffie the Body.*

my purse to put on a slice of street pizza. "Diet" or "lose weight" never came out of his mouth, and he never tricked me into exercising. Heads up, if your lover starts asking to go for walks, baby, you've packed on a few.

Maybe Quentin had a fat fetish. He wasn't jerking off while I ate shrimp lo mein or giving nicknames to my back fat rolls, but still, his unconditional love and support was sometimes unsettling. All my insecurities were tested with him, and his job at an urban men's magazines didn't help. Quentin worked with the biggest video vixens of the day.

My low self-esteem angel sat on my shoulder, chiming in. *Why would he be on set with all that T&A and want to come home to you?* The hater raised a good point. I was so fat at the time, my knees hurt. Literally, they ached if I walked or sat too long. My most embarrassing moment with Quentin: We went to see *Avatar* in a huge IMAX theater. The seats were tight, my knees pressed into the chair in front of me. Throbbing pain brought tears to my eyes, and what did my boyfriend do? He let my ham-hock thighs lie over his, massaging my knee caps until the credits rolled. He didn't just love me, Quentin adored me. Years later, I was riding on the train and saw a couple preparing to get off. She was a cute, big girl, sitting down. He was tall and thin, standing in front of her. When the train stopped at the station, he extended both arms toward her, she grabbed his hands. He set his feet, pulled her up, then guided her by the small of her back toward the sliding door. I imagined that's how Quentin and I looked to some people. Once, while walking down the street, a wino saw us walking and yelled out, "Y'all look like the number 10." Quentin turned to confront him, but I linked my arm through his. "It's okay." I was used to the fat jokes, been hearing them since I was six, but this was the first time someone wanted to defend me. I fell even more in love with him.

Even with his reassuring words and actions, it was challenging letting my guard down with Quentin. My emotions were like a feral cat who had finally found a home. Hardened by years of depravity, it was going to be a while before I rolled over and showed my belly. Quentin and I had two different love languages and expectations. I had to learn how to communicate, be affectionate, listen without trying to fix, and be patient. During one of our semiannual "state of our union" conversations, Quentin questioned if I loved him. I was dumbfounded. Of course I loved him, I cleaned his bathroom, cooked, helped him brainstorm business ideas; I took care of him when he had a cold and got him the boxing trainer he always wanted. That was love in my book. Quentin agreed those were nice gestures but he needed words, tactile connections that I stopped performing years ago. My logical mind now operated on years' worth of "if/then" scenarios, the conditional computer programming theory I learned in junior high school.

"If he doesn't call me back, then I'll block his calls."

"If he tells me he loves me, I'll say it back."

"If he makes dinner, then I'll wash the dishes."

Afraid of looking dumb, I made my love conditional. Rationed out in pieces like a fat kid reluctantly sharing their snacks. *I can't give them all my good snacks. What if I can't get any more, what will I have left for me?*

Damn, I might have just had a revelation, or it could be the vegan Ben & Jerry's ice cream talking. I'm serious about all the emotional eating this chapter has generated. Ahem, my revelation: Giving all my love to Quentin meant I would have nothing left for myself if or when our love ended. There was no telling when another man would come along. I didn't see love as infinite. I had but only so much to give because I was accustomed to not getting it from elsewhere. I was stuck operating in Ludus love for so long, I was ill equipped for Pragma love.

Love can't happen if you're holding back. It's impossible to love deeply and not be hurt. Eventually, even if everything goes perfectly, one of you will say goodbye via death. Quentin and I lasted two years. Obviously, I still reflect on that experience. No regrets, and I'm grateful for him. He succeeded in showing me how to love and be loved in more ways than one.

However, old habits die hard. I haven't been in a committed relationship since Quentin. I've dated, but it's taken me some time to trust my gut, take heed of red flags, or make myself vulnerable. I recently watched "The Power of Vulnerability," a TEDx Talk from American research professor and author Brené Brown. My millennial brother, now twenty-four (God, I feel old), suggested it to me after he witnessed my back-and-forth on how to end things with a guy I was casually dating. My instinct said, *ghost him*. But the mature adult in me said, *ghost him*.

My brother cued up Brown's talk and we watched together. The notion of one's level of self-worthiness being the driving force of having and receiving love and belonging blew my mind. And the way to tap into that was through vulnerability. The thing that I considered a weakness was actually the key to opening the greater, more fulfilling life. I don't want to do Brown's research a disservice, so go watch it for yourself. What I took away from it was that in order to receive true love I have to be patient, compassionate, and vulnerable with myself. I shunned love, wiggling from its embrace, wiping its kisses off, letting go of its hand if others were watching or hiding it with my scarf like I did with Quentin in that movie screening because deep down, that little girl who grew up bullied and overlooked didn't think she deserved it.

Time to break that cycle. I'm going to therapy to help peel back the layers and to shake all the things that kept me in a holding pattern. I am excited to love myself unconditionally and see what comes after that.

14

LET'S GO VEGAN

If memory serves correctly, here's how I've eaten since birth: carnivore, fake vegetarian, pescatarian, real vegetarian, carnivore, vegetarian, vegan, pescatarian, carnivore, and vegan. In fact, while writing this book, my diet changed several times. When I started writing, I was pescatarian. By the time we shot the book cover I was vegan. During edits, I was eating everything. (Hey, sometimes the only way to handle stress is with a plate of oxtails with extra gravy.) And by the time this is in your hands, I'll probably be vegan again. I'm always "going vegan."

I love being vegan. Within the first month, I always drop ten to fifteen. My skin glows like an inhaled cigarette. My mind is razor sharp, I never get sick, and my poops are amazing. In a perfect world, I'd be a glowing vegan who grows herbs in their apartment, reads auras, and can communicate with animals. My dream is to be vegan, living off the grid in a solar-powered home with a farm watered by rainwater. In spite of all that, the day always comes where I'll end up with a rib, wing, or shrimp in my hand.

It's a little more complicated than my lack of willpower. That's a major part of it, but other factors contribute to my repeat failures and rebounds.

YOU'RE ONLY AS STRONG AS YOUR OPTIONS

Whenever you talk to someone who's fallen of the wagon, they can tell you with all sincerity why and how they failed. Same goes for me and my love/hate relationship with veganism. Each time I fail it's because of one of three things:

1. LACK OF PROPER FOOD OPTIONS WHILE ON THE ROAD

For the last six years, I've been touring the country as a stand-up comedian. The longer I'm on the road, the harder it is to eat healthy. Forget vegan. I once asked for a salad in Wisconsin and it arrived with a half-pound of shredded cheese on top. In Nebraska, I told the comedy club I was vegan, and they set up the greenroom with coleslaw, macaroni, and potato salad all with extra mayo. When I pack food, the TSA flags my carry-on and tests my vegan pea protein powder mix for explosives. I don't know what's more embarrassing, having the bomb specialist fondle my ziplocked snacks, or an angry TSA agent checking my hair. One always happens, and I politely want to tell them, "I'm a black woman. I'm not a terrorist. The two things we don't play around with are our food and our hair. Neither of which I'm blowing up."

2. DECLINE IN HEALTH

There's more to being a vegan than not eating meat and dairy. My well-thought-out meals are often replaced by carbo loading like I'm a Kenyan marathon runner, and the weight starts to creep back on. Living proof that vegans can be fat. For a while, I refused to educate myself on the vitamins and minerals my body needed, which is how I repeatedly developed anemia. My longest vegan run started in 2015 and lasted thirty months. Toward the end, my hands and feet were always cold, my tongue was paler than Taylor Swift, sleep wasn't restful, and I became forgetful. The medical advice was unanimously, "Eat some meat!" Sure enough, I was cured with a big piece of chicken. Come on, if given the options of taking a boatload of pills every day or a two-piece meal to end your chills and tossing in bed, most of you would ask, "Where's the hot sauce?"

3. LACK OF SELF-CONTROL

Months of eating kale, quinoa, and beans grows old. Green juices are cool, but it doesn't hit the spot like a chocolate chip cookie during an emotional breakdown. Forgive me for not having the chemistry degree to concoct vegan baking recipes. I've had so many "meat defeats"— when the power of the flesh compels you to risk it all—that I look back at some of them fondly.

Franks. That's how my second vegan stint ended. Fourth of July, circa 2012, my aunt hosted a backyard barbecue. On the grill, awaiting my arrival, were jumbo footlong Hebrew National franks. *Hello, darkness, my old friend.* They teased me with their grill marks, mocking me while I chewed on pasta salad. Pasta doesn't snap in your mouth like a frank. My stomach had been on a long journey since I first quit smoked sausage. But this was a hot dog. Its unique blend of various animal parts and spices reminded me of my youth. Family reunions where I sat and ate a hot dog while my cousins ran and played. Baseball games my dad got free community outreach tickets to, I'd completely ignore the action while eating a hot dog. Oh, how could I forget trips to Coney Island where I'd eat a Nathan's World Famous hot dog while my friends rode the attractions? I was entranced by their sizzle. The meat defeats came over me.

I scanned my aunt's backyard for the perfect accomplice to do the dirty work for me. I'd been talking shit to my family for months about how great being vegan (yet again) was. No way I was going to give them the satisfaction of seeing this go down. Perhaps a little cousin could do it. Nah, they'd dime me out. I could see it now.

"Can I have a hot dog?" Their big eyes looking up at an adult.

"What you want a hot dog for, you just ate?" My family doesn't believe in wasting food on kids.

"Uhh, it's not for me." The jig is up. "Chloé wants it. She said she'd give me a dollar."

Too risky. I needed someone I could trust not to tell a soul, who wouldn't judge me and knew the perfect ratio of mustard to ketchup.

Text: *Mom, I'm upstairs. Sneak me a hot dog please.*

Of course I had to call because moms never have their phones near them.

"Hey, Dad."

"Yeah."

"Is Mom near you?"

"Yes. I'm looking right at her."

"Tell her to check her phone."

"VIOLET, your daughter said check your phone." *Click.*

The hot dog was amazing. The burps and regrets, god-awful.

CHICKEN, BEEF, OR THE END OF THE WORLD?

The phrase "vegan" was coined in 1944 by Donald Watson, a British woodworker and animal rights advocate who stopped eating meat after seeing a pig slaughtered as a teen. Watson felt a term was needed for people who in addition to not eating meat also gave up dairy. The decision to quit dairy was easy for Watson. The U.K. didn't introduce the pasteurization of milk until the 1960s. In the 1930s, 40 percent of British dairy cows had tuberculosis and 2,500 people died each year from bovine tuberculosis.

PR for his cause couldn't have been better, and thus the Vegan Society was born. Perhaps you're not an animal activist like Watson, but consider this: A vegan or reduced-meat diet may be key to reversing global warming and saving both wild and bred animals. A recent study conducted by thirty scientists and published in the British medical journal *The Lancet* warned that the steady increase in human population combined with diets heavy in meat, dairy, sugar, and processed foods would stress the planet with catastrophic results. They even suggest increasing the price of such greenhouse gas–producing foods to encourage shoppers to skip them in the aisle. Would you eat chicken six days a week if it cost fifteen dollars per pound? Researchers at the University of Oxford found that cutting meat and dairy products from your diet could reduce an individual's carbon footprint from food by up to 73 percent.

Mass deforestation for farm and grazing lands is a win for the farming industry, but the wild animals that call those places home are being wiped out, leading to what scientists are calling the sixth mass extinction in the planet's history. For most Americans, our wild animal watching is limited to shitty zoos and viral videos, so compassion for animals that aren't pets is harder to stoke. However, try driving down a highway in the middle of the country and not audibly go "aww" at the sight of cows, horses, and pigs chilling on a hillside. Well, not pigs, they don't get out much. I've driven next to a tractor trailer full of pigs and caught eyes with one. They knew this was the end. I mouthed to them, "I'm sorry," and played "Angel" in honor of their short lives.

I'm not saying everyone should give up meat, but we eat way too much of it for a society of people who sit in cubicles all day. The ancient Egyptians built the Great Pyramids and didn't eat a third of the meat we eat now. Fun fact: Egyptian laborers ate two meals a day including bread and beer. Get ready to gag: The average American will eat approximately 265 pounds of meat a year. America is the world's biggest meat producer, exporter, and consumer. It's estimated that over nine billion animals were slaughtered in the U.S. last year and, around the world, approximately seventy billion farm animals are raised for the plate each year. In November 2017, more than fifteen thousand world scientists signed a Warning to Humanity, twenty-five years after the initial warning because people don't give a damn about science. One of their warnings: Cut back on the burgers, assholes. They didn't say it like that, actually—but maybe if they did more people would pay attention.

After reaching record-breaking sales of $3.1 billon in 2017, plant-based foods replacing meat, eggs, and dairy helped make veganism the top consumer trend the following year. Watson would be proud. Today, fast-food chains are carrying meat alternatives, and more than half of adults drink non-dairy "milks." Are we surprised? More and more documentaries and books depicting the cruel and harmful effects of the meat industry and how it relates to humans pop up every week. New converts fall for the shock tactics and spread the word like a newly *deliver't* Christian.

"Oh my God, Chloé, did you see that new documentary called *Murder Meat: Medium Well?* Changed my life. I'm never touching meat again."

"Really?" Their about-face enthusiasm annoys me. "That's funny, because when I asked you to join me in my vegan detox ten years ago you told me, 'Pork ain't never did nothing to me.'"

ANCESTRAL APPETITE

Black folks' connection to soul food is strong. One of the few things black people get positive credit for, soul food is so ingrained into American history that anything that appears to challenge its traditional value is struck down in the name of Jesus. However, the foods we slave over in the kitchen and celebrate are generous remixes of what the enslaved actually ate. The 1981 book *Eating in America: A History* explains that the enslaved made it by on a diet of mainly starch and vegetables with small portions of scrap meat. Plantation owners preferred this because they noticed that "Negroes fed on three-quarters of a pound of bread and bacon are more prone to disease." Meanwhile, master and his family feasted on bacon, turnip greens, a version of corn bread, and coffee.

My ancestors saw the benefit in eating clean, yet when I tried to get my grandmother, who grew up on a farm, to eat quinoa, I almost got kicked out of the family. "What is this devil sand you trying to choke me with?" Her repulse only fueled me more. I was determined to un-shackle my family from their debilitating diets. Collard greens cooked with mysterious hunks of meat, cooked so long all nutritional value had evaporated. Don't even get me started on chitterlings. Mac and cheese oozing with enough dairy to feed a calf. Didn't they know 75 percent of African Americans are lactose intolerant? Why do you think we in-vented the term "bubble guts"? (Bubble guts: A commotion in one's stomach caused by dairy, fatty, or rich foods. Sufferers must immedi-ately locate the nearest bathroom.)

Breaking my family's cycle of bad food was my mission. I was fueled by their complacency. Over time, they applauded my weight loss and signed up for my personal trainer. They began to eat better and drop weight, but I wanted more. Food always brings a family together; it can also be the thing that gets you kicked out of the family. Christ-mas Eve 2014, I jumped at the opportunity to make dessert for the family game night. Only thing is, I didn't tell them that I would be making vegan and gluten-free treats. I wanted them to be surprised, but honestly, if they knew, they would have vetoed me. As I prepped my two big bundt pans of monkey bread—lemon with raspberry sauce and cinnamon swirl with icing—I envisioned them taking one bite, lov-ing it, and joining me in the greener vegan pastures. Now, of all the things I could have made, monkey bread requires insane amounts of butter. Keep in mind, this is before vegan butter was mass-produced. I'm not sure, but I think I used oil instead. It was ruined before it hit the oven, but my intentions were good.

All week, I'd been bragging about how amazing my monkey bread was going to be, so when I presented them at the center of the table they garnered "ohhs" and "aahhs." The first slice was telling. I had to put in all my weight to get through. I doled out huge slices that felt like three-pound weights. The room was silent. Kids weren't touching it. It was horrible. Mission abort. My family never asked me to make a dish again. I've been on ice and paper plate detail for years. To be clear, I can cook. The gluten-free cake fiasco is not indicative of my culinary abilities.

THE TEMPLE OF TEMPAH

"How can a vegan diet heal your body?" Mom asked. My parents grew up in the seventies, so I get it. Back then, holistic medicine came with antiestablishment sentiments and anarchy. I assured them I wasn't drinking the Kool-Aid, but that didn't stop them from expressing their concerns, repeatedly.

"Mom, it's only for twenty-one days, and if I like it I will keep going."

"I know, Chloé, but where are you going to get your protein from?"

"Beans, lentils." *When did you start caring about my protein intake?*

"Girl, you don't know how to make beans." She was right. My first year living with Dawn, I called back home to ask how to make Hoppin'

John for New Year's Eve. The dish is an African American tradition symbolizing wealth and prosperity for the upcoming year. I was twenty-three at the time and arrogantly thought I knew more than the woman who'd been cooking longer than I'd been alive. Soaking the peas overnight didn't sound right. I poured them straight from the bag into boiling water, and struggled to eat the rock-hard pebbles. That year I lost my job at *Lifetime* magazine. Now we know why.

To be honest, Mom had every right to be cautious about my initial interest in being vegan. This was before Instagram gurus and Facebook groups were sharing clean-eating information for the masses. Back then, the vegan lifestyle was shrouded in mystery and considered too expensive to maintain. The people who had this knowledge charged a grip. The holistic game is to be sold, not told. I spent upward of $400 for a customized foods list and herbal supplements. That's a lot of green for some greens. Maintaining the lifestyle isn't cheap either. Remember those food deserts and swamps I told you about in chapter 8, well, how much do you think an organic apple and a wilted bunch of chard is gonna run you? That's if you have any stores around that carry them. If not, add the cost of gas or public transportation to your total.

Before Trader Joe's, Fairway, or Whole Foods popped up all over Brooklyn, the only place to find most of the foods on my vegan shopping list was at the legendary Food Co-Op. Anyone worth their weight in barley knows about and was a member of this utopian supermarket. I barely had enough money to pay for the shit ton of groceries I had to now buy every week (perishables are annoying), so paying for the yearly membership fee and committing to working eight hours a month wasn't in my budget. Thankfully, I had crunchy granola friends like Genesis who offered to give me a tour and let me use her membership card. Raised vegetarian, Genesis never touched meat and successfully swayed any man who wanted to be with her to follow suit. "I tell him straight-up, if he keep eating meat, he's gonna have to brush his teeth before kissing me."

"You're gonna think they're crazy," she warned about the Co-Op folks, "but they're just friendly, so make sure you say hello. You're not going to know the brands, but don't be scared. Whatever you do, don't use a plastic bag. I brought some extra reusable ones for you."

"Reusable bags?" I clutched my imaginary pearls. "Are we homeless? Why am I bagging my own groceries?" This was 2007; people still thought recycling was for women who didn't shave their armpits and men who used a shoestring as a belt.

"Everyone you see working are actually members of the Co-Op. That's part of it, you have to commit to working a shift each month."

"Oh, how much do they pay?"

"They don't. That's how they keep costs low."

"Dude, are you in a cult?"

"No! Don't be ridiculous. You'll see, the supermarkets you're used to going to are filled with junk, sugar, and fat-filled foods that are so bad for us. The co-op provides all that we need."

"Rule number one of being in a cult is deny that you are in a cult, but I'll know, Genesis."

"Chloé, you're ridiculous."

"All I'm saying is, if there's a white woman inside with dreads, that place is a cult."

Genesis could never prepare me for the Co-Op. I was like Neo unplugging from the Matrix. The shiny, bright colors of commercial products were replaced with muted, eco-friendly packages with no names. Canisters filled with grains and beans lined one aisle. I couldn't identify any of them. What the hell is millet? I was lost, uncomfortable, filled with anxiety. Everything I knew about food was a lie. This was a safe haven in a world that was trying to kill me one fatty, salty, sugary bite at a time. Tofu, tempeh, seiten were my new friends. They cared about me and wanted me to be my best self.

SOY TO THE WORLD

Did you know most American-made vegan-friendly meat substitutes wouldn't be made possible without internment camps? Tofu wasn't produced in large quantities in America until Japanese Americans, interned after the start of World War II, grew soybeans on camp soil to supplement their daily rations. Two thousand pounds of tofu were prepared daily at one camp, feeding over ten thousand detainees. The soybean became a reliable and easily sourced crop for farmers. Corporations with their GMO patents got involved and soon America became the largest soybean supplier in the world. With that being the case, you'd think more Americans would consume soy-related products since it's grown in our own backyards. Nope, the bulk of American soybeans that remain stateside are used to feed animals, which are then killed and eaten.

In recent years, first worlders' growing interest in sustainable foods has caused catastrophic ripples in other countries. Americans go crazy for a hot, new, exotic food, driving the demand up, like quinoa from

Peru. Local supplies are sold at a markup to America, leaving the locals scrambling for a food source they've had access to their entire lives. So if you're a health-conscious eater, you may not be contributing to the killing of animals, but you could be taking food out of another person's mouth.

There are no easy answers here, people. Oxtails. Okra. Pick your poison.

THE LAST BITE

Last year, my acupuncturist heard about my rabbit-food diet and had enough. "Go eat some pho!" Anemia, my old friend, was back. Doc had been treating my nagging shoulder injury for months with little improvement. She felt my ice-cold fingertips and saw my tongue and instructed me to go to the nearest pho restaurant as soon as I left. "In Asian medicine," Dr. Pho explained, "they tell you to eat what needs repairing, so for you that's tendons." Full of guilt, I ordered a beef pho with extra tendons. Blowing on my spoon, I felt like a failure. One of veganism's biggest perks—other than good health and saving the planet—is bragging that you're vegan. *Look at me, meat eaters! I have discipline, drive, compassion.* Once the delicious slow-cooked, bone marrow broth and beef bits touched my tongue, my superhero superiority was gone. So was the inflammation. By the next acupuncture session, my shoulder improved rapidly. Once off the vegan train, I went ham—literally.

With forty on the horizon, I've cut myself some slack. Although I don't walk around in leather suits or eat milk chocolate every day, I don't want to be stoned to death by vegan purists if I do. My healthy way of living had to be realistic in order for me to be successful at it. After trial and error, I've settled on mainly eating according to my blood type. (There are books on it, check it out.) The theory behind it is interesting; your blood type holds the code that determines which foods work for or against it. People with O blood types tend to do better on a meat-focused diet while a type A person, such as myself, has optimal results on a vegan, vegetarian diet. In order not to insult anyone who has the discipline that I clearly lack or misrepresent myself, I'd like to state for the record that I maintain a plant-based diet with rare guest appearances made by fish and poultry. (I act a fool on Thanksgiving.) Another caveat, when traveling outside of the United States, best believe I'm eating whatever the local cuisine is known for. No way I'm going to Japan and *not* having Kobe beef. I spent a week in Cuba and had pork every single day, sometimes twice. Why? Because when in Rome you don't question the meat on your plate. Also, let's not act like many foreign countries don't have us beat on food-processing regulations and freshness. To that, I say bring on the cheese, pasta, meat, and bread.

My relationship with meat will always be complex. Like right now, I want lamb chops, but instead I'm going to settle for a jackfruit BBQ sandwich. One is good for a moment, the other is good for a longer lifetime.

15

A SEX GUIDE FOR THOSE WITH LOW SELF-ESTEEM

Whatever flaws you see when you look in the mirror naked, the person who wants to smash those cheeks doesn't see them or care. If someone really likes/loves you, seeing your naked body shouldn't change that unless we're talking webbed feet or a tail. Major deformities, not cellulite or uneven boobs. Fat bitches need love too.

The energy used to squeeze your eyelids closed, because for whatever reason you can't stomach watching yourself have sex, actually restricts blood flow to the G-spot, resulting in most women's inability to orgasm. I made that last part up, but who knows for sure. Next time you're getting your back blown out, look back at that booty clapping and enjoy it. Sex is beautiful, even if you don't think your body is.

These are just some of the things I wish I knew before I started having sex. Now, with over twenty years of experience under my rusted, eroded chastity belt, here are some life-changing lessons I've learned along the way.

MASTURBATE, OFTEN

Flicking your bean won't send you to hell, but it will prevent you from being sexually frustrated. If left unchecked, that frustration can lead to misdirected fits of rage. Whenever I get the urge to kick someone in the throat or yell at the top of my lungs, and I'm not PMSing, it's because I'm backed up. Before modern religion labeled it a sin, equivalent even to murder in some faiths, men and women rubbed one out without judgment. All over the world, archaeologists have found proof that ancient women enjoyed a nice hump on a hard gourd, unripe banana, and, thanks to some craftsmen, wood, ivory, jade, and metal dildos. The oldest one, found in Germany, dates back twenty-eight thousand years.

"Good girls don't touch themselves" was drilled into our heads. Even now, the subject of vibrators always reveals that one goofy broad who becomes the purity police. She giggles with embarrassment, which turns into shock and disgust. We all know this woman. She couldn't pick her pussy out of a lineup. If you are this woman, when you get home take a mirror, flash your cell phone light on your kitty cat, and study heaven's doorway. When you've built up enough confidence, talk to yourself, light a candle, play music, watch porn. Masturbation is just another form of self-care.

This feels like a great time to bow our heads and give a moment of silence to the career of former U.S. Surgeon General Joycelyn Elders, who was pushed out of office in 1994 by conservatives for condoning the idea of masturbation being taught in sex education as a way of avoiding the spread of the AIDS virus. Elders was also open to studying the legalization of drugs and the distribution of contraceptives in public schools, and was railroaded. A true legend, she was.

Young girls should be encouraged to explore their bodies and see how it works before subjecting themselves to the clumsy hands of an inexperienced or selfish lover. Once a girl is able to achieve orgasms regularly, she won't want to sleep with anyone who can't accomplish the same. For far too long, women have downplayed their sexual satisfaction in order to boost their partner's ego. We lie when they ask, "Did you come?"

Write this down: If your sexual partner, be they long- or short-term, cannot make:

a) your body tingle like a foot that's fallen asleep
b) you wetter than a melting glacier
c) your head roll back like a Pez dispenser

it is your responsibility to show them how—or at least try. But how can you do that if you don't know your own coochie cheat code? Love on yourself.

GET NAKED

T-shirts are not sexy. Walking around the house with bae's oversize shirt is cute, but once you start fooling around, take that thing off. The earlier the better. Girl, don't worry about them checking out your "problem areas." Once the dick is out, the only things they're focusing on are your face for reactions, your boobs for the jiggle, and your kitty cat, 'cause they're in it. Bras and panties moved to the side are fine, but the opti-mal setting is two uninhibited bodies touching skin to skin. Men hide behind clothes too. I've had guys keep their boxers on or hold their shirt up with their chin. *Boy, if you don't take that undershirt off. I know you don't lift weights. I felt that belly during our first hug. You're not fooling anyone.*

Yes, it sounds easier said than done, but if I can drop the potato sack, so can you. My teens and twenties were spent pulling down T-shirts, afraid they'd lift up, revealing my two bellies and he'd go soft. Silly me. I had to remind myself, the same body I was trying to conceal is the one that got him hard in the first place. He saw my body and wanted it. In fact, he had a good idea of what he was getting into be-fore I ever took off a stitch of clothing. Men can make a mental 3-D scan of anyone they are attracted to. If they can't figure out what your body looks like, they'll slide their hand around the waist, caress your back or playfully poke you in the stomach. He just took your measure-ments.

If the idea of disrobing in front of a lover gives you anxiety, practice at home. Walk around your place nude. Take a phone call naked, in front of the mirror. Look from all angles, bend over, turn around, lift things up. This is the only body you have, study it. Push your limits in public. At the gym, change your top facing away from your locker. Stop folding over like the Hunchback of Notre Dame. Those four seconds topless won't kill you.

Once you're ready for the big leagues, have your lover take pictures of you. Headless or with your face obscured is always best.

"Look at me." Mr. Friday Night and I had just finished testing the strength of his IKEA bed yet again. While I caught my breath, he got up and grabbed my camera from my purse. This was before smartphones, okay. It was 2005; I always carried around my Kodak Easy-Share.

"Are you crazy?!" I mustered whatever strength I had left to turn away from him.

"You look beautiful right now, and I need you to see it."

"I do?" I tossed my blown-out hair over my eyes and posed. *Click. Click. Click. Click.*

He took a dozen pictures, and we reviewed each one. I pointed out what I hated. He pointed out what he loved. I made sure to delete each one. All these years later, I wish I had one of those photos to remember my first step toward accepting my naked body.

LIGHTS ON

Sex in the dark is cool but so is being able to see what the hell is going on. The best intercourse involves all five senses. Take away vision and you're just feeling your way through a naked Twister game, which can be fun, but my bet is someone is gonna get elbowed in the head. If you can't bring yourself to leave the light on, here's a simple solution. If there's a TV in the room, change it to an external input channel but don't turn on the device. Let that "No Signal!" bounce around the screen, but trust me when I say that blue light is going to have your bodies glowing. Baby, you'll feel so sexy, you'll be rocking all night.

ABSTINENCE

Time-outs are perfectly normal and strongly encouraged if you feel like your product is being undervalued or diluted. Chill for a bit and come back when it's a seller's market. Use the free time for self- and home improvement. Whenever I shut down the cookie factory, I tended to my ignored to-do list and picked up skills like caulking and wood refinishing. I'd make weekly trips to Home Depot to buy supplies for all my tasks. I painted my apartment, ripped up carpet, put together furniture all by myself. I might not have been getting pounded out, but I learned how to pound a hammer. Read more, journal, meditate, take up a hobby like knitting and, of course, masturbate.

Senior year of college, a friend dared me to be celibate for a full year. His argument was that I lacked self-control, and he was halfway correct. My problem wasn't dick, though, it was doughnuts. I'd gained fifty pounds after quitting the team and all male interest had shriveled up. The prize was $100. Under the circumstances, it would be an easy win.

Abstinence is like going a long time without shaving your legs. At first you keep reminding yourself to shave. Once the hair has grown back, you're disgusted, but then you start to forget what it was like to ever have had smooth legs. You think about grabbing a razor but then you reason with yourself. *You're not the first women to have hairy legs and you won't be the last. You are fine the way you are and one day you will be motivated to shave and it will feel amazing. Do you want to ruin that long-awaited clean shave for no good reason. Make it count. Now grease your leg hair 'cause it's dry, braid it up nice, and put some sweats on. You got this, girl.*

For my twenty-first birthday I got drunk with friends at a tiny bar in the West Village. There were three days left until my celibacy challenge was over. However, I was officially an adult and as such my first adult decision was to break my celibacy . . . that night. As I blew the candles out on my Jell-O shots, a warm wave of clarity hit me. I made my wish. *Get some dick*. Over the course of 362 days, there wasn't much self-reflection, meditation, or spiritual work happening, which kinda made the whole dare fruitless. The lesson here, make sure you do this for the right reason. A $100 dare is not one of them.

PORN

Watch it. Judgment-free.

Porn, at its core, is voyeurism. We get to watch other people in unbridled acts of passion like a fly on the wall. Perhaps the thirst for such entertainment would have never arose if we did like ancient Greeks and had dinner party orgies like it was nothing. I'm telling you, it all goes back to food and the ancient Greeks. Just think about all the perversions that would no longer be taboo if sex wasn't shrouded in sin. Which brings me back to why you should watch porn. The best way to demystify something is to attack it head-on. Everything you want to know about positions, techniques, fetishes can be found in porn. There's even ethical and feminist porn with humanizing story lines, real couples, and women directors.

My initial reaction to porn was to rescue the woman, get her some clothes, and tell her she's too pretty and smart to be doing this. I questioned her upbringing, morals, self-esteem. All of that changed the night Jazz called us over to her dorm room.

"I just came back from home," Jazz explained. "My brother and I got into an argument so I stole all his porn DVDs." She was and still is one of the pettiest people I know, and I love her. She opened a black plastic bag, dozens of jewel cases fell out with black women on the cover. Our mouths were on the floor. "It's a sign. We just got finished talking about how we all wanted to get better at blow jobs. Here is our opportunity." She was right. We were seniors in college with limited experience and wanted to impress our future boyfriends. Never in our wildest dreams did we think to watch porn. We got snacks, cracked jokes, and took notes.

Even after watching with a support group, the fear and shame I associated with watching porn didn't completely dissipate. Thankfully, the internet get me together. After graduating college, I explored from the comfort of my own apartment. I'd sit at my desktop and scroll my way through thousands of fantasies. Mind you, you had to have the patience of a saint to watch. These were the early days of internet streaming. A five-minute clip could take thirty after all the buffering, an unexpected lesson in tantric masturbation.

With so many options, picking a lane was daunting but I soon settled on the search terms: *ebony, black, couple, amateur, homemade, lovemaking*. Watching "real couples" felt less lewd and more realistic. That mound of laundry in the corner, the flat sheet doubling as a curtain, a squeaky bed, and shoddy camera work. That could be me. I applauded them their fearlessness.

Lesbian porn was a close second choice. Women are gentle and nurturing, even if they are fisting each other. Professional porn does nothing for me. It's too slick, over-produced, and has terrible acting. If it's starring black people, there's always that terrible rap track that starts the scene and terrible dialogue. At first they refer to the woman as "sexy" or "baby," but by the end she's a "dirty bitch." Hard pass.

The best is when I spot an engagement ring on a professional and it's not part of the story. I imagine she got to set late because of L.A. traffic and didn't have time to find the one makeup artist on set she trusts to hold their jewelry, said screw it, and got to business biting the imaginary apple. That's the trick professional porn stars use to show enjoyment on their face. They pretend they're biting down on an apple because during sex every woman turns into a horse. All of this fractures the fantasy. She's not having fun, she's working, and her husband probably gave her a kiss goodbye and made sure she didn't forget her clear platform heels. I, on the other hand, was single and watching them for pointers so I could get a husband.

Porn stars are the real heroes, and many of us wouldn't know how to do the passion propeller without them.

WHITE GUYS

Been there done that. Twice.

For some strange reason my parents took me to see *Jungle Fever* in the theaters. At ten I was too young to leave at home, so they sat me in between them in the theater and took turns covering my eyes and ears during the sex scenes. Even as a kid, I felt the pain when Wesley

Snipes's wife kicks him out for cheating with a white woman and he has to tell his daughter he's moving out.

"But if he loved his daughter, why would he leave?" I whispered to my mom.

"It's complicated. I'll explain later," she replied.

That's how the concept of interracial dating was introduced to me. White women stealing our black men. As a kid, I knew of one interracial family, however, the mother was black and the father was white. Whenever we saw them I marveled at their union, thinking she was so noble, charitable even, to take on this swagless man. White men played the smallest role in my life. Sure, they control the country, but in my day-to-day life I only interacted with them in school, where they were a handful of my teachers, and at home, as my neighbors. Hasidic Jews don't consider themselves to be anything but Jewish; nevertheless, in a black and white world, they were white in my book and just prayed a lot. All the white boys I watched on TV—Ricky Schroder, Fred Savage, Mark-Paul Gosselaar—none of them made my heart skip a beat. I'm saying all of this to illustrate how white men were not a factor.

Then I met Boat Shoes.

Summer 1998, Boat Shoes and I met on NYU's campus. He was renting a dorm room for his summer internship. The first time he spoke to me, I stared up into his gray eyes, lost for words. On the wigger scale of 1–5—one being pre–Super Bowl Justin Timberlake and 5 being Michael Rappaport—Boat Shoes was a Robin Thicke; granted, I should deduct a point for his damn boat shoes. He peppered black slang in all the right places, rapped along with Biggie, taking extra precaution not to say the N-word, ate fried chicken, and loved a fat ass.

At seventeen, I was not ready for the vitriol we received in, all places, the West Village.

"Really, sista, that's what we doing?" A group of black men scolded me as they walked by. At lunch, our white waitress completely ignored me.

"Hiya, are *you* ready to order?" Her entire back was to me. Boat placed his order. "I'll put that right in for ya." She smiled.

"Excuse me, you didn't take her order." Boat motioned his hand to me.

This wench turned to me dramatically like Scarlett O'Hara. "Oh, I'm sorry. What would you like?"

By the end of our meal she checked on him several times, left my water glass empty, and took my plate while my fork was in my mouth. I was on my way to being a strong black woman, but I wasn't strong enough to deal with bullshit. Interracial couples got my respect; it's not for the faint of heart. Just because I wasn't ready for something serious didn't mean I was going to let my first white guy go without testing his goods. For science, of course.

Sometimes, having zero expectations is your saving grace. For all the rhythm Boat Shoes exhibited on the dance floor, we could not catch the groove. His thin lips didn't stand a chance against mine, our teeth clanged on every kiss. Down there, I was having trouble feeling anything. He was the second guy I'd been with, so the lack of friction was all on him. I didn't need a ruler to know that my white boy wonder was on the smaller side. For a week after, I kept trying to find a household object to replicate what he was working, or not working, with for my friends who wanted full details. Saltshaker? Too small.

Remote control? Child, please. With all the dick data I've collected to date, looking back, Boat Shoes was probably the average 5.1 to 5.6 inches. FYI, those are world averages and not race specific. Unfulfilled, I wrote him and white guys off.

Over a decade later, I found myself making out with a cute white guy in the back of a dark hipster L.A. bar that played underground hip-hop and had Hennessy. Their clientele was clearly smarty-arty black people and the non-black people who covet them. The heat between us was about to fry my brain. Back at my hotel he displayed his best moves and blatant black BBW fetishes.

"I love your big black lips on my cock."

Whoa, buddy. I am not your colored concubine.

"Bounce that big black ass for me, baby."

Sir, everything about me is black. No need to point out the obvious.

"Oh my God, I love your hair. Can I touch it?"

You're really lucky you got a big dick or else I would have kicked your racially insensitive ass out of here.

Split decision, folks. A real cracker crap shoot.

SIZE QUEEN

"Chloé only dates guys with a table leg for a dick." This is a running joke among my group of close male friends. I'd sit through there misogynistic jokes, post-sex recaps, and nudie pic slideshows with no judgment. But the moment I share my well-endowed playmates, these pussies find religion. "Oh my goodness, Chloé, the way you objectify men is crazy.

You're the smart one. The feminist. You treat men like meat, reducing us to our sex organs." Well, they don't put it as eloquently. What they really said was, "Ill, no one wants to hear about all the donkey dick you're getting."

"I can't help it if I attract men who are packing pipe," I'd reply. "I'm blessed." Yes, I know how ri*dick*ulous it is to bring God into this, but he saw me fit to take in and nurture some of the biggest sperm cannons he created. Who am I to reject God's will? My girlfriends listened with jealousy and awe at my tales. I was a mandingo whisperer; with one look I could tell what a man was working with. The most common mistake made when trying to size up a package is looking at the crotch of his pants. Unless he is wearing sweatpants, a clingy fabric, or tailored slacks that are too small, you won't be able to see a dick print. Jeans are stiff, and the crotch space is already a part of the pants' construction. Therefore, based on the size of his waist and what hole the belt is in, that gap you see in the front could be surplus of denim, air, or, worse, balls. Dick prints can be misleading. Some are showers, others growers. Growers always make it a point to tell you they are before you see it for yourself. Usually it's sandwiched in between laughs, tossed into the convo like a football flag on the play.

I have two tried-and-true ways to settle one's dick dilemma: dick energy and directness. Men either possess big-dick energy or little-dick energy. Catch those vibes early by watching his body language and you'll save yourself some disappointment. At their core, each is powered by a very simple motivation.

Big-Dick Energy: Never wants a problem

Little-Dick Energy: Always asks if there's a problem

Let me paint the scene. You're at a party and two guys bump into each other, spilling one's drink. They briefly lock horns like wild bulls, but one steps back. Seeing that the matter is minuscule, nothing some club soda or a dry cleaner can't fix, he's willing to concede and go back to his two-step. The other bull isn't having it. He digs his heels in, puffs his chest, and gets louder. He thinks he looks macho but he's really an insecure Chihuahua, all bark and no bite. He's showcasing classic little-dick energy, the need to overcompensate for a lack of confidence. The other gentleman, who brushed off the clash and went back to enjoying himself, displayed big-dick energy and probably has a tripod in his pants. Disclaimer, BDE can also be projected by men who have money. Don't fall for it. The ugly guy in the exotic car taking up two parking spots in the lot. The showoff who takes you shopping so you can watch him buy expensive things for himself. The idiot who makes sure to tell you how much everything in his house costs. The guy in VIP throwing money in the air. All of that is LDE masked as BDE. Their confidence is bought, but the dick won't be able to deliver. Oh, BDE guys also tend not to be the best dressers. Sure, they apply themselves when it matters, but on the daily they aren't killing time in the mirror. Whatever doors their clothes won't open, their big-dick energy will.

Directness is your best weapon. When in doubt about what energy team your prospect is on just ask, "How big is your dick?" There's no right or wrong time. Whisper it in his ear at dinner. Yell it over loud music on the dance floor. My personal favorite, ask when he's hijacked a nice "get to know you" conversation, turning it into an interrogation about your favorite sex positions and craziest places you've done it. Cut him off and ask, "How big is your dick?" Since he wants to be inappropriate, show him you can play the game too. If he takes long to answer, there's your answer. BDE knows how big it is in inches and centimeters. If you are feeling cocky, pun intended, ask him to pull it out. I've never had a guy refuse. BDE will be proud to do it, knowing they have a drool inducer. Even LDE will try to talk himself out of it but will eventually relent. Try to keep a pleasant look on your face no matter what comes out. Ghost him after, but in the moment, stroke his ego even if you don't want to stroke his dick.

Sadly, the time is approaching for me to take off my size queen crown. The way my health insurance is set up, my premium won't cover dropped cervixes and vaginal rejuvenation. Big johnsons are fun when you're young, but I'm almost forty. My best snatch-snapback years are behind me. I'll gladly retire on a nice respectable penis that taps all the important angles and doesn't have to leave a police report behind for the coroner.

FUCKBOIS

For time, space, and minimum headaches I will only address fuckboi behavior in the bedroom. Avoid these types at all costs.

Slippers: Removes condom without you knowing, usually during doggy-style. This can be avoided by (a) keeping the lights on or (b) reaching down and feeling for a condom.

Lickers: Resorts to oral sex to prevent from cumming too fast or to cover up their (hopefully) momentarily lost erection. Not the biggest problem if you like superfluous saliva everywhere.

Stickers: Determined to enter your anus without warning, the proper setup, or lube. The one-thrust bandit will feign ignorance like he had no idea where he was aiming.

Limpers: Unable to keep their dicks hard, especially after talking big. Often blames it on work-related stress when it's probably because their diet is trash and their dick arteries are clogged up with french fry grease and beer.

SEX WITH FRIENDS

There's only one outcome to this. You'll agree to cross the line and promise it won't change anything. That's a lie. Within weeks, one person will realize they had feelings all along or that the arrangement is so stress-free and comfortable that they trick themselves into thinking it can transfer into something more permanent. The friendship will never be the same but you will try to keep it going. Texting on birthdays, commenting on posts, inviting them to events they never show up to. Years later, they've moved on, married, maybe with kids. You run into them and their other half and are introduced as an "old friend." You smile at each other knowing all that your *friendship* included, your gaze lasting moments too long. No need to ask for their info, you have it but don't use it because you know the friendship you had can't be replicated, even without the sex. It was nice to see them though.

THE PERFECT FUCK BUDDY

* No public outings. Watch a movie at home and order in.

* Personal conversations are limited to information you'd share at a cocktail party with strangers. Focus on current events.

* All communications are centered around meeting up. Avoid "good morning" texts or "where you at?"

* No pictures.

* Do not follow each other on social media.

* All mention of past relationships are strongly discouraged. You should never answer the question, "So why are you single?" from a person who wants to fuck but doesn't

want to date you. They're just being nosy and trying to gauge how nuts you are.

*   Unprotected sex is NEVER an option. Be smart.

*   Call it quits around the seven-month to one-year mark. Anything after that and all the Eros fade away, along with the chemicals in your brain that thrive of its passion. You'll want more, something with substance, a real relationship not because you love the person, but because you want a return on your time invested. Congrats, you've just ruined your arrangement. It's over!

THERE'S NO ROOM FOR SHAME

The world would be a much better place if women were encouraged and allowed to enjoy sex. A woman's right to choose, use, sell, and protect her body has transformed into a publicly traded commodity. Her value is determined by a set of draconian standards better suited to accommodate the male ego than the woman's emotional and physical needs. If a woman feels she's sexy, they call her a slut. The undermining is so strong that other women join in on it. The berating continues until it's drilled into the subconscious.

You don't have sex; sex happens to you.

Good girls don't make sexual demands; they take them.

No man wants a woman who has more sexual partners than him.

Ladies, it's time to hurt some feelings, chuck those T-shirts, charge those vibrators, and guide that careless partner who thinks foreplay should only take the time it takes for him to reach for a condom and open it. I understand that not everyone reading this is a woman, and if you aren't, I hope you have the confidence to let the women in your life be great in the bedroom.

Happy woman, happy world.

16

I'M A COMEDIAN

ife has a way of showing you where you need to be.

In the midnineties my elementary school bestie, Shelly, and I would have our annual New Year's Eve slumber party. We would dress in matching flannel pajamas and stuff our faces with takeout. Dessert was cake and ice cream mixed together in our bowls until it became a soup. We'd curl up on my living room couch and watch HBO's *Def Comedy Jam* marathon. Martin Lawrence, Mo'Nique, Bernie Mac, Adele Givens, and dozens of other black comedians knocked my fuzzy socks off. Most of their jokes went over my pubescent head, but I admired their charm and fearlessness. Fast-forward to high school. During all those summer days spent hanging with Indigo in the West Village, it never dawned on me that we were on NYU's campus. I was too busy trying to make eye contact with boys in Washington Square Park to notice the big white-and-purple flags that flew overhead. Then in 1998, I moved into NYU's Hayden Hall, literally across the street from Washington Square Park, which I walked through to get to a class. On an off night from basketball, some girls on the team suggested a comedy club around the corner. Twenty years later, I now perform regularly at that club—the Comedy Cellar.

———

Chloé, how the hell did you get your start in comedy?

Good question. However, I'm afraid my answer is going to be all logic and zero Hollywood magic: I took a stand-up comedy class while working as an editor at VIBE *magazine.*

Overworked and underpaid, I often spent twelve hours in the office and on more than one occasion spent the night—asleep at my desk or *on* a conference table—to meet a deadline. Between the crazy work hours, nearby bank robberies, 24/7 aroma of Popeyes chicken (our offices were above one on 125th Street in Harlem), dope fiends defying gravity on the corners (our office was also near a methadone clinic), and the aggressive African hair braiders who harassed me to use their services every morning as I walked out the train station, I was ready for a change. Adding insult to insult, there was the glass ceiling that I'd been pressing my nose up against since the day I started there. The year was 2009, pay gap and gender discrimination was the same as it is now. After a year on staff, I learned that a male coworker, years my junior in both age and experience, was making the same as me. When I went to the three men above me, with a list of my job accomplishments and attributes to inquire about a promotion, they smiled in my face, asked me to leave so they could discuss it further, and eventually offered me an increase of $5k and a title change. It was made clear this wasn't a real promotion. They just wanted to shut me up.

Letting go of my Pulitzer aspirations, corner-office dreams, and company-card wishes was going to be hard. Reluctant to do so, I convinced myself to give journalism one more chance. I'd been through digital, newspapers, and magazines. The last stop on the career train was being in front of the camera, broadcast. What better to prepare me than a stand-up comedy class. At the end of the six-week course, I'd be a witty talking head/correspondent. My only requirement for my new dream job was having to show up, talk shit, get paid, and go home. Unbeknownst to me, I was describing a comedian.

My first day of comedy class, I walked in and took a seat at the back. Folks there were either on a mission to be the next Seinfeld or just wanted a reason to get out of the house. All in all, the twenty-five of us were nervous, anxious, and thinking of better ways we could have spent $325. I especially felt guilty because Quentin, who I was with at the time, had paid for me. He saw the light in my eyes while we talked about it and, without hesitation, handed me his debit card and said, "Go for it." (To be fair, I also changed his life while we were together.)

Our instructor, Patricia, was a veteran who'd appeared on all the late-night shows. The job must've paid well because we were terrible. Each week we fine-tuned jokes to be performed at the class graduation. Once in a while, she couldn't contain her disgust with a joke. Lots of shit and dick jokes come from new comedians. You're grasping at straws up there. Everyone thinks they're funny until it's time to be funny. Patricia encouraged us to dig deeper.

"Nothing is funnier than real life," she explained. "Talk about what makes you, you." *I came here to learn how to be funny. Not talk about myself.* When graduation rolled around, I stuck to jokes about the weather, my name not being stereotypically black, and some other goofy stuff. Trembling with nerves, I jotted down my jokes on the side of my hand. I left the mic in the stand. After each punch line, while the audience laughed (which they did, a lot!), I'd peek down at my next joke. Those five minutes changed the course of my life.

———

"Women aren't funny!" is propaganda pushed out by the male ego agenda. Generally speaking, men don't want women to be funny. In their mind, humor is the one thing they all possess and can activate at will. Of all the things for one group to want ownership over, why humor, you ask? Like a Swiss Army knife, humor has multiple uses. It can disarm, insult, charm, compliment, or impress. To be the funniest person in the room is to also be the most powerful. Women have to use their beauty to get the same result. Even if a woman is clearly the funniest person in the room, men are silently saying to themselves, "I'm funnier." *Sir, 99 percent of the time, you are not.*

I vividly remember interviewing John Legend while at *VIBE*. He was promoting his 2010 collaboration album with the Roots. As a budding comic, I was compelled to ask everyone I interviewed something comedy-related.

"Who makes you laugh?" I asked.

Without skipping a beat he replied, "My girlfriend, Chrissy, is the funniest person I know. She makes me laugh like no one else." I was shocked. Keep in mind, this was pre-Twitter. Back then she was viewed as the pretty swimsuit model who delivered smoldering looks, not wisecracks. That was the first time I'd heard a man make such a statement without a self-serving footnote. *She's funny, but ya know, I've been known to say a gut buster or two myself.* Sadly, there aren't enough John Legends in the world.

Like most professions, comedy is male-dominated and full of double standards. The road leading to the stage and sold-out shows is not for the faint of heart. Which is why not a lot of women stick it out. Many won't make it past the open-mic phase. An honored rite of passage, open mics are like gator-filled swamps. They're necessary in order to cultivate friendships, support groups, sworn lifelong enemies, and of course better jokes. This was my breeding ground. At twenty-nine, I was the new kid on the block.

The routine was frustrating. Sign-up sheets were posted as early as 2:00 p.m. The goal was to sign up for as many mics as possible, bounce around to each one, and get up. This was the only way to get multiple spots in an evening. Timing was everything. I'd rush downtown from the *VIBE* office and meet Hannah, my first friend in comedy. Hannah was white, from a hippie Upstate family, and talked about her feelings a lot. She was a full-time creative, so she could run over and sign us up for mics in the afternoon. Younger than myself, Hannah helped me slow down to smell the shitty roses. Before her, I'd go to open mics after work and introduce myself with a handshake like I was in a business meeting. You know, like an adult. They looked at me like I had two heads. For many of them, it was their first physical contact of the day. I could tell by their faces they wanted to know why I was chasing my dreams when I had a job with benefits. *Yes, but comedy is better.*

After sitting through a few mics, you start to notice a trend. People go for dirty and offensive material early and often. Since the majority of comics were men, they displayed their toxic masculinity in the form of rape, dick, masturbation, and anime jokes. Lots of what we call today "incels" on the scene. In 2010, we just called them unfunny weirdos. (Google "incel" and "mass shootings.") Unable to play nice with others or take responsibility for their terrible jokes not working, real comedy clubs didn't book them. Oh, this is the best. Guys like them loved to describe their style as reminiscent of their comedy gods Mitch Hedberg and Bill Hicks. They were on a mission to write the best rape joke or die trying. If you ever expressed your disdain for their material, they'd team up and blast you for not understanding comedy.

———

Over the last ten years, I've been shut out, heckled, sexually harassed, and manhandled by male comics. Most of these incidents happened within the first three years. Some offenses were minuscule. Like the time I was waiting to perform at my first weekend show. It was a weekly urban show where the lineup was all black and maybe one Latinx person. Usually comedy clubs have a formula to make sure their shows aren't just white guys. A "diverse" lineup includes one woman and one person of color. If a comic checks both boxes, that's even better. This strategy meant a lot of black and brown comics had a hard time getting stage time. So clubs allowed race-specific shows to take place once a week. They always had interesting names. *Melanin Mondays. Too Cara-*

mel Tuesday. African Diaspora Wednesdays. The club would be swarming with urban comics. It was every bit of a hangout as it was a place of business. Comics who weren't on the show came to hang out and size up the competition. Left to myself, I stood in the hallway leading to the showroom awaiting my turn. Behind me, two older male comics chatted.

"Would you?" I heard the taller one say.

"Yeah," said the other. "You?"

"Man, I'd climb that so fast." *Are these muthafuckas talking about me?* I looked over, locked eyes with them, and gave a nervous smile. *Yup, they're talking about me.* If this was the real world I would have cussed their asses out. If this was *VIBE*, I'd have them written up with HR, who would at least entertain me and pretend they would do more about it. But this was the comedy world. If I spoke up, I could've risked being blacklisted.

"Oh man, you heard of that new chick, Chloé? She's nuts. Totally lost it at the club the other night. Said we shouldn't *objectify* women, and show respect. That bitch dumb." I'd be cast off, left to perform in weird alternative comedy rooms or feminist shows. My material would feel like a TED Talk and instead of laughs I'd ask you to join my latest cause. I bit my tongue, went up, had a cool set, and came back several more times. After seeing me do well, they stopped talking about how big my tits were.

My scariest run-in happened once I started to gain traction. Comedy was generating income, my calendar was filling up. While I'd been attracted to some of my fellow comics, better judgment prevented me from pursuing anything. Then I met another comedy late bloomer. Like me, he came from corporate. We shared tactical advice and exchanged flirting glances. The thought of hooking up lingered in the air but was never spoken.

He invited me to do a show. I arrived to find him drunk backstage, which shocked me. He wasn't the messy type. I go up, do my time, and as I'm putting on my coat in the greenroom, he offers to walk me out. We take a service hallway to the street exit. Before I reach for the door, dude gently pulls me toward him. Face-to-face, he slurs, "Yo, why you be playing games?"

"Excuse me?" I smile.

"I mean, what's up?" He walks me back to the wall and has me pinned. "You know we feeling each other. Give me a kiss." He lunges in, the force smacks the back of my head on the wall. He pulls back and has my red lipstick all over his face. I go to move his arms but he's holding my coat sleeves below the elbow. I'm restricted but use my chest to push him back. Even more turned on, he slams me back on the wall. Now, I try to reason with him. Low tones, calm voice.

"Yo, what are you doing?"

"You playing games!" His hot alcohol breath makes my eyes water. A woman who was in the show turns the corner and spots us.

"Oops, I'm sorry." She thinks she's witnessing a hookup, not an attack. She goes into the bathroom and comes back out when she hears the commotion of me trying to release from his grip and aggressive kissing. Initially, I don't ask her for help because (this sounds terrible) she is smaller than me. *If I can't manage this man, what was she going to do?* But now I call out to her. "Can you tell him to stop?"

She sees the confusion and fear in my eyes. "Let her go!" All five foot five of her wedges in between us. Once he steps back, he snaps out of it, hands me $50 for my spot, and walks back to the greenroom wiping my lipstick off his face. A couple of days later, he texted to apologize and offered me spots on more shows.

————

In 2013, I took the leap and became a full-time comedian. This wouldn't have been possible without a college agent seeing my first cable TV set. Chuck sent me a Facebook message and asked if I'd be interested in touring campuses across the country.

"Do you have an hour (of material)?" he asked during our first phone call.

"Oh yeah!" I lied. I had maybe fifteen minutes at best. Comedy sets are in increments of 5, 10, 12, 15, 20, 30, 45, and 60 minutes. It takes a good comic years to fine-tune the perfect hour, which is why you don't see many comics with one-hour specials. With three years in the game, there was no way I was close to having an hour, but I'd figure it out on the way. Within weeks, I went from getting paid $25 for a 10–15-minute spot in the city to making $1,300 for an hour-long college show. I was building up my 10,000 hours and my bank account. (I've made more money telling and writing jokes than I ever made as an NYU-educated journalist.)

Others were starting to notice too. In the spring of 2014, I was invited to fly out to L.A. and audition for the reboot of NBC's *Last Comic Standing*. The new season was being executive produced by Wanda Sykes. I was gassed. *Oh my God, Wanda Sykes is going to see me perform?* I was so grateful for the opportunity, on my walk back to my hotel, I took a selfie with the biggest smile to commemorate the moment. I had heard Wanda laugh. That was all the validation I needed. Oh, making it to the semifinals was amazing too. *Last Comic* raised my profile and my college rate.

Everyone has either given or received a motivational pep talk about following one's dreams, but I'm here to tell you, I never dreamed this big. A universal nudge turned into a push, then a bungee jump. My worst nights onstage are still more fulfilling than most jobs I've ever considered. Something needs to be said about the cost of peace of mind. Doesn't matter if I'm telling jokes to three thousand people or thirty, the woman I am on that stage is all the best parts of me, even the best of the worst parts. Onstage Chloé is sweet, kind, caring, confident, an enforcer (to folks who want to heckle), and in awe of the world. I've learned more about myself and the human condition through interacting with thousands of people over the years. I see it as an extension of my journalism career, my second act, if you will. I'm still telling stories and impacting lives. I'm enjoying the time that I've been allowed to explore this new adventure. I told myself that before I "make it" I need to be mentally and emotionally ready. No point in rushing to fail.

17

NOT SASSY ENOUGH

Before I got good at stand-up, people were quick to give me unsolic-
ited career advice.

"You should be on *Saturday Night Live.*" *Why didn't I think of that?
Oh, let me call up Lorne right now.*

"When I'm gonna see you on TV?" *Right after I see myself on TV, and
let's be honest, there are like 200 million channels. Even if I was on, you
probably wouldn't be watching.*

I was more than content with being a comedian, but that wasn't
enough for everyone else. Why stop at telling jokes, they said, be an
actress. There's only one issue with that; when it comes to 99 percent
of the black women roles I come across, I'm not black, loud, brash, or
no-nonsense enough. Yes, I get it's all acting. However, when the people judging my take want to tell me how to wave my finger or move
my neck for a line that simply says, "Excuse me," you start to under-

stand why the acting world didn't wow me. Sad part is, once you stick your toe into the world of entertainment, you want to try everything and see what speaks to your heart and bank account.

I left my full-time job at *VIBE* magazine for an editorial director position at a digital start-up for black millennials. We weren't calling them that at the time. It was 2012. I think the official language was "smart, upwardly mobile, young African Americans with disposable income." I thought working from home on a website would give me all the time I needed to tell jokes. I was so wrong. The owner was a taskmaster and micromanager. He monitored our emails and work-provided laptops. Messy. I tolerated it because up until that point, it was the highest-paid job I had, with a starting salary of $72,000 with bonuses. The old Chloé would have worn a diaper and chained herself to her desk to meet all the daily targets. Comedy Chloé didn't give a damn about this job and set out to get laid off. Important emails would get replied to after half an hour, phone calls rang to voice mail, work was completed but with 65 percent effort. It was the type of calculated decline that gets you cut from the team but not bashed or blacklisted. Over time, my employer felt it was best the site went in a different direction, and that was without me. All that mattered was I'd be able to collect unemployment for several months. Comedy wasn't paying, but I loved it. Acting, on the other hand, did. If I landed a role it came with at least a couple hundred bucks. *Shoot, how hard is it to memorize some lines?*

TAKE ONE

Hello Chloé,

I came across your comedy videos and thought you'd be
perfect for a role we're auditioning for. It's a reality show with
a former A-list celebrity and we're casting their best friend.
We're looking for someone who is larger than life, not afraid to
keep it real, and hysterical. Non-union.

Translation: black, loud, and fat. Casting emails are easy to decipher once you learn the code. I read the email again: *"We're looking for someone who is larger than life, not afraid to keep it real, and hysterical."* I'm all those things, especially the large part. I was pushing 275 pounds. Since it was a reality show, there were no lines to learn or, in my case, forget in front of the camera. I got this in the bag. I took the train into the city with loose change I found in my futon because, you know, *dreams and rent.*

Inside the waiting room, multiple variations of me awaited their turn. Tall, short, thick, thicker, thickest. Chocolate brown, light brown, dark brown. We all had the look of a cute friend who wouldn't overshadow the star. Frazzled, I wrote my name on the sign-in sheet and grabbed an empty seat. I'm sorry, did I say seat, I meant flimsy folding chair. How was I supposed to calm my nerves when all I could focus on was not breaking my chair? When you're officially heavy, you develop the ability to telepathically communicate with inanimate objects that may be threatened by your size. Be it a stool, bench, couch, or in a car, plane, or bus seat, you feel the moment, like a pit in your stomach, when whatever you're occupying is close to its breaking point. You hear a creak or a crack, a snap, even a pop. Before abandoning ship, you start a dialogue, trying to negotiate. *Chair, please don't break on me. Please, please, please. Okay, I'll adjust my weight to this side. Is this side better? Wheww.* Now I'm holding my breath. Heavy people hold their breath in these situations because in our minds a massive exhale may further jeopardize things. Your body must stay as compact as possible, thighs together, ass clenched, whatever core muscles available are activated. Think I'm exaggerating? Next time you see a big person sitting in an uncomfortable seat, look at their relief and audible exhale once they stand.

"Chloé?"

I grabbed my purse and color headshot I printed out at home and stood to my feet. *Exhale.*

"Follow me this way."

———

During the silent and golden age of Hollywood, films with an all-black cast were known as "race films," not to be confused with blackface, where a white actor like Judy Garland or Fred Astaire pretended to be black in a major motion picture film. Race films were shown at "black only" theaters or segregated ones, but at certain times, usually matinee and midnight screenings.

In the early days, roles for black women were either that of the help or the temptress. The first black woman to win the Oscar for Best Supporting Actress was Hattie McDaniel in 1940 for playing a maid named Mammy in *Gone with the Wind.* For every Hattie McDaniel, who famously said she'd rather play a maid on film than be one in real life, there was a Lena Horne, whose beauty and singing voice meant she complemented the white cast but was limited to being a lounge singer who entertained them but rarely interacted with them. The intermingling of races was heavily restricted in Hollywood movies; Southern audiences would walk out of the theater or become violent. The studios' solution? Give black actors solo scenes that would be cut from the film when it showed in the south.

As Hollywood progressed, so did the types of roles black women played. By the 1950s the mammy and background beauty evolved into several still-problematic archetypes.

Mammy: Overweight, dark-skinned woman, domestic worker who cooks and cleans with a smile on her face. Her purpose in life is to make others, usually her white employers, happy. Aunt Jemima, the Popeyes spokescharacter, Annie, and the Pine-Sol lady are all modern examples of Mammy. Let's not forget the highly acclaimed and problematic 2011 film *The Help*. Even Viola Davis felt compelled to apologize for her part in the modern mammy porn.

Jezebel: Named after a blood- and power-thirsty queen in the Bible whose beauty, enhanced with cosmetics, hypnotized men into doing her bidding even at the risk of their own lives. By this definition, *Scandal*'s Olivia Pope was a jezebel. Come on, don't act like she wasn't fucking the president of the United States and getting people kidnapped while her hair and outfits slayed.

Matriarch: Another physically big woman who cooked and cleaned, but unlike Mammy, she was wise and devoted to the protection and upliftment of her family. Tyler Perry's Madea is the overexaggeration of this.

Tragic Mulatto: Biracial beauty queen who always manages to have far more European attributes than black (i.e., fair skin and long curly hair). Caught in between two worlds, she finds herself the object of both black and white men's affection while being hated by women.

The Angry Black Woman: Brash and bitter. Perhaps the most notorious black female archetype not only perpetuated in media but also in everyday life. Originally this archetype was referred to as Sapphire, a character on the 1950s hit TV show *Amos 'n Andy*, who was overbearing, insufferable, emasculating, and undesirable.

———

Led to a small black box theater, I'm greeted by one of three white women sitting behind the camera. "Hi, Chloé! So nice to meet you." The tiny platform stage creaked with every shift of my weight. "We're going to ask you some questions, get your advice on different situations women find themselves in. Basically, it's girl talk."

"Got it." I smiled and nodded. My replies were informative, concise, witty, and not good enough. They wanted jarring, crass, outrageous. Oh, and arm movements. They specifically told me to move my arms like those reality-TV people do in their confessionals. No one talks like that in real life. But I had to remember, this wasn't real life.

"Think bigger," one of them said. "We want you to fill the frame."

Ten years of being a journalist who prided herself on being an objective fly on the way did not prepare me for this. Yes, physically I was big, but that didn't mean I had the personality to match. I'd spent years successfully minimizing my presence. My polished disposition frustrated them. I couldn't see their faces, but I could feel their disappoint in my inability to deliver. With no other direction left to give, they pulled out the big guns.

"Okay, Chloé, your answers are great but, ehh, we need to see more sassiness."

"Yes!" the others agreed. All three of them broke into a side conversation about sass.

"That's the perfect word. I was looking for that this entire time."

"Chloé, can you be sassy?"

Sassy sas·sy /'sase/
adjective: **sassy**; comparative adjective: **sassier**; superlative
adjective: **sassiest**; lively, bold, and full of spirit; cheeky.

The sassy black woman combines attributes from mammy, jezebel, and the angry black woman. She's caring but not a pushover. She's flirty but not a whore. She's direct but not "call the cops" threatening. All of this makes her the perfect supporting character. She's the sassy, loud, tell-it-like-it-is coworker or best friend. She has a catchphrase and rolls her eyes and neck for punctuation. She's the comedic relief, devoid of shame. The type to throw herself on a man she knows she'll never get and bounces back from rejection because she's emotionally impenetrable. Above all, she is loud and at times embarrassing.

The sassy black friend's look depends on who she is playing opposite. Yes, there is a science to it. If her screen mate is a white woman, the black friend can be gorgeous like Stacey Dash in *Clueless*. Dash's character was rich, pretty, and petite and, in my opinion, better all-around than the lead. She was also black, and in a white film, the black friend, no matter how stunning, is never a threat to the white main character's story. However, if both women are black, the sassy black friend must be a big girl. Her weight is the reason she isn't seen as a threat to the cute, slim, black female lead. 2017's *Girls Trip* slightly broke the mold by featuring four black women. The sassiest of the group was the comedic foil, undercutting the most tense situations, but at its core the film was about the married, slim, and super successful Ryan, played by Regina Hall, and the larger, single, and broke Sasha, played by Queen Latifah. I bet Latifah went into the first meeting and told them she wasn't going to be the stereotypical loudmouth. She did that already in *Bringing Down the House*. Never again. The Queen is a jazz singer now.

The role I was auditioning for was opposite a petite black woman, hence why all the women in the waiting room were stressing out the folding chairs. I'm big but I don't have a big personality. When I speak, it's because I have something constructive to say, not a desire to be seen and heard at all times. Yelling isn't part of my everyday emotional range. I can accomplish the same things as a sassy black woman, without the bravado, but Hollywood doesn't like their black women subtle.

Hi Chloé—
I spotted you at a comedy show the other night and would love for you to come in and read for a recurring role. Her name is Tanya, 30s, single, who is always looking for a hot date. The perfect *sassy* wingwoman, life of the party. She's the lead's neighbor.

Pass.

Hi Chloé—
We're looking to cast the role of Gaby. She's the lead's cubicle mate/office manager who keeps everyone in check with her *sassy* attitude and street smarts . . .

Delete.

Hello Chloé—
Are you available to come in and read for Joanette, the *sassiest* teacher at Thomas Elementary . . . ?

I'm good, love, enjoy.

———

Nell Carter was a Tony– and Emmy Award–winning theater actress and singer. She started her career in 1970, eventually landing on TV with a starring role in the 1980s hit sitcom *Gimme a Break!* The official description of her character, Nell Harper, lists her as a housekeeper, which was just a nicer way of saying mammy at the time. The show's plot could have been plucked out of Hattie McDaniel's era. Nell Harper, a singer, befriends a white woman after running away from her Southern home at eighteen. *Black best friend? Check.* When Nell's white bestie falls ill with cancer, Nell promises to move in and help take care of her family, which includes a stern police chief husband and three teen daughters. *Caregiver and domestic? Double check.* Nell's character occasionally broke out in song. *Shuckin' and jivin'? Check.* All that was missing from this racially insensitive gumbo was blackface. Oh, wait, there was an episode when one of the characters, a young Joey Lawrence, wore blackface to perform at Nell's church event. *WTF? Check.*

Don't get me wrong, I'm glad Nell was able to star in her own hit show for six seasons; however, this did little to advance the image of black women in American homes. Even though it was 1981–1987, people still found comfort and joy in watching a black woman dote on a white widower and his three kids. The only other black maid on TV at the time was Florence on *The Jeffersons* (1975–1985) whose "don't give a damn" attitude shattered the mammy mold. As a kid sitting in front of the tube, I missed all that made *Gimme a Break!* problematic. I'm also the only person I know who loved Richard Pryor's film *The Toy.* I stumbled upon it one Saturday afternoon as a kid and became obsessed with it. I won't ruin the plot, but my parents had a hard time convincing me that people, especially black people, hated the film. It's Richard Pryor! Living in a Hasidic Jewish neighborhood and attending all-black schools meant I was naive to a lot.

I watched *Gimme a Break!,* wishing I could sit on Nell's lap and be engulfed by one of her hugs. I bet they were so warm, like fresh-baked cookies, her boobies soft like pillows, and she smelled like cinnamon or fried chicken, since she was always cooking something for her white family. My mother's hugs were great, but my mom was slim. Slim hugs are no match for big-woman hugs. Their arm flab warms your neck like a chinchilla scarf. Why am I going down memory lane? Because Nell was the quintessential Sassy Black Woman, and for decades Hollywood wanted to cast this type of character, and in a small way they still do.

Auditioning made me take myself seriously as a product. No one wants to think of themselves as being bought and sold, but that's all entertainment is. Are you sellable? Will you generate big money? I'd been approaching these roles as a realistic extension of who I am, which is why I rarely booked anything. Serious actors make themselves a vessel for the character to pour into. I'd read over lines, compelled to change them because "a real black woman wouldn't say no crap like this." I was too tied to reality. That's why I stunk at improv.

Three years into doing stand-up, fully committed to living the dream, I applied for and received a diversity scholarship to a respected improv company. Quickly, I connected with the other two cynics in the class. The three of us sat in the back corner, cutting each other looks at the fantasy fuckery going on. Improv is the world of "yes, and" building on whatever is presented to you. However, I was taught long ago not to just go along with things. *That's how my people ended up on a boat in the Middle Passage.*

"Everyone, let's get in a circle." Our instructor was an improv vet who dressed like a hipster greaser. We moved our rows of chairs out of the way and joined in the middle of the classroom like kindergarteners. I'm in my thirties; this feels dumb. "Okay, we're going to take turns tossing a baby. Imagine there is a six-month-old baby and we're tossing it in the air and across to someone. Great, now I'm gonna add a knife into the game. Remember you are catching a knife and a baby, those catches should have two different reactions." After each class I walked out with a knot in my chest. I needed to yell, "The emperor has no clothes on!" Something about playing games with grown-ass people four hours a week felt insane. Then it dawned on me. I'm not fitting in because I'm a black woman and improv is about feeding your imagination, which if you are a person of color navigating this unfair world, you don't have time for. I call it the "luxury of imagination." White people have all the time in the world to play fantasy games, like Dungeons & Dragons and Quidditch, because they aren't bogged down with constantly validating their existence to the world.

Being black in America means always being aware of your surroundings, how you carry yourself, approaching every situation with caution even if the danger is not yet present. To be black in America means you must master all five senses and develop the sixth, intuition, to keep your ass out of harm's way. Improv was asking me to suspend reality, be vulnerable, and just go forward aimlessly. I felt like every time I stepped into class my ancestors collectively shook their heads in disappoint. *Child, we didn't die for you to toss a fake baby in the air. The revolution ain't going to be a game.*

"Chloé, you're a tree."

"Okay, but like, we're in a Laundromat, so how about I be a person since we're folding clothes."

"Chloé, remember, the only rule to improv is 'yes, and . . .'"

"Yes, and I don't want to be a tree."

Committed to moving past my mental blocks, I started raising my hand first to play in a scene. I was getting the hang of it until Mac started being my scene partner. Mac was an early-twentysomething white woman with greasy hair that always looked two days away from forming dreadlocks. She dressed like Stevie Nicks, which earned her the nickname Fleetwood Mac or Mac for short from my cynical friends and me. At first I thought it was a fluke, but my friends confirmed that she waited for my hand to go up before raising hers. Okay, she's on my dick. No big deal. I'll yes and roll with it. Teacher Greaser would throw out a scenario. "Ladies, you are in a coffee shop. Go!" I pull up a chair and mime reading a book while drinking a coffee. Up walks Mac.

"Hey, *GIRLFRIEND*! What up?"

Game over. What the fuck is this black voice she's doing. Before I can open my mouth, here goes the teacher.

"Chloé," he's pleading with me. His experience teaching at this school, dealing with other diversity scholarship winners, he knew I was about to lose it on Little Dirtilocks. "Remember, the game here."

I shook it off. Let's try again. I looked up at her annoying face.

"Hi, how are you today?" I'm deliberate and proper in my response.

"You know how hard it is for us out there."

"No." I pause my character. "I do not know."

"Chloé, 'yes, and,' let's stick to the 'yes and.'" The teacher was on the edge of his seat, hoping I would move past Mac's black woman cosplay and find the true life-altering lesson of improv. I was happy to disappoint him.

"What is she doing?" I needed answers. Mac played innocent, claiming she was just getting into character. It felt like they were gaslighting me. I wasn't crazy. These improv people were crazy, living in their heads because their real lives lacked adventure.

After Improv 101, I appreciated acting a little more. Acting has clear parameters. No matter how far you take things emotionally, there are still lines on the page that guide you until the end. In my opinion, improv had no map, no end, no emotional motivation. Improv will have you drive over a cliff to see how far the "game" can go. I'm too old for that crap. I need to know where we going, why, and who all is coming. Are those people friends, family, coworkers? So many questions for your dumb little "yes and . . ." asses. Again, luxury of imagination.

If I was going to be more serious about acting, I had to address my weight. I refused to be typecast as the mammy. As a new actor, your look is everything until people learn to appreciate your skill and the uniqueness you bring to a screen. Otherwise you walk into an audition needing to check off boxes. Black, fat, loud, funny, sassy. Thing is, I wasn't fat *fat* anymore. After breaking up with Quentin and seeing how big I was on my early comedy tapes, I hired a trainer and lost most of the love weight I put on, leaving me in this in-between stage that could make it hard for me to land roles. "You're too small to play the fat sassy friend and too big to play the token black friend. You either need to gain weight or lose more weight." Those were real words of advice. As much as I wanted to argue this theory, I couldn't.

Black women on TV and film still largely fell into two body types—plus-size or petite. I wasn't about to gain fifty pounds just so I could play the sassy school guard on a Nickelodeon show, nor was I disciplined enough to lose another fifty so I could land the role of a sassy secretary in a white law firm on NBC. Whichever way you look when you break into Hollywood, that's the look you have to keep for a long time. Take Halle Berry. We all looked at her crazy when she tried to grow her hair out. She had to rock with her Mario Bros. mushroom cut for decades, and even now when you see her with long hair you have to remember, oh, yeah, that's Halle Berry. Why do you think actors spend so much money on looking youthful, or getting the same exact highlights and haircut? You freeze yourself in time. Signature looks are key. If I broke onto the scene as another big girl, the only way my weight loss would be accepted was if I became a spokesperson and client of a weight-loss program. Sorry, I'm not about to count points and dance in a commercial to elevator music while eating a dry, low-fat, sugar-free cookie just so the world will accept me shedding pounds.

After breaking my neck and undermining my integrity for way too many soul-crushing auditions, I had to come to terms with the fact that I wasn't willing or able to deliver the industry's off-base definition of a black woman. It was best that I focused on comedy. It was the one place the world couldn't tell me what or how to be.

18

EAT LIKE AN AMERICAN

O ver the last seven years I've crisscrossed the country telling jokes at comedy clubs and colleges. Mostly colleges in small towns with one stoplight and an annual harvest festival on Main Street. Never in my wildest dreams did I think I'd step foot in Wyoming, Iowa, Minnesota (other than going to a Prince jam session at Paisley Park), Kansas, Oklahoma, Nebraska, Wisconsin, North and South Dakota. These flyover states are known for their crop fields, cows, and conservatism. Why did they want to hear jokes from a black woman from Brooklyn? Simple, I check off two boxes. The bulk of my bookings were for February, Black History Month, and March, Women's History Month. My first college tour, I drove around in subzero temperatures completing twenty-eight shows in thirty-two days. People always ask what's the hardest part about being on the road. Is it doing an hour of jokes in front of audiences big or small? Hecklers? Driving hours to the next gig? Being alone? Racism? I've had a few instances where the hairs on the back of my neck stood up, letting me know it was time to get my black ass up out of there. All those things were manageable. The most difficult part is finding good food.

Dairy-free? Don't step foot in Wisconsin. Meatless? Skip Texas. Hate restaurant chains? Just cry in a corner of your hotel room and drink your salty tears. Throughout my travels, I found Americans eat like crap. I would love to host a travel show called "Can a Bitch Get a Salad?" I'll drive around in a Prius and challenge local restaurant cooks to build me their best salad. The winner gets a crown made of carrots. Get it—carrots, carats. I'm here all night, folks.

Driving past endless farmland, reality hits. We grow a lot of food in this country, yet our plates look the same—battered, fried, drowned in butter, and lacking nutritional value. Days away from home, reaching my takeout-food limit, I began craving fresh fruit and vegetables. I mean, junkie detox craving brussels sprouts, mangos, kale. It got so bad, I would've sucked dick for a plate of fresh asparagus. Why was it so hard to get my hands on these things? Why did people look at me like I was crazy when I asked them not to put cheese sauce on my steamed broccoli?

Economics are a key factor, the lower the income, the poorer quality foods we eat. Another is the fact Americans believe they're invincible. In Iowa I drove past a massive highway billboard that read: EAT MEAT, READ THE BIBLE, CARRY A GUN. *Uh, two of those things can kill you. I'll let you pick which two.*

The biggest thing to divide this country won't be race, religion, politics, or LGBTQIA rights. It will be food. Nothing enrages a red-blooded American more than someone telling them how and what to eat. When First Lady Michelle Obama launched her "Let's Move" initiative introducing schoolkids to healthier lunch options, she was roasted on social media and talk shows. The sentiment was, "How dare this woman tell my kids to eat a whole serving of fresh fruit and lean protein." Her plan was torpedoed by local school districts that served the new nutritional requirements via spoonful's of gray and brown mush.

When I first hit the road, I searched for nearby eateries that'd been featured on Guy Fieri's *Diners, Drive-Ins and Dives*. Clearly, my interest in being a food tourist meant putting my vegan aspirations on hold. Who knows the next time I'll be able to try a ten-pound blooming onion. Besides the Mall of America, Paul Bunyan statues, and Lewis and Clark landmarks, local signature dishes were a big draw. Wisconsin produces about 30 percent of America's cheese. That's two billion pounds a year. No way I can leave without trying cheese curds.

Oh, and they come in flavors. Yes, I'll take a bag of ranch and dill to go.

Touching down in the twin cities, I must try both restaurants that claimed to have invented the heart attack–triggering Juicy Lucy.

Oh, the burger is cooked with a chunk of cheese inside so when I bite into it there's a lava of melted cheese coming toward my face? I'll have it with bacon, thanks.

What's this restaurant chain I see stretching from Ohio to Idaho? Culver's.

Oh, they're known for their homemade ice cream custards. I'll take a large.

Funny story, I spilled a Culver's chocolate milkshake all over the passenger seat of my rental car. When the Styrofoam cup tipped over, I said to myself, *You weren't supposed to have that shake.* Another sign. I was wearing my workout clothes but had not worked out. Thank the Lord the seats were leather or the car return would have been embarrassing. I used all the towels in my room to soak up the mess and had no choice but to chuck them for fear housekeeping would think I'd shitted myself.

After about a year of treating myself to the greasiest, cheesiest, sweetest concoctions I had had enough. My breaking point: biting into a Green Bay "butter burger" and realizing the secret ingredient was just an extra pat of butter on top of the butter-fried meat patty. I left the restaurant ready to fight. All this shitty food was changing me. I'd become agitated, short-tempered, and melancholic. I felt stuffed all the time and I was; meat was winning the battle with my digestive system. Typically it can take twenty-four to seventy-two hours for the human body to break down meat, but I felt like I was passing kidney stones. Gym workouts became critical to my physical and mental well-being, giving me the energy I needed to get through the day and onto the stage.

Americans spend over $605 billion a year eating out. That's about $3,000 per person, and we're not talking gourmet, Michelin-star meals. That's $3,000 worth of drive-thrus, BBQ, value meals, nuggets, fries, soda, and sweets. In 2012, the American Heart Association conducted a survey that broke American's dietary patterns into five categories:

Southern: Fried, processed meats, and sugar-sweetened beverages

(Ethnically) Traditional: Chinese and Mexican food, pasta dishes, pizza, soup, and other mixed dishes including frozen or takeout meals

Healthy: Mostly fruits, vegetables, and grains

Sweets: Large amounts of sweet snacks and desserts

Alcohol: Proteins, alcohol, and salads

Demographics and socioeconomics heavily influence the type of diet people eat. Poor diets lead to anxiety, depression, and hyperactivity.

* Blacks were more likely than whites to eat a Southern dietary pattern.

* Men, people making less than $35,000 a year, and those who weren't college graduates were more likely to follow the Southern pattern of eating. Women, those who made more money, or those who were more educated did not.

* Blacks tended to avoid the alcohol dietary pattern.

* People ages 45 to 54 tended to eat a traditional dietary pattern.

* Those 75 years and older were likely to not eat the traditional dietary pattern.

* College-educated adults tended to not eat the Southern dietary pattern.

Whew, that's a lot to *digest*. Pun intended. I'm here all night, folks. Now you see why they love me in Nebraska.

EXOTIC EATS

I have a confession to make. I, Chloé, a black woman, do not care for soul food. I can count on one hand how many times a year I sit down to a meal of corn bread, sweet tea, collard greens, candied yams, and a meat that's either fried, smothered, or both. I don't fry any foods and have never made baked mac and cheese. No, not even a vegan version. Revoke my black card if you must, but understand that living above the Mason-Dixon Line, it's easy to stay clear of soul food. However, Italian, Mexican, Chinese, and other ethnic foods, not so much.

There are over 59,000 Mexican restaurants registered in America. That doesn't account for all the fast-food chains and mom-and-pop spots that feature a taco trio or chicken tortilla soup on their menu. Cultural appropriation led to Americans' new favorites days: Taco Tuesday and Cinco de Mayo. The latter originally commemorated the Mexican Army's victory over the French Empire at the Battle of Puebla, on May 5, 1862. Now it's a commercialized reason to get "white girl wasted" on Coronas and margaritas while wearing sugar skull T-shirts. Adding insult to injury, Taco Bell was recently voted the "Best Mexican restaurant in America" by the Harris Poll, a nationwide consumer survey of favorite brands.

When I read that I laughed, thinking about the sci-fi film *Demolition Man*, which takes place in 2032. In their world, Taco Bell had become a fancy five-star restaurant. Hopefully, life doesn't imitate art.

Mexico should have built a wall protecting them from us over a century ago. A third of the United States was Mexico until we stole Texas, which lead to the Mexican-American War in 1846. Two years later, the victorious U.S. government paid Mexico today's equivalent of $15 million for California, Nevada, Utah, most of Arizona, half of New Mexico, a quarter of Colorado, and a small section of Wyoming. Now we can't escape quesadillas, and "that'll be extra" guacamole at every low-end food joint. Nachos, fajitas, and hard taco shells were invented in Texas, hence the fusion food Tex-Mex. We've been remixing Mexican food to fit our taste buds for years, yet convince ourselves that every time we sit down for a burrito we are somehow participating in a cultural acceptance.

"How is everything?" a tiny Latinx waitress with the name tag Vanessa says, smiling at me. Traveling alone in the whitest parts of the country, "ethnic" restaurants are the only way to see people of color in concentrated numbers. I chat them up for as long as I can, which is easy once I slip in that I'm visiting from New York. "Oh, I've always wanted to go there. What are you doing here?"

"I'm performing tonight at the college. Stand-up comedy."

"Wow, I've never met a comedian before." Vanessa pulls a chair out and joins me. I switch to journalist mode.

"What brought you to Wyoming?" I'm always puzzled where immigrants choose to settle down in. She has no accent, her family has lived in these parts for three generations. This restaurant is a family business. They're cool with all the other families who run Mexican restaurants across town. "Do you like it out here?" I always expect the answer to be no.

"It's a good place to raise a family," Vanessa says, refilling my water. That's the most popular response I get. It's also a loaded one. Vanessa and others like her don't live in lily-white redneck areas because it brings them joy. They live here for the opportunities. I believe we're still calling it "the American dream." Silently, we exchange a deep and knowing gaze, like people of color in white spaces often do.

Touring red states during the two years leading up to the 2016 presidential campaign was very hard for me. Everyone knew this country wasn't perfect, but seeing massive Trump signs in cornfields, on car bumpers, and in business windows was a smack to the face. *These people are racist*. Their hurtful ideology was front and center. Just hearing his name in conversation, or worse, seeing a red hat triggered me. *These people are racist*. Ethnic restaurants became a safe haven. Unless when I walked in, all the waitstaff was white. *I know you don't want Mexicans taking your job, but did you have to take theirs?* That's the other thing, Americans round these parts consider anyone who hails from a Spanish-speaking country to be Mexican. For the sake of running a successful restaurant, the staff go along with it because the last thing a close-minded guest wants is a geography lesson served with their Mexican fried ice cream, which ironically was created by a Japanese chef using tempura batter.

Asian food is always my first choice when on the road. I'm not alone; Chinese is the most popular ethnic cuisine in the country, followed closely by Mexican. Strip malls are filled with Chinese buffets, pho spots, Japanese hibachi grills, and sushi shops. If you're lucky, you can get all of the above at one place. Before I forget, which one of you is willing to tell these Asian restaurants to chill on using "oriental" in their name? I cringe whenever I see it. Part of me wonders if they are pandering to a racially insensitive base on purpose. If so, it's fucking genius. Get that money!

"Hi, I'd like the tom yum soup, vegetable lo mein, broccoli in garlic sauce, and a Thai iced tea with no milk." In most cities, these spots offered the best clean eating I was going to get.

"Where you from?" My waiter was an older Chinese man. "You not from here, I can tell." He was also very astute. We were in North Dakota. Sticking out like a palm tree, I go through my whole "I'm visiting from New York" spiel.

"We don't make things spicy here. They"—he looks around at the white people surrounding us—"don't like spice." That was his warning for me to lower my expectations. His customers can't handle complex flavors. This was not going to be New York–quality Chinese food. "Don't worry, I make it spice for you." Boy, did he ever. There was so much chili in my dish, I finished in tears. Through my blurred vision, I saw him give me a thumbs-up and a smile.

———

The Pekin Noodle Parlor in Butte, Montana, which I have not had the pleasure of dining at, claims to be the oldest operated Chinese restaurant in the country. It was opened by Chinese immigrants in 1911, who flocked to America following famine and political strife in their native land. The gold rush and budding railroad industry of the late 1800s attracted male Chinese laborers to the Midwest and West Coast. By 1870, nearly 10 percent of Montana's population was Chinese American and with them came their food, which they modified to appeal to the bland palates of their new neighbors. Chop suey, a menu staple invented in America, translates to odds and ends, scraps of vegetable and meat cooked together to make food stretch. Americans ate it up.

In 1882, frustrated with the influx of Asian immigrants, the United States passed the Chinese Exclusion Act, a federal law signed by President Chester Arthur banning Chinese immigrants from entering the country and those already residing here from becoming citizens. Chinese women had already been banned seven years prior via the Page Act. You get it, because if you stop the women from coming over, you prevent population expansion. By the early 1900s, the gold and railroad rush dried up. Chinese men picked up menial jobs in the food and service industry. Soon, they became the targets of down-on-their-luck white Americans who blamed the Chinese for lowering wages. *Crazy how history repeats itself.* The ban on Chinese immigrants would be upheld by the government until it was repealed in 1943, which changed the law to allow 105 Chinese people to enter each year. There was one loophole to this absurdly racist political agenda—merchant status. Enter Chinese restaurants. By 1915, the federal court ruling added restaurants to the short list of approved visa-earning jobs. This allowed Chinese Americans to travel back and forth to their home country and new Chinese immigrants to apply for merchant visas as long as they were coming here to own and operate a restaurant. Both options led to chain migration that saw Chinese restaurants explode. By 1920, Americans were eating $77.9 million worth of wok creations a year, which increased to $154.2 million ten years later.

Of course, it wasn't easy. We're dealing with racists here. They made it really hard to qualify. Merchant visas required the establishment of "high-grade" restaurants that offered a fine-dining experience. Only one person, the investor/owner, would qualify for the merchant visa and had to show twelve to eighteen months of managerial work at the business that couldn't include line cook, waiter, or cashier work. Lastly, each visa application had to be cosigned by two white references. Several Chinese families would pool their money together to open fancy "Chop Suey Palaces," each taking turns running it to solidify their boss status. Once one person met the time requirement, the reigns were handed over to another. They were determined to earn their American dream, one chop suey at a time.

CART ATTACK

Sadly, one cannot live on Asian, Mexican, or soul food alone. At wits end, I resorted to making meals in my hotel room like an prison inmate. I've crafted meals with the microwave, coffeepot, iron, blow dryer. I'm a real Lady MacGyver but none of those meals would've been possible without Walmart. Let's be clear, I have a love/hate relationship with the retailer based on its atrocious wages, anti-union, gun-selling, crippling-impact-on-local-retailers practices. But when you are in a town that only has a Walmart and it stays open twenty-four hours, it becomes the most wonderful store in the world. Walmart has saved me from starvation many a night. My go-to meal is a box of salad, steamer bags of mixed veggies, salad dressing, vegan Ben & Jerry's ice cream, and if I'm deprived of protein, a rotisserie chicken, lemon pepper of course. I can see why Walmart shoppers have a hard time giving up meat; a whole chicken is $4.98. It's always $4.98. Then there's the bakery section. When Walmart introduced the Patti Labelle sweet potato pie, I was touring along the northeast and lost my mind. We don't have Walmart in New York City. I posted a picture on my social media and instantly, my DMs were filled with orders. I'd go online to see which location had them in stock and clear them out. Always the businesswoman, I sold for a respectable markup. I was pushing pies like a trap star.

Growing up with bodegas, the 178,000-square-foot supercenter was a portal into a different world. Each aisle was a revealing look at America. Each shopping cart filled with what fueled or, rather, plagued us. Yes, I'm hinting at the horrible eating habits and poor-quality food options the majority of us are subjected to, but this goes deeper than being one of the fattest countries in the world. You don't notice it at first, what with the waving flags, big cars, large iced coffees, sports jerseys, and selfies, but look closely and you'll see a malaise growing like mold. Melancholy is in the air. Americans are miserable, and it might be because of what we put in our bodies.

I feel you shaking your head at me. *Chloé, you're doing too much.* Hear me out. You ever eaten a big meal and felt gross afterward? That feeling of discomfort, disgust, and slothfulness dampens your mood. Now imagine eating like that every day. That occasional slump becomes your new normal and the only way to feel better is eating sugar.

Repeat this cycle long enough and, over time, your arteries are clogged, your poop is harder than a roll of quarters, and you've got gout.

Each year over 610,000 people die in the U.S. due to heart disease. The nation's number one killer—responsible for 1 out of 4 deaths—includes heart attacks, strokes, heart failure, angina, arrhythmias, and high blood pressure. Cancer is the second most common cause of death, with diet-related cancers accounting for an estimated 30–35 percent of total cancer cases.

We pride ourselves in being #1 in the world, but that #1 also applies to us being the most depressed nation. Americans consume the most antidepressants in the world? Make that make sense. What are we so unhappy about? I'm telling you, it's the food and whatever chemicals are in it. It has to be. Who hasn't eaten an entire pizza pie and immediately wanted to go jump off a bridge? I once cried while eating a sleeve of cookies, paralyzed by depression and feeling guilty about eating the cookies, which led to further depression and more cookie eating, thus more guilt. By the time I've finished eating the crumbs off my shirt, I've gained weight and my doctor is telling me my cholesterol is high. It's the circle of strife we know all too well.

I ♥ FINLAND

Disneyland lied. It's not the happiest place on earth, Finland is. The northern European country is also the healthiest. *Gee, I wonder if there's a connection between the two.* It wasn't always this way. In the 1970s, Finland held the world record for heart disease. Determined to save lives, the government created incentive-driven programs to get people off the couch and outdoors. Communities competed to see who moved the most, lowered their cholesterol and lost weight, for prizes that included cash and cruises. Public spaces were designed to accommodate walking, biking, and ski pathways. Senior citizens were given free bike riding lessons and snowshoes with cleats, so they wouldn't slip on the ice and hurt themselves during the cold months. Farmers, formerly paid according to the fat content of their products, were now compensated for leaner meat and low-fat milk. A country of heavy smokers, the government banned all cigarette advertising. And it worked. In addition to being fit and happy, Finns have universal health care and a national education system that covers daycare to postgraduate degrees.

Could the same happen in America? It's not like we don't have the money. 2017 figures place us #1 in military spending ($825 billion), medical research ($172 billion), robotics ($790 billion), fast food ($198.9 billion), and cheese sales ($17 billion). Health care is a whopping $3.5 trillion a year. That's a lot of free education and snowshoes.

AS AMERICAN AS _____

Apple pie, the hallmark of America isn't American at all. The fruit originated in Asia, brought over and planted by early European settlers, who used it to make apple cider, the preferred drink over water. *I know their piss stunk.* Later, they planted apple and other trees as a way to lay claims to land. An early recipe for apple pie dates back to 1500s England. Yet here we are and it has become a marker of patriotism. Saying something was "as American as apple pie" meant it was pure, wholesome, valuable. We're such fatties, our gold standard marker is apples cooked in butter and sugar and placed over a buttery, high-calorie crust.

ROOM FOR MORE?

Comedy has taken me to nearly all fifty states, allowing me to interact with a wide variety of people. I've concluded America is full of contradictions.

* We're the largest exporter of food in the world, yet 40 million Americans have trouble securing food.

* We would rather overmedicate than eat in moderation and exercise.

* We save cats, dogs, and horses; but not cows, pigs, and chickens.

* We love ethnic foods, but not necessarily the people who make them.

Americans love God and country. After my travels, I can confidently add to that: food and guns. (Imagine my shock the first time I saw a man with a gun on his hip inside of Applebee's. How dangerous is it to get a two for $20?) We want to present ourselves as impenetrable, but it's all smoke and mirrors. We're afraid of change, slaves to tradition, even if they're slowly killing us from the inside out.

There's always a silver lining. America is still a young country with room for improvement. Dare I say it? Change can be as simple as what we put in our mouths. Idyllic, I know, but ask Finland how's it going.

19

TO CHEAT OR NOT TO CHEAT

Can you be woke and have plastic surgery?
I'm asking for a friend.

Society has come a long way on its views toward cosmetic surgery. Once a tightly guarded secret among the rich and famous, elective plastic surgery has become so mainstream and affordable it's easier to count the number of people who haven't gotten "a little work done." On any given day, a picture of a woman angled with her perfectly augmented ass positioned toward the camera with a face that bashfully says, "Oh, this old thing?" appears on my social-media feed. The caption is always part Nietzsche, part NeNe Leakes, and the "likes" are in the thousands or millions if you're a Kardashian.

♡ ○ ◁   ⊓

75,947 likes
Influencer101: Life is like a play. Give it 100% before your
curtain call. Don't you want to receive your standing ovation
from the bitches who loved to hate on your success?!
#mynewbikini #thongsong #selfcareNsunscreen #IDrinkWater

This IG model has a stomach so flat you can bounce a Bitcoin off it. My thumb hovers over her alluring smile but I dare not double tap—I'm judgmental and jealous. Would I be frolicking on a beach if my entire stomach fit under a string bikini bottom? Yes. Would my quality of life be better if my boobs sat up at attention instead of swaying toward my solar plexus? Yes. Would I be happier, funnier, more fulfilled? Maybe.

I'm not saying all people with body fat below 25 percent are living their best lives. However, a majority of my lifelong insecurities stem from having a body fat index over the 32 percent obesity mark. I can't imagine what it feels like to have self-esteem issues that aren't weight related. I've always had boobs and an ass, but they were often overshadowed by loose and ill-fitting clothes, casualties of Operation: Hide Yo Gut. Girdles, Spanx, and now the popular yet organ-shifting latex waist trainer are uncomfortable and cumbersome. Colombian fajas seem like a good idea until you need someone to help snap you into it. Sure, the results are amazing, but after a few hours sitting in one, my vagina went numb. Nothing worse than walking around in public trying to wake up your lady wallet. I have a drawer full of control-top, tummy-flattening cellulite casings in a range of sizes to fit whatever my current waistline is. Then there's the oils, ointments, and creams. I have a basket of those, too. They all promise targeted weight loss in the abdomen. I'd buy so many rolls of plastic wrap, for tummy wrapping, you'd think I was a drug dealer packing up kilos. If a nonsurgical product promised results, it was worth a try. "I *just* want to lose my stomach."

Just. That word undermines the task at hand as if it's an easy, small feat. If I were to achieve a flat stomach I'd have to eat six times a day and workout with military discipline. Flat stomachs are not in my DNA. The only person to have a flat stomach in my family was my grandfather. He ate one big meal a day, and long after retirement kept busy via manual work around the house. One summer day we were locked out of his house and he refused to let me climb through the five-foot-high window. "Push me up," he told me. He was eighty-two years old.

No number of crunches, planks, or knee rises were going to get me to a flat tummy. Well, yes, I'm sure there is a number, but I don't want to do them or count carbs or stop eating junk food when I emotionally need it to soothe my soul. My current workouts keep me in a sweet spot, although my 32.8 percent body fat means—at my current size 14—I'm technically obese. But my last annual checkup results (RIP, Obamacare) showed that I was perfectly healthy. What do I believe; the highly regarded BMI test or my own knees?

In the 1830s, Belgian astronomer, mathematician, statistician, and sociologist Lambert Adolphe Jacques Quetelet created the simple equation of dividing a person's weight by their height squared to determine who was fat and who wasn't. Originally known as the Quetelet Index, now called the BMI, it was accepted all over the medical world and is still relied on heavily today. Keep in mind, Quetelet's SAT math problem doesn't factor in bone density, muscle mass, water weight, age, et cetera. Folks in medicine know that it's outdated and gives inaccurate readings, but they'd rather torture us instead of implementing a more reliable tactic.

I'm not obese. I know what obese looks, smells, and sounds like.

I'm fat. Correction, I consider myself fat. The change in my language is new. Friends and family have made it clear that I'm not allowed to call myself FAT anymore because I'm not. Meaning I should check off "average" or "a few extra pounds" if I were filling out a dating profile.

"You've been fat," explained Jazz. "You're not fat now." She would know, we've been friends since I was seventeen at NYU. I hated to admit it, but they were right. Now I'm only comfortable saying I'm not fat because the standards changed. We're dominated by extremes. They're so extreme—rail-thin or extra-large—that folks in the middle like me are a fading blip on the social radar. (Like the American middle class.) The monster that I made myself out to be was nowhere as scary as I thought. I'm not gross; I'm not perfect either.

Perfection is expensive. If you didn't pay for it through blood, sweat, and tears, you better have the cold hard cash to actually pay for it. The wealthy snuck away for a few weeks and came back with new faces and waists. Whispers traveled but confirmations were rare. Living in California, the plastic surgery capital of the U.S., porn stars had access to the same doctors that injected and corrected Beverly Hills. Plastic surgery was for rich white people, a couple black celebs who made it and wanted to change their noses, and sex workers who needed to stand out. We judged them for being blinded by vanity. We look down our birth noses at them, convinced we were better people for being able to love what we got in the body lottery. Correction, we weren't better, we couldn't afford it.

———

We have war to thank for modern-day plastic surgery. After the Civil War, soldiers left deformed on the battlefield became the first guinea pigs for new reconstructive surgeries that repaired bullet-riddled noses, chins, and eyes. Both world wars created more ex-servicemen who needed mending. The medical field stepped up to the challenge and techniques that served as the precursor to the flashy reality-TV show cosmetic doctor was born. The study of reconstructive surgery—the predecessor to plastic and cosmetic surgery—has been around for centuries. The Edwin Smith Papyrus, the oldest known medical text, dates back to ancient Egypt, 2500 to 3000 BC. In it, healers explained how to fix broken noses. In the 1500s, Gaspare Tagliacozzi, an Italian surgeon, documented his plastic surgery procedures in a highly acclaimed book, earning him the title of plastic surgery's godfather. Tagliacozzi perfected his technique by dissecting the corpses of prisoners that were provided to him by the Brotherhood of the Death, an organization that took it upon themselves to comfort those sentenced to death and provide their burial and death records, granted after Tagliacozzi picked them apart.

Like history often likes to do, Tagliacozzi is credited for something he didn't really invent. The first plastic surgeon on record is actually Sushruta, an ancient Indian healer who lived in 600 BC. *Sushruta Samhita*, a Sanskrit text, details his discovery of over 1,100 illnesses, their treatments, the use of cadavers, reconstructive techniques such as skin grafting and cleft palate unification, as well as the description of medical tools that are still used today. Europeans who traveled to India learned of Sushruta and brought his book back, jump-starting their medical studies including those of Tagliacozzi. "Plastic surgery" didn't get its name until 1798, its origin being the Greek word *plastikos*, which means "molding" or "shaping."

So men were the main beneficiaries of early plastic surgery due to their panache for violence and, subsequently, wounds. Feeling left out, women started undergoing breast augmentation in the late 1890s. The first recorded instance of breast reconstruction happened in Germany, where a doctor inserted fat from the patient's hip into her breast, which had a benign tumor removed. Early cosmetic fillers would be banned by today's medical board. Doctors injected turn-of-the-century titties with paraffin wax, beeswax, vegetable oil, ivory, and glass. Side effects included blindness, tissue-eroding ulcers, deformity, and in some cases a complete breast removal in order to save the woman's life. The first doctor to bring breast augmentation to the United States stuffed his ladies with celluloid, silk floss, and silk, giving a new meaning to a "smooth chest." The first silicone breast implant was used in 1962, and the rest is breast history. These women didn't have social media or twenty-four-hour access to TV and film, yet they still felt the need to compare and improve themselves. (We're doomed.)

Sarah Baartman, better known as Venus Hottentot, was a South African Khoikhoi woman born in the late 1700s. Her natural, large buttocks caught the attention of an English doctor who brought her back to England and proceeded to tour her around as a freak-show act for years. Baartman stood naked before gawking onlookers who paid two shillings. It cost more to poke her with a stick or their finger. Abolitionists, alarmed by Baartman's mistreatment, took her employers to court, but a contract—that Baartman mostly likely wasn't aware of—was produced and the case dismissed. Sold to various owners afterward, Baartman's case was the catalyst for scientific racism. In 1815 she died penniless in Paris from an unknown illness. After her death, Baartman's dissected organs, genitalia, and buttocks were displayed as bias proof of her sexual primitivism and intellectual equality with that of an orangutan. In 1994, President Nelson Mandela requested her remains be returned to her home country, but it took years of legal negotiations with France. Baartman was formally buried in South Africa in 2002, over two hundred years after she left.

Kim Kardashian allegedly broke the internet, posing on the 2014 winter cover of *Paper* magazine greased up and naked. Her ample augmented booty front and center. "White women are getting their bodies done to look like black women," said my cousin Dawn, trying to help me make sense of it. "Now black women are getting their bodies overdone to look like white women who wanna be black. All this to attract men who don't give a fuck, 'cause pussy is pussy." Well damn.

Between 2005 and 2013, the American Society of Aesthetic Plastic Surgery found that black patients increased by 56 percent. In 2016, 8 percent of all plastic surgery procedures were for black patients. Looking for answers, I turned to Maxwell, a longtime friend and professional photographer. He's seen the change in black women's bodies up close. "I think black women don't feel loved and appreciated, so they'll go anywhere for acceptance."

The most disrespected person in America is the black woman.
The most unprotected person in America is the black woman.
The most neglected person in America is the black woman.
                                                    —Malcolm X, 1962

Black women are trained to be proud and, of course, strong. We have to be, for all the reasons Malcolm X mentioned. Part of that pride had been body acceptance. So what, you're shaped like a refrigerator box? Keep your hair and nails done and be the cutest refrigerator box on the block. No butt, accentuate your breasts. No breasts, toot that booty out. Got neither, learn to rap and win guys over with your spunky attitude until you have the money to pay for enhancements. Shout out to Lil' Kim. Can we talk about the Queen Bee for just a second?

Kimberly Denise Jones, we owe you an apology. For years we roasted you for getting surgery, attacked your looks, accused you of self-hate, and downplayed your accomplishments all because we didn't like your face. All these things may be true, but you know what else is true? It's none of our business what you choose to do to your own body. If you like it, we should love it. That's my revelation. For far too long black women's bodies have been seen as public domain. First as property, then as a source of community and spiritual strength. When one of us breaks away to redefine herself, we see it as a personal attack on the rest of us, the sisterhood. *If she isn't okay with herself, does that mean I have the freedom to voice my displeasure with my body?* Lil' Kim walked so we could run to the operating table. That includes a lot of your favorite artists today. In fact, one can argue that most current female artists, sadly, wouldn't have a career if they didn't have enhancements—boobs, hips, ass, lips, nose. And that's just the female rappers. At least they are open about it. You can make more music when you don't have to spend time ducking questions about your ass shots.

Around the way, girls are going under the knife and launching careers as "models." Black women are safely making money from their new-and-improved bodies on their own terms. Don't hate on the hustle. Think about it this way, college or an office job isn't for everyone. Who needs $100,000 of college debt when you can get a 360° makeover for $30,000, pay in monthly installments, and land on a reality-TV show earning $1 million a season? Talk about a return on your investment. Of course, the rush for the new black body—breast implants, tummy tuck, Brazilian butt lift—has some downsides. Women who can't afford professional treatments have resorted to deadly and illegal injections with substances found in home improvement stores. Those who survive are left with debilitating scars and lingering health issues. The other, less severe issue is uniformity. Too many women look the same, like they took a deep breath and forgot to exhale. Like a ball of Play-Doh that's been squeezed in the middle by a toddler. Like an hourglass with too much sand.

It's funny the things that get embedded in our minds from childhood. My young aunts had a VHS copy of Alice Walker's *The Color Purple*. For some strange reason, it was one of the few films Grandma let them watch. It was 1987, and I was starting to gain weight and feel ugly. On weekends we'd sit on the floor in front of the one TV in their brownstone and watch it. They knew all the words. My favorite part was the singer and temptress Shug Avery telling the homely, unattractive, and abused Celie (played by Whoopi Goldberg) that she was in fact beautiful. Standing before a mirror, the two black women barely surviving in the Jim Crow South share a raw moment uncovering Celie's confidence. Briefly, we see Celie straighten her back, lift her head, uncover her big toothy grin, and soak in who God made her to be. Just as soon as her self-esteem rises to the surface, it retreats and doesn't come out until years later in a confrontation with Celie's common-law husband and abuser, Mister. (Don't let this brief summary stop you from watching the full film. I'm leaving out a lot. Cue it up for Black or Women's History Month.)

After decades of abuse, Celie stands up to Mister at a family dinner and declares before leaving him for good, "I'm poor, black, I might even be ugly, but dear God, I'm here. I'm here." Even at age six, I was wowed by her resolve. *Will this be my new response to bullies on the playground? I think it may be.* (It did not have the same impact.) Cut to present-day Chloé recanting this early lesson on body image and self-esteem under the lens of 2019, where options are readily available. Would Celie still feel the same after seeing the thousands of manufactured beauties, their tagged surgeons, and pay websites and email for bookings? If Celie was a woman of today, she'd start a crowdfunding page highlighting her hard-knock life with a goal of $20,000. She'd chronicle her total body makeover—from plastic surgeon consultation to postsurgery recovery—on her IG story. Of course, once she's all healed up she's gonna come out as bi-curious and open an Etsy shop for her trouser business, where she modeled all the online looks.

Both of these scenarios play in my head whenever I ask myself, "Would you change anything about yourself?" The noble part of me (a.k.a. Old Celie) wants to tell myself to kiss my FUPA and go about living my best life. My ego (New Celie) is pricing plastic surgeons and creeping on several plastic surgery message boards. Reality is, the social responsibility of being a strong black woman used to mean not changing what makes you, you. If you did, you'd be seen as a sellout, self-hating, less of a woman. *Why would people trust you when you didn't believe in yourself?* When I start to seriously entertain the thought of undergoing cosmetic surgery I always minimize it to make myself feel more at ease. *I don't even need much. I just want to lose my stomach.* The guilt of letting the sisterhood down always wins. Sistas who told the world to kiss your Brazilian butt lift, I applaud your courage to defect. For me, it is moral tug of war. Personally, I don't know which side is going to win.

Can you be a strong black woman if you can't accept your flaws?

I'm asking for myself.

conclusion

I'm no food guru, life coach, or empowerment princess. Don't worry, I won't be hitting the road charging obscene amounts of money for three-day women-only healing weekends with flower crowns. No, I'm not advocating for unrestricted caloric intakes or telling people to eat their weight in vegan fried chicken. (Be careful with that soy.) The title *F*ck Your Diet* was my genuine response to learning that diet books are massive sellers. The D-word has been toxic to my mental and physical well-being since my double chin sprouted in elementary school. I grew up thinking something was genetically wrong with me. How was it that diet pills or magic shakes didn't working for me? (I've spent hundreds on chalky powders that taste like an ashtray.) Why did I gain weight when I cut carbs? Would I ever master the Master Cleanse, or was I using the wrong brand of cayenne pepper? I've lost, gained, and lost countless pounds over the years, but the psychological impact was much harder to shake. This had to be my fault.

WHAT I (NOW) KNOW

1. Food isn't my mortal enemy. Pie isn't on a mission to give me diabetes.

2. I'm smart, but I'll never really grasp the concept of calories.

3. Instead of going on a "diet," go on a cleanse to reset your body and taste buds. A cleanse is an act of love and forgiveness. A diet is an act of punishment.

4. American cuisine is very limited, which is why we are constantly trying to reinvent the wheel. Seriously, how may flavors of potato chips do we need?

5. Allow yourself to indulge every once in a while. Hold the guilt.

This isn't exactly an un-diet book, but it is a little nudge and push for you (and me) to stop putting faith in an industry that feeds off our misery and to start making better choices about how we spend our energy. (You know how many perfectly good tans I missed out on while wearing a T-shirt over my bathing suit?) Initially, my mission was to share funny essays, a blooper reel of my food-related hijinks. I never imagined this would venture into systematic oppression, political agendas, conspiracy theories, sex tips, and traumatizing relationships. Then, there was the data. While reviewing numbers and scientific reports (please go check out the appendix), I began to forgive myself for all the self-hate I harbored. The odds were long stacked against me, against all of us.

To live in America means to buy into a system that doesn't have your best health interests in mind. Our food industry will gaslight you into thinking your extra pounds are the result of a lack of self-control and not the addictive additives or empty calories they fill our food with. Then the medical industry racks up on all the pills and surgeries needed to keep us barely functioning. That's why I say *F*ck Your Diet.*

Okay, now here is the part where I'm supposed to spell out the bigger implications of the research and history I covered, or lay out the next steps for your personal journey and, last, highlight the lessons you should have learned in case they escaped you. (At least that's what my Google search for "How to Write a Conclusion" said.) As you can now see, this isn't a self-help book. I don't have any answers. However, I do have a life of highs and lows centered around my unhealthy relationship with my body. Now's the time to take the pressure off. Yes, the grass is greener on the other side, but my grass would be green too if I started watering it. Let's start by removing the stigma around "diet" and focusing on health and quality of life. That's what I hope to convey. Perfection comes at a high price, but being comfortable with who you are is priceless.

WHAT I HOPE

1. You don't feel sorry for me. My pain is my past and I don't need a hug or a shoulder to weep on when you see me.

2. I've given you reason to reexamine the things you thought made you undesirable or unworthy.

3. Kathy Ireland reads this book and agrees with everything I said, while we eat some of her fruit ambrosia on the deck of her multimillion-dollar estate.

4. More people get full-length mirrors in their bedrooms, stand in front of them naked, and do that head tilt as they realize they're nowhere near as monstrous as they thought. They'll say "hmph" and put on that skintight T-shirt anyway.

5. You have a great (well-balanced) meal and/or great sex at least once a week.

THE CAMERA ADDS TEN POUNDS

In the spring of 2019 I made my late-night talk show debut on *The To-night Show* with Jimmy Fallon. A major feat for any comedian. As I stood behind the curtain waiting for my name to be announced, I had a moment of Zen. I thanked my ancestors, the alpha and omega, and my team for putting me in position. I'd gotten to this moment by turning my painful memories and insecurities into jokes. Fun fact: Network TV won't let you mention suicide even if the joke is hilarious. I had to change that punch line to something more clever and less sad about my knees.

From the stage, I could see Mom and Dad seated in the stands, beaming. I felt amazing. I looked amazing, too. My fuchsia off-the-shoulder jumper was custom-made. I'd gotten "oohs" and "aahs" from anyone who laid eyes on me that day. My shoulders were back, head high. By the time I finished and Jimmy walked over holding the cover of this book in his hands, my out-of-body experience was complete. After the taping, I had twenty-four hours of euphoria, which culminated with a viewing party for friends and family the following night. The next morning, I woke up and went straight to the comments section to see what the world had to say. I know, I know. Bad move, but I had a good reason. This was my first impactful comedic showing to the world. Sure, *Last Comic Standing* was a big deal, but this was Johnny Carson's *Tonight Show*. So many iconic comics had stood where I was. Five minutes of pure Chloé was beamed into millions of homes around the globe. I'll never get people's honest reactions to me after this. They will have heard of me, or seen me somewhere, and have an angle. These commenters had nothing, no twisted agenda. I wasn't troll-worthy yet. These were just opinions, the kind you'd get in a blind focus group. Call me a sadist, but I scrolled, liked (even the negative posts), and replied for the first twenty-four hours.

Overall the feedback was positive. Some people didn't think I was funny at all. That's fair. My experience as a former fat kid, now single woman isn't everyone's cup of tea. Especially white men who can never extend themselves to understand someone who isn't exactly like them. One person said they hated my voice. Never heard that before. I'm scrolling, scrolling, scrolling, then I see:

"Oh no, what is she wearing."

"That outfit does nothing for her!"

"Who dressed her?"

They didn't outright say it but they kinda did. The body shaming was thinly veiled. Here's the deal, my longtime frenemies North and

South Belly weren't going to let me get all the shine. They conducted a sneak attack and reared their ugly heads onto the screen. I was surprised to see them as well. During my fittings, then in my greenroom mirror, and in the pictures taken minutes before I walked out, the bellies were nowhere to be found. But once those HD cameras and LED lights landed on me it was a different story. For the record, I had on brand-new, top-of-the-line shapewear. I was rolled tighter than a Snoop Dogg joint, yet comfortable. That's all I could ever ask for, but it wasn't enough. The first time I watched I was too focused on my words to see my midsection. Then I watched again and stopped the clip the second I saw South Belly. *Damn. That's unfortunate. Oh well. Nothing I can do about it now.*

If this was years ago, I would have wiped the entire experience from my mind. *No one is going to take me seriously looking like that! It's fine. I'll just be fat. That's not the worst thing in the world. It's not like I'm doing drugs.* Thank the Lord, I'm not going out like that anymore. I'm done waving my white flag. This book-writing thing reminded me just how strong I've always been. We underestimate ourselves because it's not every day we're asked to wax poetic about our life's highlights and lessons. I once read somewhere that everyone shouldn't write a book. While that may be true (I know coming from me that is rich), everyone does have a story.

This book serves as my ultimate act of self-care. Thank you for sharing it with me.

acknowledgments

I've always wanted to give an acceptance speech like a rapper at the Grammys who's nervously shifting in his first-ever pair of hard-bottom Italian designer shoes. So here goes.

First and foremost, I'd like to thank God. For without him, nothing is possible. To my mom and dad for doing the dirty and having me. I owe you a house once my money comes in. Shout-out to my brother, Chad, who let me use his name on *The Tonight Show* and gave me loving pats on the back while I sat at my desk pulling my hair out. To my extended Stevens/Kinscy/Hilliard family, who prayed for me even when I didn't answer their phone calls 'cause I was going after my dreams. To Vallene, you're my sister and the best hype woman. Brooke and Nicole, thank you for busting my chops and checking me when I'm tripping. To the Six Foot Nothing Crew: Monroe, Derek, Dave, Reggie, and Menuhin. Thank you for backing me up in this crazy comedy world and listening to me when I am constantly trying to expand your minds and get you to become better allies. To Miles, it's time for us to dream up new dreams. Isn't this crazy?! I'm ready for my wig now. To my darling May, thank you for always offering to beat someone up for me and your 9:00 a.m. calls to just say "I love you." To Elisheba, thank you for inviting me to my first sleepover and being a true friend ever since. Hey, Waris! Shout-out to my CPC-02 crew: Rakia, Zakia, and Darah. Our committee meetings were where I first realized my stories were crazy from your gut-busting, headshaking reactions. Shout-out to Bethany for years of finding sheer joy in my dysfunction and making me an auntie. I see you, Monique. Staten Island, stand up! Tatum, what can I say, we go back like babies with pacifiers. B. G. all day! Let's see, I don't want to forget about anyone. *Orchestra starts playing music* Oh shit, the sign is saying wrap it up. *Takes deep breath.* Okay, I have to thank the people at *Brooklyn Magazine* for including me in the 2016 list of "The 50 Funniest People in Brooklyn," which was read by Robert Guinsler, who then reached out to me and asked if he could be my book agent and if I had any book ideas. A big thank-you to my manager, Marlene, for replying to my 3:00 a.m. texts on how we can take over the world. Okay. Okay, I'm wrapping up, damn! Thank you to my editor, Natasha Simons, who took a chance on me and gently walked me through the process of cutting myself open and bleeding onto the page. *Music gets louder, I'm just rattling off names now until they cut my mic off* Yamaneika, Zainab, Keith, Aida, Shawntaye, Tarik, Mary P., S. Dot, my NYU teammates, Mr. Forde, Aminah for being the plug from day one. All the other people who like my shit on the regular and bought this book and not the bootleg, and my dog, Winnie, whose love is pure and is gonna be crushed when I kick her out of my bed for my future husband. We did it!

appendix

POINTS WERE MADE

In case you thought I made stuff up, here are my sources.

Prologue

Dr. Kellogg was a man of good intentions and a boatload of money. Too bad his quest for health inadvertently led to a billion-dollar industry that pushes empty calories and sugar.

Dr. Howard Markel, "How Dr. Kellogg's World-Renowned Health Spa Made Him a Wellness Titan," PBS, August 18, 2017, www.pbs.org /newshour/health/dr-kelloggs-world-renowned-health-spa-made -wellness-titan/.

Judith V. Sayad, "W. K. Kellogg Foundation." *Encyclopaedia Britannica*, January 13, 2016, www.britannica.com/topic/W-K-Kellogg-Foundation/.

Priceonomics. "The Surprising Reason Why Dr. John Harvey Kellogg Invented Corn Flakes," *Forbes*, May 17, 2016, www.forbes.com/sites /priceonomics/2016/05/17/the-surprising-reason-why-dr-john -harvey-kellogg-invented-corn-flakes/#1384b6469970/.

Chapter 1: Ronald Reagan Can Do His Own Push-Ups

Presidents who force kids to take a timed fitness test are bullies. Yeah, I said it.

President's Council on Sports, Fitness & Nutrition, "Our History," U.S. Department of Health and Human Services, HHS.gov, March 13, 2018, www.hhs.gov/fitness/about-pcsfn/our-history/index.html.

Robert H. Boyle, "The Report that Shocked the President," *Vault*, August 15, 1955, www.si.com/vault/1955/08/15/604917/the-report-that-shocked-the-president/.

Chapter 2: Starving Kids in Africa

Here in America, folks go hungry due to poverty, but even on our worst day we haven't had to deal with the ravages of famine, drought, and civil war. There's so much more to unpack, and I don't want to trivialize it.

Edmond J. Keller, "Drought, War, and the Politics of Famine in Ethiopia and Eritrea," *Journal of Modern African Studies* 30, no. 4 (December 1992): 609, https://doi.org/10.1017/s0022278x00011071.

"Facts About Hunger and Poverty in America," Feeding America, www.feedingamerica.org/hunger-in-america/facts/.

Tehila Sasson, "Ethiopia, 1983–1985: Famine and the Paradoxes of Humanitarian Aid," *Online Atlas on the History of Humanitarianism and Human Rights*, December 1, 2015, https://hhr-atlas.ieg-mainz.de/articles/sasson-ethiopia/.

Chapter 3: Let Them Eat Ketchup

Before President Reagan, Americans were nowhere near as big as we are now. That is not a coincidence.

E. Douglas Kihn, "The Political Roots of American Obesity," Truthout, May 4, 2013, https://truthout.org/articles/the-political-roots-of -american-obesity/.

Jonathan Harsch, "Reagan Cuts Eat into School Lunches," *Christian Science Monitor*, September 17, 1981, www.csmonitor.com/1981 /0917/091746.html.

Richard Dukon and Elizabeth Chuck, "Dalene Bowden, Idaho Cafeteria Worker Fired Over Hungry Student's Free Meal, Offered Job Back," NBCNews.com, www.nbcnews.com/news/us-news/dalene-bowden -idaho-cafeteria-worker-fired-over-hungry-student-s-n485441/.

Chapter 4: Champions Train; Losers Complain

Learn more about two American tennis legends. Don't wait for Black History Month either.

Althea Gibson and Edward E. Fitzgerald, ed., *I Always Wanted to Be Somebody* (New York: Harper Collins, 1958).

Raymond Arsenault, *Arthur Ashe: A Life* (New York: Simon & Schuster, 2018).

Chapter 5: Fuck Kathy Ireland

For shits and giggles, go read the full Jennifer Aniston cover story.

Julie Jordan, "Jennifer Aniston Is PEOPLE's 2016 World's Most Beautiful Woman!" *People*, April 20, 2016, https://people.com/bodies /jennifer-aniston-is-peoples-2016-worlds-most-beautiful-woman/.

People Magazine Most Beautiful People #1s
(People of Color marked with *)

DATE	PERSON	AGE
June 1, 1990	Michelle Pfeiffer (1)	32
June 7, 1991	Julia Roberts (1)	23
May 4, 1992	Jodie Foster	29
May 3, 1993	Cindy Crawford	27
May 8, 1994	Meg Ryan	32
May 8, 1995	Courteney Cox	30
May 8, 1996	Mel Gibson	40
May 12, 1997	Tom Cruise	34
May 12, 1998	Leonardo DiCaprio	23
May 14, 1999	Michelle Pfeiffer (2)	41
May 8, 2000	Julia Roberts (2)	32
May 14, 2001	Catherine Zeta-Jones	31
May 13, 2002	Nicole Kidman	34
May 12, 2003	Halle Berry *	36
May 30, 2004	Jennifer Aniston (1)	35
May 8, 2005	Julia Roberts (3)	37
April 28, 2006	Angelina Jolie	30
April 27, 2007	Drew Barrymore	32
May 2, 2008	Kate Hudson	29
May 11, 2009	Christina Applegate	37
April 30, 2010	Julia Roberts (4)	42
April 15, 2011	Jennifer Lopez *	41
April 27, 2012	Beyoncé Knowles *	30

DATE	PERSON	AGE
April 26, 2013	Gwyneth Paltrow	40
May 5, 2014	Lupita Nyong'o *	31
April 24, 2015	Sandra Bullock	50
April 20, 2016	Jennifer Aniston (2)	47
April 19, 2017	Julia Roberts (5)	49
April 18, 2018	Pink	38
April 24, 2019	Jennifer Garner	47

"People (Magazine)," Wikipedia, May 11, 2019, https://en.wikipedia
.org/wiki/People_ (magazine)#100_Most_Beautiful_People/.

See how many people are in the world and where they live.
"Current World Population," Worldometers, www.worldometers.info
/world-population/.

In addition to his groundbreaking doll test, Dr. Kenneth B. Clark wrote several books about race, poverty, and the black experience in America.
Kenneth B. Clark and Gunnar Myrdal, *Dark Ghetto* (New York: Harper
& Row, 1965).
Kenneth Bancroft Clark and Jeannette Hopkins, *A Relevant War Against
Poverty: A Study of Community Action Programs and Observable So-
cial Change* (New York: Harper & Row, 1970).
Kenneth Bancroft Clark, *A Possible Reality: A Design for the Attainment
of High Academic Achievement for Inner-City Students. With the As-
sistance of the Staff of the MARC Corporation* (New York: Emerson
Hall, 1972).

Kenneth Bancroft Clark, *Pathos of Power* (New York: Harper & Row, 1975).

Kenneth Bancroft Clark, *Prejudice and Your Child* (distributed by Harper & Row, 1988).

Chapter 6: Watch Out for the Big Girls

Rumors of a Philippa Schuyler bio pic starring Alicia Keys have been swirling around for a decade. In the meantime, read about the child prodigy's amazing life.

Kathryn Talalay, *Composition in Black and White: The Life of Philippa Schuyler* (New York: Oxford University Press, 1998).

Teen Pregnancy Rates* While I Was at I.S. 383 (1991–1994)

1991	1992	1993	1994
115.3	111.0	108.0	104.6

Teen Pregnancy Rates by Race

	1991	1992	1993	1994
Black	222.3	216.6	209.9	198.7
Hispanic	169.1	169.7	165.8	164.4
White	96.6	92.3	90.0	87.8

*All Rates per 1,000 Women

Kathryn Kost and Stanley Henshaw, "U.S. Teenage Pregnancies, Births and Abortions, 2010: National and State Trends by Age, Race and Ethnicity," Guttmacher Institute, May 2014, www.guttmacher.org /sites/default/files/report_pdf/ustptrends10.pdf.

Chapter 7: What Would Janet Jackson Do?

Fad diets have been around for centuries, but they are fads for a reason.

Grapefruit Diet, a.k.a. Hollywood Diet

This diet will not be beneficial to anyone over a long time as the extremely low calorie intake could lead to malnutrition and many health problems. The grapefruit diet also does not require exercise.

The Cabbage Soup Diet

Consuming only cabbage soup over a short period of time may lead to weight loss, but it will be mainly water weight. It's not recommended for extended periods of time.

The Tapeworm

This is an infection and some first-world luxury nonsense. Here's just some of the dangers:

* Blockage of bile ducts, appendix, or pancreatic duct

* Neurocysticercosis, a complication of the brain and nervous system that can cause dementia and vision issues

* Disruption in the function of various organs in your body, including the lungs and liver

* Weight gain while infected, as a tapeworm can increase appetite

* An increased craving for carbohydrates

* Death

CDC Violence Prevention: Intimate Partner Violence
A hub of information on how to spot, prevent, report, and heal from an abusive relationship.
"Intimate Partner Violence," Centers for Disease Control and Prevention, last reviewed October 23, 2018, www.cdc.gov/violence prevention/intimatepartnerviolence/index.html.

Teen-Dating Violence Facts

* Nearly 1 in 11 female and approximately 1 in 15 male high school students report having experienced physical dating violence in the last year.

* About 1 in 9 female and 1 in 36 male high school students report having experienced sexual dating violence in the last year.

* 26 percent of women and 15 percent of men who were victims of contact sexual violence, physical violence, and/ or stalking by an intimate partner in their lifetime first experienced these or other forms of violence by that partner before age eighteen.

* The burden of TDV is not shared equally across all groups—sexual minority groups are disproportionately

affected by all forms of violence, and some racial/ethnic minority groups are disproportionately affected by many types of violence.

"Preventing Teen Dating Violence," Centers for Disease Control and Prevention, last reviewed March 12, 2019, www.cdc.gov/violence prevention/intimatepartnerviolence/teendatingviolence/fastfact .html.

Chapter 8: Hoop Dreams

I watched a viral video of a grade school girl dunking on a boy in their classroom. I replayed it several times with happy tears in my eyes.

"Benefits—Why Sports Participation for Girls and Women," Women's Sports Foundation, August 30, 2016, www.womenssportsfoundation .org/advocate/foundation-positions/mental-physical-health/benefits -sports-participation-girls-women/.

For a city of over 8.5 million people, New York City is plagued with food deserts.

Cynthia Gordon et al., "Measuring Food Deserts in New York City's Low-Income Neighborhoods," *Health & Place* 17, no. 2 (March 2011): 696–700, https://doi.org/10.1016/j.healthplace.2010.12.012.

Grace Chen, "How Diet and Nutrition Impact a Child's Learning Ability," *Public School Review*, updated December 24, 2018, www .publicschoolreview.com/blog/how-diet-and-nutrition-impact-a -childs-learning-ability.

Noah Yonack, "In Brooklyn, Poor People Travel 3x Farther than Rich People to Get to the Grocery Store," *SafeGraph*, December 27, 2017, blog.safegraph.com/brooklyn-food-desert-c2cf580945c3.

What are food swamps and how are they making people sicker?
Olga Khazan, "Food Swamps Are the New Food Deserts: It's not just a lack of grocery stores that's making us fat. It's an overabundance of fast food," *The Atlantic*, December 28, 2007, https://www.theatlan tic.com/health/archive/2017/12/food-swamps/549275/.

Chapter 9: Fat as Shit

Five Weird Facts About Catherine de' Medici

1. Orphaned as an infant, the Medici heiress was hidden from the public who, by the time she was eleven, wanted her killed or deflowered to prevent her royal ascension.

2. Once married to King Henry II of France, the unattractive and petite Catherine drilled holes into the roof of her husband's mistress's house, to watch them in action.

3. She's alleged to have been a master poisoner and is believed to have killed a nemesis via a pair of gifted perfumed (poisoned) gloves.

4. She was very into astrology and called on the legendary mystic Nostradamus for personal horoscopes.

5. During her ten-year-long bout with infertility, Catherine relied on unconventional homeopathic recipes like drinking mule urine and spreading cow dung on her floor. At twenty-four, she had the first of her ten children.

Leonie Frieda, *Catherine de Medici: Renaissance Queen of France* (New York: Harper Perennial, 2006).

Emma Wynne and ABC Radio Perth, "A Short History of the High Heel," ABC News, November 12, 2017, www.abc.net.au/news/2017-11 -13/why-do-we-wear-high-heeled-shoes/9135936/.

Chapter 10: Real Women, Yeah Right!

Top-Selling Traditional Women's Magazines, 2018

BETTER HOMES AND GARDENS	7,628,025
GOOD HOUSEKEEPING	4,232,948
FAMILY CIRCLE	4,017,226
PEOPLE	3,425,166
WOMAN'S DAY	3,135,358
COSMOPOLITAN	3,037,932
SHAPE	2,556,050
O, THE OPRAH MAGAZINE	2,396,473

The biggest lie an American woman tells is her size.

Kate Zernike, "Sizing Up America: Signs of Expansion From Head to Toe," *New York Times*, March 1, 2004, www.nytimes.com/2004/03/01 /us/sizing-up-america-signs-of-expansion-from-head-to-toe.html.

Deborah A. Christel, and Susan C. Dunn, "Average American Women's Clothing Size: Comparing National Health and Nutritional Examination Surveys (1988–2010) to ASTM International Misses & Women's Plus-Size Clothing," *International Journal of Fashion Design, Technology and Education* 10, no. 2 (August 2016): 129–136, https://doi.org/10.1080/17543266.2016.1214291.

Find out your true size via the Size Matching Report.
www.sizeusa.com

Chapter 11: The $1,500 Mistake

Fitness equipment sales are in the billions.
Ankita Bhutani and Pallavi Bhardwaj, "Fitness Equipment Market Statistics 2018–2024 Global Industry Report," *Global Market Insights*, updated November 2018, www.gminsights.com/industry-analysis/fitness-equipment-market-report/.

Chapter 12: The Time I Almost Died

R.I.P. Sakia Gunn.
Ronald Smothers, "Teenage Girl Fatally Stabbed at a Bus Stop in Newark," *New York Times*, May 13, 2003, www.nytimes.com/2003/05/13/nyregion/teenage-girl-fatally-stabbed-at-a-bus-stop-in-newark.html.

Racial bias leads to poor medical assessments and treatment for patients of color.
Kelly M. Hoffman et al., "Racial Bias in Pain Assessment and Treatment

Recommendations, and False Beliefs about Biological Differences between Blacks and Whites," *Proceedings of the National Academy of Sciences* 113, no. 16 (April 2016): 4296–4301, https://doi .org/10.1073/pnas.1516047113.

Bijou Hunt and Steve Whitman, "Black:White Health Disparities in the United States and Chicago: 1990–2010," *Journal of Racial and Ethnic Health Disparities* 2, no. 1 (September 2014): 93–100, https:// doi.org/10.1007/s40615-014-0052-0.

Monique Tello, "Racism and Discrimination in Health Care: Providers and Patients," *Harvard Health Blog*, January 16, 2017, www.health .harvard.edu/blog/racism-discrimination-health-care-providers -patients-2017011611015/.

Superbugs are being created on American farmlands.

Holly Williams, "Could Antibiotic-Resistant 'Superbugs' Become a Bigger Killer than Cancer?" *CBS News*, www.cbsnews.com/news /could-antibiotic-resistant-superbugs-become-a-bigger-killer-than -cancer-60-minutes-2019-04-21/.

Katie Couric, "Animal Antibiotic Overuse Hurting Humans?" CBS News, February 9, 2010, www.cbsnews.com/news/animal-antibiotic -overuse-hurting-humans/.

"Living Near Livestock May Increase Risk of Acquiring MRSA." *Science-Daily*, October 10, 2012, www.sciencedaily.com/releases/2012/10 /121010131337.htm.

Mark Bittman, "Breeding Bacteria on Factory Farms," *New York Times*, July 9, 2013, opinionator.blogs.nytimes.com/2013/07/09/breeding -bacteria-on-factory-farms/#1.

Chapter 13: The Power of Love

Brené Brown, "The Power of Vulnerability," TED.com, www.ted.com
/talks/brene_brown_on_vulnerability/.

Chapter 14: Let's Go Vegan

Donald Watson's vegan society was found in 1944 and is still going strong.
www.vegansociety.com

Turns out, Egyptians may have been drunk when they made the pyramids.
Micheline Maynard, "Veggies May Be Healthier, but in 2018, Americans Will Eat a Record Amount of Meat," *Forbes*, January 2, 2018,
https://www.forbes.com/sites/michelinemaynard/2018/01/02
/veggies-may-be-healthier-but-in-2018-americans-will-eat-a-record
-amount-of-meat/#25ef0df819b9/.
Stephanie Butler, "Eat Like an Egyptian," History.com, updated August
29, 2018, www.history.com/news/eat-like-an-egyptian/.

World Scientists' Warning to Humanity: A Second Notice
PDF of the letter
http://scientistswarning.forestry.oregonstate.edu/sites/sw/files
/Warning_article_with_supp_11-13-17.pdf.
Michael Symonds, "Faculty of 1000 Evaluation for Reducing Foods En-
vironmental Impacts through Producers and Consumers," *F1000—
Post-Publication Peer Review of the Biomedical Literature*, 2018,
https://doi.org/10.3410/f.733362404.793552433.

Michele Simon, "Plant Based Foods Sales Experience 8.1 Percent Growth Over Past Year," *Cision PRWeb*, September 13, 2017, https://www.prweb.com/releases/2017/09/prweb14683840.htm

Soul food and milk are killing African Americans. (Not really, but close.)
Susan S. Lang, "Lactose Intolerance Seems Linked to Ancestral Struggles with Harsh Climate and Cattle Diseases, Cornell Study Finds," *Cornell Chronicle*, June 1, 2005, news.cornell.edu/stories/2005/06/lactose-intolerance-linked-ancestral-struggles-climate-diseases/.
Waverley Root and Richard De Rochemont, *Eating in America: A History* (New York: Ecco Press, 1981).

The dark history of soybeans in America blew my mind.
William Shurtleff and Akiko Aoyagi, "History of Tofu—Page 5," SoyInfo Center, www.soyinfocenter.com/HSS/tofu1.php.

Chapter 18: Eat Like an American

Which of the five American food patterns do you follow?
"Dietary Patterns Exist Among US Adults Based on Demographics," *ScienceDaily*, March 13, 2012, www.sciencedaily.com/releases/2012/03/120313190052.htm.

Y'all really spending big money on Taco Bell.
"CHD Expert Evaluates the Mexican Restaurant Industry, the Second Most Popular Menu Type in the USA," CHD Expert, www.chd

-expert.com/blog/press_release/chd-expert-evaluates-mexican
-restaurant-industry-second-popular-menu-type-usa/.

Melody Hahm, "Taco Bell Is 'America's Favorite Mexican Restaurant,'"
Yahoo! Finance, May 8, 2018, https://finance.yahoo.com/news/taco
-bell-americas-favorite-mexican-restaurant-153058944.html.

Reade Pickert and Scott Lanman, "Americans Are Spending Like Crazy
at Restaurants," *Time*, August 15, 2018, https://time.com/5368424
/americans-spending-like-crazy-at-restaurants/.

When you try to be racist but your kids end up loving kung pao chicken.

Godoy, Maria. "Lo Mein Loophole: How U.S. Immigration Law Fueled
a Chinese Restaurant Boom," *NPR*, February 22, 2016, www.npr
.org/sections/thesalt/2016/02/22/467113401/lo-mein-loophole
-how-u-s-immigration-law-fueled-a-chinese-restaurant-boom/.

Finland, you're doing amazing, sweetie!

Douglas Broom, "Finland Is the World's Happiest Country—Again,"
World Economic Forum, March 21, 2019, www.weforum.org/agenda
/2019/03/finland-is-the-world-s-happiest-country-again/.

"Fat to Fit: How Finland Did It," *The Guardian*, January 15, 2005, www
.theguardian.com/befit/story/0,15652,1385645,00.html.

Federal Spending: Where Does the Money Go?
2015

"Federal Spending: Where Does the Money Go," National Priorities Project, www.nationalpriorities.org/budget-basics/federal-budget-101
/spending/.

2017

"The Federal Budget in 2017: An Infographic," *Congressional Budget Office*, March 5, 2018, www.cbo.gov/publication/53624/.

Chapter 19: To Cheat or Not to Cheat

Women have been getting botched boob jobs for centuries.

JR Thorpe, "The History of Breast Implants & Enlargement, From Cobra Venom to Silicone Gel," *Bustle*, September 14, 2015, www.bustle .com/articles/110248-the-history-of-breast-implants-enlargement -from-cobra-venom-to-silicone-gel/.

Sydney Whalen, "13 Things You Didn't Know About the History of Plastic Surgery," *Zwivel*, July 28, 2017, www.zwivel.com/blog/plastic -surgery-a-look-through-history/.

Her name was Saartjie, not Venus Hottentot. Put some respect on her name, and body.

Rachel Holmes, *The Hottentot Venus: The Life and Death of Saartjie Baartman; Born 1789–Buried 2002* (London: Bloomsbury, 2007).

"Sara 'Saartjie' Baartman." *South African History Online*, June 11, 2018, www.sahistory.org.za/people/sara-saartjie-baartman.

As social stigmas wane, more folks are going for their perfect body.

American Society of Plastic Surgeons, "New Statistics Reveal the Shape of Plastic Surgery," American Society of Plastic Surgeons, March 1, 2018, www.plasticsurgery.org/news/press-releases/new-statistics-reveal -the-shape-of-plastic-surgery.

"Cosmetic Surgery National Data Bank Statistics," *Aesthetic Surgery Journal* 36, issue suppl_1 (April 2016): 1–29, https://doi.org/10.1093/asj/36.supplement_1.1.

"Cosmetic Surgery National Data Bank Statistics," *Aesthetic Surgery Journal* 38, issue suppl_3 (July 2018): 1–24, https://doi.org/10.1093/asj/sjy132.

The BMI model is biased . . .

"Body Mass Index—BMI," World Health Organization, accessed May 15, 2019, www.euro.who.int/en/health-topics/disease-prevention/nutrition/a-healthy-lifestyle/body-mass-index-bmi/.